The Social Structure of Modern Britain

BY

E. A. JOHNS

M.A.(Soc.), B.Sc.(Econ.), A.C.I.S.,
M.I.P.M., A.M.B.I.M., Dip.Ed.

Principal Lecturer in Management (Behavioural Sciences),
Faculty of Management, Slough College of Higher Education

THIRD EDITION

PERGAMON PRESS

OXFORD · NEW YORK · TORONTO · FRANKFURT
SYDNEY · PARIS

U.K.	Pergamon Press Ltd., Headington Hill Hall, Oxford OX3 0BW, England
U.S.A.	Pergamon Press Inc., Maxwell House, Fairview Park, Elmsford, New York 10523, U.S.A.
CANADA	Pergamon of Canada Ltd., 75 The East Mall, Toronto, Ontario, Canada
AUSTRALIA	Pergamon Press (Aust.) Pty. Ltd., P.O. Box 544, Potts Points, N.S.W. 2011, Australia
FRANCE	Pergamon Press SARL, 24 rue des Ecoles, 75240 Paris, Cedex 05, France
FEDERAL REPUBLIC OF GERMANY	Pergamon Press GmbH, 6242 Kronberg-Taunus, Pferdstrasse 1, Federal Republic of Germany

First edition 1965

Second edition 1972

Reprinted 1974 and 1975

Third edition 1979

British Library Cataloguing in Publication Data

Johns, Edward Alistair
The social structure of modern Britain. – 3rd ed.
(Pergamon international library).
1. Great Britain – social conditions – 1945 –
I. Title
309.1′41′0857   HN385.5   78-40531

ISBN 0–08–023343–0 (Hard cover)
ISBN 0–08–023342–2 (Flexicover)

Printed in Great Britain by William Clowes & Sons Limited London, Beccles and Colchester

FOR

ANNABEL,
ADRIAN AND CHRISTOPHER

Contents

Introduction to
the Third Edition

THE process of continuous social, economic and political change has now overtaken the second edition of this book and made necessary a further complete revision of the original text. In undertaking this work, I have taken the opportunity to critically evaluate some of the assumptions and generalizations—often based on inadequate samples or on information obtained from highly atypical groups—incorporated in the earlier edition simply because of the absence of any evidence constructed on more enduring foundations. The rapidly accumulating body of reliable published information on such matters as family life, social class, voting behaviour and so forth has enabled me to feel much more confident that this new edition gives a reasonably authentic picture of the British social structure.

Specifically, the content (although arranged in the same general format as the second edition) includes references to and detailed accounts of recent work on, for example, population trends (especially birth rate fluctuations), the relative influences of heredity and environment on intelligence (highly relevant to the impact of egalitarian social policies), the significance of early socialization and parent–child relationships in the subsequent development of the individual, the changing role and expectations of women in society, the Nuffield College Social Mobility Project, the social and educational performance of the comprehensive school, and the attenuated role of religion in British life. The book also incorporates up-to-date statistical information, not only on the more obvious areas like births, deaths, immigration and the like, but on such lesser known (but no less important) topics as leisure behaviour, income and wealth, recruitment to Oxbridge, and trends in criminal and other deviant activities.

The book also tries, where possible within its self-imposed concentrated framework, to place existing aspects of social structure into an historical and comparative context. When we place many of the practices and conventions, which we take for granted, into historical and cultural perspective, we can more easily see that our current norms have no particular sanctity. I hope that this new edition, like its predecessors, will continue to arouse and stimulate an interest in the fascinatingly complex problems of our social structure, while also developing that attempt at scientific detachment which, in my view, is the mark of the true sociologist.

E. A. J.

Introduction to
the Second Edition

FOR some time it has been apparent that *The Social Structure of Modern Britain* needed to be brought up to date to take account of social, legal and other changes that have occurred since original publication. The entire text has been rewritten for this edition, which takes account of developments in divorce law and practice and recently published research material on the validity of the *embourgeoisement* thesis, the effects of comprehensive education, and the causes of cross-class voting behaviour. To these examples of additional material could be added many others, as the reader will find. Where possible statistics have been related to current data, and two important new sections have been added to the book. In the chapter on demographic trends, a discussion of the effects of immigration has been included, while consideration of social controls (Chapter 6) incorporates an examination of criminal behaviour, the causes of crime and the aims of the British penal system.

In many ways the book now presents a more rounded and comprehensive picture of the fabric of British Society, though as is inevitable with an introductory text, it should guide the reader towards some of the more specialized sources which explore particular aspects in more detail.

E. A. J.

Introduction to
the First Edition

THIS book is about society in general and English society in particular. In one single volume it is not possible to give more than a very elementary account of the manifold aspects of our social structure, and it has been necessary to omit entirely some problems—those of urban sociology and of industrial relations, for example—in order to devote sufficient attention to, say, social class and educational selection in this country. Society is like a huge and complicated jigsaw; each of the chapters in this study concerns one or more of the pieces. I hope that when the whole has been joined together some view of contemporary English society will emerge which, if not entirely complete and comprehensive, will at least be an accurate reflection of our social background.

For obvious reasons, each component of society is here treated virtually in isolation, so that separate sections are allocated to political, religious and other facets; but it cannot be too strongly emphasized that in practice none of these elements operates in such isolation. All social processes exert influence over, and in turn are influenced by, other social processes, so that although different sociologists at different times may place very great stress on the ascendancy of individual social forces, they can never afford to ignore the countervailing importance of sociological pressures as a whole. To this extent, the chapter divisions which follow represent an artificially contrived breakdown of the social structure, but I must plead (in mitigation) that without some such system of classification it would not be possible to study society at all. In addition, everyday observation suggests that there is some justification for referring to specifically economic, political, educational and other categories as a basis for further inquiry. These descriptive divisions, of course, have no objective reality of their own: just because the class structure has a persistence beyond the lives of particular individuals, this does not mean that it is a real entity in itself, for its perpetuation depends solely on the actions and attitudes of its constituent parts. British sociology has an empirical tradition which lends itself easily to the study of social structure, that is, the way in which the broad pattern of the community exhibits regularities and organization, whether formal or informal. If society is a jigsaw, it is the task of this book to determine the shape of the pieces and then to examine the content of each in some detail; I hope that the questions raised here will prompt many readers to search for further enlightenment among the more specialized works available. Indeed, the growing number of sociological publications is strong evidence, I feel, for the increasingly constructive interest which many people, whether laymen or experts, are taking in the future shape of their own society.

The plan of this book was prepared with the idea that it would act as a basic source of material for the "Elements of Social Structure" optional paper in the University of London B.Sc. (Economics) degree, together with the "Social Structure of Modern Britain" paper in Part II of the same course and the B.A. and B.Sc. (Sociology) degrees. In addition, it will be found useful by those studying for the academic post-graduate Diploma in Public Administration (also a London University qualification), and by students of any branch of sociology, whether motivated by examination requirements or simply the layman's desire to acquire an understanding of the subject's main principles.

I am deeply indebted to Dr. A. H. Richmond, Professor of Sociology, York University, Toronto, for his constructive advice and criticism in the preparation of this book.

January 1964   E. A. J.

CHAPTER 1

Demographic Features of British Society

And God spake unto Noah, saying, Go forth of the ark, thou, and thy wife, and thy sons, and thy sons' wives with thee. Bring forth with thee every living thing that is with thee, of all flesh, both of fowl, and of cattle, and of every creeping thing that creepeth upon the earth; that they may breed abundantly in the earth, and be fruitful, and multiply upon the earth.

(Genesis viii. 16–17)

Is not a country over-populated when its standards are lower than they would be if its numbers were less?

(John Maynard Keynes)

Population Trends in the Twentieth Century

Apart from one unavoidable interruption in 1941, an unbroken series of decennial censuses stretches as far back as 1801. Although the first four are not strictly comparable because they do not include those members of the army, the navy, and the merchant service who were at home on the date of the census, the results can be regarded as valid for all normal purposes. Certainly it is clear that the period since 1801 has been characterized by an enormous expansion in the population of England and Wales, particularly in the early years of the last century. The reasons quoted for this are many and varied. Much emphasis has been placed, for example, on the culmination of that era in which agriculture was the basis of the social structure. It has been argued that the urban industrial worker found it easier, when the limitations of a peasant economy were removed, to set up a household of his own at an early age. Furthermore, the economic value of children in the first half of the nineteenth century must have encouraged large families to some degree. The most potent factor, however, was the significant fall in infant mortality.

According to an estimate for London published in the *Lancet* in 1835, the death rate for children was halved between 1750 and 1830. In the

1

period up to 1750, nearly three-quarters of all children died before reaching 5 years of age; 100 years later the proportion dying was under one-third. Why did this falling mortality rate occur? Various explanations have been offered, including the spread of a purer water supply (although cholera epidemics broke out periodically throughout the century), vaccination, the general advance of medical knowledge and midwifery techniques. As regards public health facilities, it is likely that after 1815 there was actually a worsening of conditions in the rapidly developing factory towns, for reasons which L. C. A. Knowles[1] sums up as follows:

> As there were no building restrictions houses were run up in any fashion, often back to back. There were no regulations to prevent over-crowding or cellar dwellings. There were no arrangements for disposing of the house refuse which always accumulates, ash-pits overflowed and spread a "layer of abomination" about the courts and streets; there was no system of main drainage and no system of sanitation. An adequate or clean water-supply laid on to the houses was rare until after 1850. The well and pumps were quite insufficient for the numbers who wished to use them and the river and canal water was polluted and disgusting.

In fact it would not be correct to assume that squalid housing was purely an industrial, urban phenomenon. As Gauldie[2] shows, life in rural and pre-industrial society was "nasty, brutish and short". It was the poorest of the rural poor for whom the towns had (literally) a fatal attraction. The consequence of the shift in population and the increased need for cheap accommodation was homelessness, the overcrowding of newcomers into dwellings vacated by the middle classes and "respectable artisans" and much low quality speculative building. Inevitably, the supply of housing to those with lower incomes became separated from the more profitable end of the market. Not only could the poor afford less, they were likely to economize on housing to obtain food and other necessities and thus, in the long run, became accustomed to paying less, and unwilling to pay more, for their housing. This upper limit on the demand price combined with the need to make profit tended to produce low quality dwellings and to make working class housing an unattractive field for investment.

A society which extolled the virtues of "self help" and the private

[1] Knowles, L. C. A., *The Industrial and Commercial Revolutions*.
[2] Gauldie, E., *Cruel Habitations: A History of Working Class Housing 1780–1918*, Allen & Unwin, 1974.

ownership of property found no difficulty in rationalizing the housing situation as the natural and just consequence of improvidence and low standards. Only slowly was it appreciated from the evidence of statistical enquiries, government committees and individual commentators that poverty, disease, brutal working and living conditions formed self-perpetuating circumstances from which escape was well-nigh impossible. Contemporary thinking suggested that a solution lay in better public health which would improve workers' incomes and ability to pay the rent. After a good deal of legislation—itself a result of Christian philanthropy combined with hard-headed self-interest—it turned out that public health was a symptom rather than a cause. While incomes and employment fluctuated, rents continued to rise and the lot of slum dwellers worsened.

Before the eighteenth century, people were under-nourished and prey to infective diseases. According to McKeown,[3] improvements in medicine were not an important causal factor in the subsequent fall in mortality, because "the health of man is determined essentially by his behaviour, his food and the nature of the world around him, and is only marginally influenced by personal medical care". The main contribution to the reduction in death rates came from a decline in the mortality from infective diseases, in particular the airborne diseases such as tuberculosis and several childhood diseases, although proportionately the fall in mortality in the nineteenth century was more striking for the waterborne diseases of cholera, diarrhoea, dysentery, typhoid and typhus. For the nineteenth century, therefore, and even perhaps for the eighteenth, reductions in mortality had less to do with medical improvements than with changes to environment and nutritional standards. At one time, for instance, infant survival was adversely affected by the fact that many expectant mothers had to work until the day of the birth of their children. In the mines, women often suffered distortions of the spine and pelvis which caused great difficulty at childbirth.[4]

---

[3] McKeown, T., *The Modern Rise of Population*, Edward Arnold, 1976.

[4] According to one woman quoted in the Report on Mines of 1842, a vast number of women "have dead children and false births, which are worse, as they are not able to work after the latter. I have always been obliged to work below till forced to go to bear the bairn, and so have all the other women. We return as soon as able, never longer than ten or twelve days; many less, if they are much needed."

Until the outbreak of World War I, the average size of the family had been fairly high, although the trend was obviously towards a reduction in the number of children. For those married in the period 1861 to 1869, the mean ultimate family size was 6.16; for couples married between 1900 and 1909, the equivalent figure was 3.3 children.[5] But the war had a far-reaching effect on family size, not only from the point of view of those husbands and fathers (both potential and actual) who were killed, but also because the ones who returned tended to have either very few children or none at all. Up to 1914 the average annual increase of the population, calculated in 10-year periods from official figures, had fluctuated around 1 per cent. After 1918, however, the figure fell to less than half, and did not rise again until after World War II. Since fewer babies were being born, it followed that older people would constitute a higher proportion of the total. In due course, it was argued, the population would actually decline, both absolutely and relatively, compared with the world at large.

Yet in fact the 1951 Census showed that the population of England and Wales was nearly 44½ millions (compared with 41½ millions in 1939) and, as if to emphasize the dangers of extrapolation even more strongly, the figures indicated a continuing rise. Subsequently, the birth rate dropped steadily from a peak of 18.5 births per thousand population (England and Wales) in 1964 to 16.2 in 1970, followed by a further fall in 1974 to 13 per thousand.[6] According to the 1971 Census figures, the total population of the United Kingdom (as distinct from England and Wales alone) was just under 55½ millions in 1971, compared with nearly 53 millions in 1961, 38 millions in 1901, and over 6½ millions in 1700. The official forecasts suggest that this will reach just over 59 millions in 2011, with more than 23 millions of the population aged over 45 and the beginnings of a big increase in pensioners. Specifically, the number of those aged over 75 will increase by 30 per cent from 2½ millions in 1975 to 3 millions

    [5] Figures from the Registrar-General, *Statistical Review*, 1957, Part III, Commentary. The original data were obtained at the 1911 Census and the 1946 Sample Family Census of the Royal Commission on Population.

    [6] *On the State of the Public Health*, H.M.S.O., 1976. A rate of 14 births per 1000 gives exact replacement; in other words, zero population growth. Thus the figures for 1974 suggest, for the first time, the real possibility of a population decline.

in 1986 and to $3\frac{1}{4}$ millions in 2001. It is predicted, too, that the birth rate in England and Wales will continue to fall but then rise in the 1980s, followed by another cyclical decline and a further revival. Such predictions, as their nature suggests, incorporate the long-term assumption on fertility that the large family is seen as an anachronism. However, extrapolations of existing birth rates are inevitably prone to considerable error. It is interesting to note that the United Kingdom is among the least accurate of nations in terms of population forecasting: a recent O.E.C.D. survey showed that Britain had under-estimated its future birth rate by 8 per cent compared with an average degree of inaccuracy of 5 per cent in Western Europe.

What really matters in the long run, however, is not birth rate but change in average family size. For exact replacement this has to be 2.1 children per family (the extra 0.1 accounting for deaths before the age of 50), yet Britain has only just dropped below this level apart from a brief period during the depression of the 1930s. In the post-war period there have been two peak periods for the production of children: the immediate post-1945 years and a rather more puzzling increase in 1955. It seems probable that the unexpected rise in births which took place in 1955 and shortly afterwards could be explained simply in terms of a fall in the average age for marriage, though other factors undoubtedly played a part. These included the introduction of family allowances, the increase of child allowances for income tax, extensions to social security benefits of all kinds, the absence of economic slumps, the slow but steady increase in real incomes and the influx of immigrants.

Some remarkable things have been happening to the distribution of population, too. The growing number of people living in cities and conurbations is probably the most important factor in the human geography of the modern world. As nodes in communication networks of all sizes, cities provide vital links for the economic functioning of regions, and are exceptionally fertile seedbeds for contemporary economic growth. They create special social environments in their own residential areas, and by functioning as centres from which social change is diffused they influence society well beyond their own limits. They act as centres from which political power is exercised, again operating on a variety of scales.

It was in Britain that the process of urban growth in the nineteenth century took place earliest and involved the largest proportion of the total population.[7] At the outset, the industrial system was based on coal and iron, with the main population centres located in the northern counties, South Wales, and the Scottish industrial belt. In modern times, however, coal and iron play a much smaller part in determining the location of industry: electricity, gas and oil have replaced coal as a direct source of power. Industries now tend to regard ports and markets as more potent factors in determining their choice of site. As a result, between 1921 and 1934 the population of London and the South-east rose by nearly 14 per cent, whereas the numbers in South Wales fell by 5 per cent. The South—already far more densely populated—gained no less than five times as much population in the period 1951–61 as did the North. Specifically, the South-east is grabbing the lion's share of this increase. Hertfordshire grew at a rate of 3.65 per cent *each year* over the same 10-year period, compared with 0.33 per cent per year as the rate of increase for the South-east region as a whole.

The social facts behind such economic changes in the first four decades of the twentieth century constitute a curious mixture of expansion and depression, especially in the interwar years. True, there was an overall and widely diffused improvement in living standards due to economic growth, the decline in world food and raw material prices, and the declining size of families, but at the same time Britain's socio-economic profile was only marginally altered. The highest peaks of wealth had been decapitated by World War I but little redistribution of wealth took place after the sudden collapse in 1921 of the post-war economic boom. Although poverty was undoubtedly receding, a substantial minority—perhaps a quarter of the population—still faced real hardship that varied from relative deprivation to actual malnutrition, and many working-class households sank below the poverty line at such times as child-rearing and old age, when their earning power reached its nadir. One group in particular was at greater risk than ever before: the workers in Britain's staple industries—textiles, coal, shipbuilding—which had lost markets owing to wartime dislocation and price competition from the Japanese and others. This structural unemployment in the industrial North hit those "highly specialized and regimented industrial communities with a pronounced 'work ethic' " where unemployment was

[7] See Tranter, N. L., *Population Since the Industrial Revolution: The Case of England and Wales*, Croom Helm, 1974.

"the ultimate tragedy in social and economic terms."[8] In contrast, the South and Midlands where, before 1914, work had been more casual and less well paid, attracted the newer and more flexibly-located industries. It should be added, too, that it was mainly the middle class which, enjoying better job security and stable prices, was able to taste those first fruits of affluence from the boom sectors of the economy. The price of the motor car halved in a decade, and a third of the nation's families lived in their own houses by 1939, properties mainly of middling rateable value and located in suburbs which had been colonized for housing by suburban railways and buses.

Currently, the evidence shows quite clearly that the British people have lost their earlier habit of concentrating themselves in large urban centres. Whereas in 1851 the population of England and Wales was evenly divided between urban and rural areas, the proportion had changed so much by 1901 that 75 per cent lived in towns; and in 1955 this had increased to more than four-fifths. The Census of 1961 showed that almost exactly half the population lived in the six conurbations (Greater London, West Midlands, Merseyside, South-east Lancashire, West Yorkshire, Tyneside and Clydeside) or in the other cities whose populations exceeded 100,000. Yet while the population of the United Kingdom increased by $2\frac{1}{4}$ millions in the 10 years from 1951 to 1961, almost the whole of the increase took place outside the conurbations and cities. Inside the latter, the population increase amounted to a mere 0.1 million. In the 5 years to mid-1970 the only metropolitan county to increase its population was West Yorkshire, and Greater London lost more than 500,000 people between mid-1970 and mid-1975.

With the continuing expansion in private motoring and the maintenance of subsidies for public passenger transport, it is unlikely that the trend to the outer suburbs, to the countryside or to small towns will be either checked or reversed. Already over 40 per cent of the United Kingdom population live in rural areas or in towns with a population of less than 50,000; by 1983 the ratio may well be as high as 50 per cent. Dr. Mark Abrams has declared that "from being Europe's first example of a highly urbanized society Britain may well become its first model of a predominantly suburbanized community, with a majority of its people

[8] Glynn, S., and Oxborrow, J., *Interwar Britain: A Social and Economic History*, Allen & Unwin, 1976.

trying to enjoy simultaneously some of the advantages of rural life (fresh air, gardens, privacy, quiet) and some of the advantages of metropolitan life (rapid access to a variety of high quality social and cultural services and a wide choice of occupational opportunities)."[9]

Finally, it is worth noting that there is some basis in fact for the popular identification of North and South, bounded by a line drawn from the Severn to the Wash. According to regional statistics, the North— especially the North-east, Yorkshire and Humberside, is dirtier and less healthy. Its households receive comparatively more in social security money but earn less on average each week and are more likely to have a wage earner unemployed. Wealth and high incomes remain concentrated in the South-east, but regions of population growth since 1970 (and, it is thought, for the next two decades) are East Anglia, the East Midlands and the South-west, such growth being mainly the result of migration.

Socio-economic Aspects of Population

Changes in the age structure, geographical distribution and social habits of the population have important implications for public finance and welfare policy. For this purpose the population can be subdivided into three broadly distinct categories:

1. Those below working age—calculated as all individuals below the age at which it is permissible to leave school.
2. Those of working age—the age group 16–65 for men, and 16–60 for women.
3. Those above working age—65 for men and 60 for women.

Since 1964 the birth rate in Britain has fallen by a third, at a time when more women have been getting married younger. The characteristics of the population have also been changing, with a sharp increase in the proportion of those in retirement (a 37.5 per cent increase between 1951 and 1974) and the proportion under the age of 15 (a 16.5 per cent increase). Over the same period the number of people of working age has increased by only a little over 3 per cent.

[9] Abrams, M., "Britain: the next 15 years", *New Society*, 7 November 1968, pp. 670–3.

The numbers in the group below working age have clearly increased substantially. The minimum school-leaving age has been raised periodically and opportunities for further and higher education have been made available to a larger proportion of 16-year-olds. Unfortunately it is this group which presents the greatest problems in terms of forecasting, since nobody knows precisely how the birth rate will fluctuate in years to come. Most projections see an increase in births in the 1980s simply because women born in the 1950s and early 1960s 'boom' will be entering the reproductive phase. Yet this upward trend, due to start in the mid-1970s, has not happened yet. Fewer babies were born in Britain in 1975 than at any time since the 1930s, and although 500,000 people have been added to the population since 1970, most of the increase occurred before 1974 and the population has virtually stopped growing since then. In the year ended March 1976, deaths exceeded births by a few thousand, the first time that has happened in peacetime since central records were first introduced 140 years ago.[10]

Such global figures conceal the fact that the decline in births has been principally concentrated in families where the husband is in unskilled or only partly skilled work. While there has been virtually no change in the total number of births in social classes I and II—people in professional, managerial and senior administrative occupations—births in social classes IV and V fell by about a third. Premaritally conceived legitimate first births have declined for all social classes. Between 1970 and 1975 they fell from 15 to 8 per cent of all legitimate births for the non-manual social classes, and from 31 to 23 per cent for the manual classes. A steep decline in the proportion of recently married couples starting a family in the early years of marriage is reflected in the general movement towards smaller families. It is worth noting, too, that the lower social groups, who have tended in the past to use less reliable methods of contraception and to have a higher number of 'unplanned' pregnancies than other social groups, have begun to adopt more satisfactory methods, particularly the contraceptive pill.

After about 1990, forecasting births becomes prohibitively difficult, since up to then the numbers of potential mothers are known with some certainty—they are alive now and the number of survivors can be

[10] *Population Trends 7*, H.M.S.O., 1977.

estimated quite accurately. But after 1990 the number of mothers is itself dependent on the survivors of births in 1970 and thereafter, which introduces a dual degree of probability into the situation. Even if it could be predicted with certainty that the population would remain static, or even fall, it is not clear what effect that would have on economics and social life. "Some are optimistic, believing that it would produce a mirror image of the effects of population growth—less pollution, noise and congestion; more resources to devote to severe pockets of deprivation and to improve standards; higher *per capita* incomes. Others believe it would produce problems totally new in character which will at least maintain, if not increase, pressure on public services."[11] Perhaps the best response to uncertainty about demographic trends is a high degree of flexibility in social policy decisions, with a need for workers to accept greater occupational and geographical mobility, and so forth. Fewer school teachers are already being produced; plans for new towns are being reviewed; and housing policies must take account of the fact that families seem to want fewer children.

At the other end of the scale, the number of "pensioners"—men aged 65 and over and women aged 60 and over—is also expected to rise, from 8.8 millions in 1970 to just over 10 millions by the end of the century. The sex balance in this group is weighted in favour of women principally because they tend to live longer; their average expectation of life is 75.5 years compared with just over 69 for men.[12] Partially the rising numbers of elderly people in the population can be explained by reference to improved medical techniques leading to longer life expectancy. Thus the number of people aged 85 and over increased by 17 per cent between mid-1970 and mid-1975, raising the total in the age-group to 515,000.

Because the population has been ageing rapidly—as the very high numbers of children born at about the turn of the century now enter the ranks of the elderly—the balance between the producers of resources and the dependent sections of the population is less favourable today than at

[11] Buxton, M. and Craven, E., eds., *Demographic Change and Social Policy: The Uncertain Future*, Centre for Studies in Social Policy, 1976.

[12] 1975 figures (Office of Population Censuses and Surveys). It is worth recording that the greater longevity of women only begins to tell at ages over 45; up to that point it is offset by the fact that more boys are born than girls. From the point of view of pensions policy, the life expectancy of a man aged 65 is 11.95 years, whereas that of a woman aged 60 is 19.11 years.

any time since the early 1930s. An improvement is in prospect, however, that will continue to the end of the century and beyond. This is because, although the number of over-75s will rise from about 2.8 million in 1976 to about 3.4 million in 1991, pensioners will increasingly be derived from those born in the inter-war years, when birth rates were very low; and the present fall in the birth rate means there will be far fewer children to support. At the same time, the calculations may be upset, at the upper end of the dependent sectors of the population, by the trends towards earlier retirement at ages like 60 or 55.

Arguably the most important section of the population comprises those aged roughly between 16 and 65 (60 for women), since these are the economically active people upon whose efforts all others at the lowest and highest ends of the age ranges must depend. In 1965 there were 41.9 millions in the working-age group, a figure which rose to 42.7 millions in 1970. Estimates for the future give totals of 45.4 millions in 1980 and 53.8 millions by the end of the century[13]—a steady if not striding growth. In 1966 about 93 per cent of men and 50.5 per cent of women between 15 and 64 in Great Britain were economically active in remunerative word (this includes those temporarily out of work or sick). In addition some 23.3 per cent of men and 6.7 per cent of women aged 65 or more were still economically active.

A useful general indicator of the dependency structure of the population is the number in the dependent age-groups (all under 16; and 65 and over for men, 60 and over for women) for every hundred in the working age groups. A rise in this ratio indicates a rise in the numbers of dependants in the care of each "supporter". The ratio was 68 in 1970 (after being 62 in 1965) and is expected to rise to 73 in 1980, only to fall back a little to 71 by the end of the century. Relatively speaking, in other words, a smaller number of productively employed citizens is being called upon to support a larger number of dependants. In view of such developments, it seems unlikely that the nation could afford anything other than cost-of-living increases for pensioners.

---

[13] These figures have been calculated on the basis of an official school-leaving age of 15 and must therefore be adjusted downwards slightly to take account of the rise to 16. Moreover, the degree of uncertainty in the forecasts after 1990 increases sharply because of their dependence on guesses about the post-1976 birth rate.

On the other hand, the quantitative shortage of manpower in the economically active sector of the population is more apparent than real. For one thing the extent to which people of working age are already actually employed varies quite a lot from country to country, and this degree of activity is largely (though by no means exclusively) a function of the extent to which women work. Apart from the possibilities inherent in increasing the proportion of women in employment (provided that such an increase is not accompanied by a commensurate reduction in opportunities for males), it is also feasible that the more rapid introduction of automation in British industry may enable productivity to rise without a corresponding increase in manpower requirements.

Population changes are also bound to produce changes in family life. Of the 16.9 million private households counted in 1966, about 15 per cent consisted of one person only, 30 per cent of two persons, 21 per cent of three, 18 per cent of four and 16 per cent of five or more. It is slightly surprising that this distribution hardly differs between the conurbations, the cities, the small towns and the villages. In England and Wales, for example, the proportion of people who live alone only ranged from 5 per cent in the conurbations down to 3.5 per cent in rural localities. Similarly the proportion of people living in households of five people or more ranged only from 28.6 per cent in the conurbations up to 30.4 per cent in rural areas. The differences are too small to have any real meaning but the predominance of smaller households does suggest that grandparents live apart from their children, a tendency which is likely to continue.

Current projections envisage a crystallization around three very different family types. Of the total 20 million households in 1985, nearly a quarter will consist of one or two persons and contain someone of pensionable age; one household in every ten will contain no more than a man or woman (usually the latter) of pensionable age living alone. Another third of all households will be those where the mother is under 40 years of age and is primarily engaged in bringing up her young children while trying to manage on the income provided by one wage-earner in the family. The third distinctive family type will be that where the parents are aged between 40 and 54, the children have grown up, and the wife has a paid job. This will represent about 20 per cent of all families.

Trends in Fertility

One of the most conspicuous features of recent developments in the family is the growth and acceptance of the idea and practice of voluntary family limitation. Parents may deliberately control the number of births in their family with reference to the conditions and opportunities they can provide for their offspring, and the kind of life they themselves wish to lead. The undeniable decline in family size, since that era when the Victorians and their immediate predecessors reared families of an average size larger than those of any other period in British history, can be broadly illustrated by the fact that in 1881 the average family had between five and six children, whereas now it has around two.

A possible cause of the change in the nineteenth century was probably the sharp fall in infant mortality. The birth rate was indeed very high and was rising up to the end of the 1860s, but what made the average family so unprecedently large at that time was the sudden propensity for survival among these numerous offspring. Hitherto, it had not been unusual for parents to lose at least half its total number of, say, 10 to 12 children in infancy or early childhood. This appalling situation was alleviated by improvements in standards of housing, sanitation, feeding and medical knowledge generally. Any fall in infant mortality was first felt among the middle classes, since typically they enjoyed a higher standard of living and were better placed to take advantage of any improvements in social conditions. So it was not surprising that, having recovered from the initial shock of retaining 8 children out of 10, they were the first to take some positive action towards birth control.

The idea of family limitation was gaining ground in the last quarter of the nineteenth century. Although most of the propaganda on the subject was directed towards the masses, it somewhat naturally took effect first among those who could easily read and understand it. Ironically, then, it was the wealthy upper and upper-middle classes—with the least economic incentive to control their families, at least in the objective sense—which first began to do so. Thence the habit spread downwards to the middle classes proper, and finally to the skilled manual and lesser clerical workers. The twentieth century has completed the conversion of the middle classes to a small family pattern. When the Royal Commission on Population produced its report in 1949, it was still true that the higher occupational groups practised birth control more diligently than the lower categories. Among couples married between 1900 and 1930, for instance, the families of manual workers were consistently about 40 per cent larger than those of non-manual workers. Statistical and anecdotal evidence from most of the post-war empirical research carried out in Britain supports the same conclusions. Willmott and Young tell of a social worker in Bethnal Green who persuaded a woman to have a contraceptive cap fitted. Two months later she was again pregnant, saying: "My husband wouldn't have it. He threw it on the fire."[14]

Despite the arrival of the contraceptive pill (and its relatively classless impact), surveys still show that a high proportion of married women— ranging from 30 to 50 per cent—have had "accidental" or "unplanned" pregnancies even when using some kind of birth control method. In many of these cases, the pregnancy is unwelcome because it occurs too soon, in which circumstances the problem could be resolved by improved spacing. Two highly divergent approaches to the study of fertility— including the associated questions of "accidental" pregnancies and spacing—have developed over the past 20 years. From economics has come a rapidly growing body of theoretical work that attempts to link changes in fertility to economic factors. From sociology have come empirical studies of people's preferences and intentions about family size and spacing, contraception, and of the social and economic influences upon them. Both approaches share a common weakness: neither is concerned to make any detailed study of the way in which men and women think about having children and make decisions that result in a particular pattern of childbearing. The first, because in the search for some *general* theory of fertility it makes *a priori* assumptions about decision making; the second because its primary aim is to find links between fertility and structural features of society and this tends to direct attention away from the individual actor's ideas and beliefs. Thus neither approach, by itself, provides a satisfactory explanation of changes in fertility, though sociologically-oriented studies tend ultimately to be the more fruitful.

Luker's firmly sociological analysis, for instance, while based on work done in California, sets out to answer the question why so many women

[14] Young, M. and Willmott, P., *Family and Kinship in East London*, Routledge & Kegan Paul, London, 1957.

who have access to both contraceptive knowledge and supplies nevertheless take risks and seek to terminate their ensuing pregnancies.[15] The
commonsense idea is that women with contraception available will use
it in preference to abortion as a means of fertility control—hence the
derived assumption that women who do not do so are behaving irration-
ally. But Luker shows that the women studied had been acting rationally
in the Weberian sense of consciously using means appropriate to their
goals. Luker uses the model of classical decision-making theory to demonstrate the rationality of the women's behaviour in terms of their perceptions of the probabilities of various outcomes and of the costs and
benefits of contraception and of pregnancy. The key elements of the
cost-benefit analyses presented are the perceived short-term costs of using
contraceptives, perceived potential benefits of pregnancy, the low or uncertain perceived probability of becoming pregnant, and the discount-
ing of the future costs of pregnancy. In these terms, failure to use effective
contraception cannot simply be attributed to lack of information, individual personality disturbance, or technological factors, and until this is
recognized, attempts to reduce unwanted pregnancies may prove fruit-
less. The main usefulness of Luker's approach is that it casts doubt upon
the validity of much of the conventional wisdom on the relationship
between the contraception and abortion. Some of the implications of
Luker's work—for example, that freely available abortion may decrease
effective contraceptive use by reducing the perceived costs of pregnancy
—are far-reaching and require further study.

Cartwright's study of family size and spacing is more authentic if only
it supplies evidence from a firmly British context. Based on a 1973 survey
of a national sample of 1473 mothers and 263 fathers, all of whom had
recently had a legitimate child, it concentrated on three topics: intentions about family size and spacing; the factors that might be related to
these intentions; and the use of and attitudes to contraception and
abortion.[16] The author carried out a similar study in 1967–68 and a
comparison of the data from the two undoubtedly provides some extremely useful information. It shows, for instance, that between 1967–68
and 1973—a period of continuing fertility decline in England and Wales

[15] Luker, K., *Taking Chances: Abortion and the Decision not to Contracept*, University of
California Press, 1976.
[16] Cartwright, A., *How Many Children?*, Routledge & Kegan Paul, 1976.

—the size of the family people intended to have declined; the use of the pill increased considerably; in 1973 it was used *less* by the wives of men in professional occupations than by other wives; and mothers were less hostile to abortion than in the earlier study. But when it comes to the question of identifying the influences on intentions about family size and spacing, the study is far less satisfactory. The deficiencies of Cartwright's approach is illustrated by the attempt to examine the influence of housing on intentions. The author is able to show that those who were purchasing their house on a mortgage wanted fewer children than those in a council house. Cartwright goes on to speculate that housing may affect family size either because it is easier for larger families to get a council house *or* because "couples with a mortgage may feel somewhat less inclined to take on further responsibilities in the form of a larger family."

Although the use of contraceptive devices is not in itself a *cause* of birth control, but simply a *means* whereby the desired degree of family limitation may be obtained, it is true that the increased availability of chemical and mechanical methods of contraception has further contributed to the ideology of the small family. Contraceptives are available at most chemists and hairdressing shops for those not too embarrassed to ask for them, and there is no shortage of advice on how to use these implements. About 300,000 people seek guidance each year from the 400 clinics of the Family Planning Association, all of which are voluntarily staffed, most subsidized by the National Health Service and located on local authority or hospital premises. It should perhaps be noted in this context that the F.P.A. is not solely concerned with encouraging family limitation: it also conducts research into infertility on the grounds that 10 per cent of all marriages in Britain are involuntarily childless, a disappointing and frustrating situation which can lead to divorce.

What were the motives prompting the middle classes to limit the size of their families from about 1875 onwards? The Royal Commission on Population lists a variety of explanations including, for example, the progressive emancipation of women and their attainment of equality with men in many fields. Certainly financial considerations could not have been paramount, for although the middle classes suffered a slight reversal of their economic fortunes in the 1870s—when the rate of increasing prosperity merely slowed down a little—their affluence in absolute terms was never seriously threatened. On the other hand, those living at the time may well have interpreted their situation in more in-timidating terms, as they did not have the benefit (as we do) of historical hindsight. From being an economic asset in the early years of the nine-teenth century, too, children rapidly became a financial liability. Rural prosperity decayed (and it became more difficult to rear a large brood), factory legislation limited and finally prevented the exploitation of child labour in industry, and education became compulsory. These changes probably affected the higher income groups some time before the last quarter of the century. As Banks[17] argues, although no single factor in the upbringing of children became markedly more expensive in this period, the cumulative effect of the increased cost of all the factors together was quite considerable. Even before education became com-pulsory, the gradual introduction of competitive examinations had made it more important for entrance into "gentlemanly" jobs. This in itself would not have been a major element in making children an economic liability, but it became so when the purely social differential was harder to maintain. At that stage, outlay for the children's future could no longer be skimped. This decision to restrict the size of one's family in order to provide all the children with "a good start in life" is to be distinguished as a motive from the restriction of families in order to maintain the material standard of living of the parents.

This latter consideration must be of vital importance in view of the fact that, other things being equal, the competitive struggle for goods and services is a race in which the advantage lies with the childless couple. Added to this are the extraneous influences of increased leisure oppor-tunities coupled with the large number of leisure pursuits being com-mercially exploited. Since all these cost money, the economic incentive to limit families is further intensified. As the leisure activities, clothing fashions, and general style of life of the wealthier sections of the commun-ity permeate through to the masses, aided by the large-scale media of communication, so these characteristics become more visible and more desirable. It may be true that the conscious desire to achieve upward social mobility is a comparatively recent phenomenon, but it is a pre-requisite of achieving such an aim that the individual should adopt the ethos of the social group he wishes to enter. Because the neo-Malthusian

[17] Banks, J. A., *Prosperity and Parenthood*, Routledge & Kegan Paul, 1954.

birth-control propagandists directed their warnings on the dangers of excessive fecundity mainly to the poor, it is scarcely remarkable that increasing numbers of "status-dissenting" lower-class people began to regard the practice of "breeding like rabbits" as an undesirable habit to be avoided at all costs.

Again, the considerably improved status of women did more than weaken the traditional supremacy of the male. It also concentrated anxious attention on the welfare of expectant mothers and young children. The old attitude of "If the women complained, it was hold your noise and give her another baby"[18] has been generally replaced by an arrangement where, in Ronald Fletcher's words, "Women now enter marriage on a completely voluntary basis and on an equal footing with their male partners. This improved status has meant, of course, that many women no longer wish to be confined to a life of child-bearing, child-rearing, and domesticity."[19] Initially, the feminist movement was directed largely against the subordinate status of women in the middle classes but, as in so many other social changes, its effects were eventually felt in all sections of the community. The emancipation of women had economic implications, too, inasmuch as if wives demand to pursue their own independent aims and interests, these may cost money and the family may feel compelled to sacrifice the desire for more children.

In 1949 Lewis-Faning reported to the Royal Commission on Population that early marriage was one of the most important factors tending to produce a large family, and this view was accepted by the Commission.[20] Certainly there may have been some truth in this assertion during the nineteenth century, when the rapid development of industrialization forced a decline in the number of apprenticeships offered and a compensating increase in the proportion of urban workers who began to earn a full wage when scarcely out of adolescence. The 1840 *Report* of the Poor Law Commissioners remarks that many 18-year-olds "assumed the most important office of manhood" and consequently had adequate time to acquire a vast collection of children. More recently, on the other hand,

---

[18] An informant quoted in Young, M. and Willmott, P., *op. cit.*
[19] Fletcher, R., *The Family and Marriage*, Penguin Books, 1962.
[20] Lewis-Faning, E., *Family Limitation and its Influence on Human Fertility during the Past Fifty Years*, Papers of the Royal Commission on Population, H.M.S.O., 1949.

couples have been concentrating their births into the early years of marriage, which has given the short-term illusion that the birth rate is rising at a far higher rate than is, in fact, the case; this can be contrasted yet again with the current position, still characterized by small numbers of children, but now postponed until later in the marriage. The result is that there is virtually no correlation between numbers of children and marriage duration—and in logic, there is no reason why there should be.

Because childlessness in early marriage has become much commoner in the past few years, the big question facing demographers has been how far this is a postponement of child-bearing, and how far it represents a real reduction. Certainly there has been a marked decline in childless and one-child families, after 10 years of marriage, among couples who were married between 1951 and 1964. For every 100 women who married at ages 20–24 in 1951, there were 14 still childless and 27 with only one child after 10 years. The equivalent figures for those married in 1964 were down to 9 and 17. There has also been a drop in the proportion of families having four or more children, and an increased proportion of two-child families.

Successive Census reports since World War II have continued to draw attention to differential fertility rates between the social classes. The 1951 figures, for example, showed that class V families, in the Registrar-General's fivefold classification, averaged 3.18 children compared with 1.88 for class I households. In general, therefore, the data point to an inverse relationship between family size and family income: in other words, the bigger the family, the poorer the home. True, the variations have become less marked in recent years, but nonetheless there is still a substantial difference between the average fertility of the various social classes and the social consequences of this fact should be considered.

Before 1939, because of the widespread belief that the population was being recruited largely from those parents with below-average intelligence, it was predicted that the ability of the country as a whole, as measured by I.Q., would decline by about two points per generation. After the war, however, similar studies (chiefly on Scottish school-children) in fact revealed a slight gain in average intelligence, at least as measured by tests. This does not necessarily mean that the original hypothesis was wrong, for the reliability of tests (as indicators of innate intelligence) might be questioned. Post-war children may be more familiar with such tests and such sophistication would produce mis-leadingly high scores. But more important than any of these methodo-logical arguments is the fact that a redefinition of intelligence itself has largely demolished the pessimistic arguments on the relationship be-tween "innate" ability and differential fertility. In the words of the *Newsom Report*:[21]

> Intellectual talent is not a fixed quantity with which we have to work but a variable that can be modified by social policy and educational approaches . . . the kind of intelligence which is measured by the tests so far applied is largely an acquired characteristic. This is not to deny the existence of a basic genetic endow-ment; but whereas that endowment, so far, has proved impossible to isolate, other factors can be identified. Particularly significant among them are the influences of social and physical environment; and, since these are susceptible to modification, they may well prove educationally more important.

At one time it would have been arguable, moreover, that class position (determined primarily by occupation) had little to do with innate intelligence and more to do with the operation of luck and other random factors, like inherited wealth and family relationships. Today, with recruitment and selection procedures focussing on the possession of academic and professional qualifications, there is greater justification for supposing that social groupings in Britain can be differentiated by intelligence (or, to be more precise, the particular attribute measured by intelligence tests). Any positive correlations between occupational cate-gories and I.Q. scores, however, have to be interpreted with great caution. First, they can only be averages within a very large statistical range; second, any relationship between I.Q. and social class is much too weak to be of any use for predicting the intelligence of any individual. Analysis is further complicated by the continuing dispute on the precise extent to which intelligence is acquired or inherited, ranging from ex-treme hereditarians like Jensen of Harvard, who suggests that between 80 and 90 per cent of the variability in human intelligence derives from heredity, down to authorities like Fehr of the University of Illinois with a heredity element of 38 per cent. Broadly in the latter camp, for instance,

---

[21] The Newsom Report, *Half Our Future*, a report of the Central Advisory Council for Education (England), H.M.S.O., 1963.

is Husen,[22] who takes issue with the validity of the actual data presented by Jensen—representative groups of twins—and argues that Jensen's heritability estimate of 80 per cent should be reduced to somewhere between 40 and 60 per cent.

Even so, according to Husen, since the task of the educator is to bring about worthwhile changes in a growing individual, and since modifications due to environmental influences are the only ones that can be directly observed and measured, the burden of proof as to how genetic factors hinder educational efforts should lie with the heredity school, not with the environmentalists. As he points out, a Swedish study found that the average increase in I.Q. due to length of formal schooling was between 10 and 16 I.Q. points—a decisive significance which could determine whether a student was eligible for higher education or not. By contrast, majority opinion (not necessarily correct simply because it is in the majority) among scientific circles now agrees that, within British or white American populations, about four-fifths of differences in I.Q. are of genetic origin and only one-fifth due to the environmental influences of all kinds to which the individual is exposed from conception onwards.

If this is so, then we would expect that genetic factors are bound to play a considerable role in determining an individual's class membership. In turn, therefore, what can be achieved by equality of opportunity? One of the more modest aims of the drive towards equality of opportunity has been to ensure that one's chances of success in life should not be adversely affected by being born into a lower class: and there is much evidence that success (measured in occupational status terms) is largely dependent on ability regardless of class. On the basis of established I.Q. differences between the classes (and bearing in mind that these differences are simply *averages* within very wide distributions), very few children of unskilled parents are likely to have an I.Q. which reaches the average I.Q. of the children of higher professional parents. Equally, very few children from the higher professional class will have lower I.Q.s than the average I.Q. found among the children of unskilled workers. Thus if equality of opportunity (in this modest sense) is working, it would be necessary both that a fairly large number of children changed from the class to which their parents belonged (some moving up and some down);

[22] Husen, T., *Social Background and Educational Career*, O.E.C.D., 1972.

and that, as adults, proportionately more children of upper-class than of lower-class parents found themselves in the upper classes and proportionately more children of lower-class than of upper-class parents found themselves in the lower classes.

Both of these things occur. The observed social mobility in Britain is, in fact, about 30 per cent per generation. Furthermore, both upward and downward mobility are highly correlated with the difference between the individual's I.Q. and the mean I.Q. in his parents' class. If social mobility based largely on I.Q. (though, of course, other factors are also involved) were not happening, then the phenomenon of regression to the mean[23] would soon iron out all class differences in I.Q. But individuals with high and low I.Q.s are not born at random into the different classes. That is why it is no criticism of the workings of equality of opportunity to point out that proportionately few of the children of working-class parents do well at school or get into university or obtain high incomes. This is exactly what would be expected from equality of opportunity; though no doubt inequality of opportunity between the classes exacerbates the situation.

Another, more radical interpretation of the aim of equality of opportunity is that it provides a means for eradicating the inequalities of achieved standards of life. As equality of opportunity by itself is unlikely to enable such an end to be attained, then society would have to seek alternative means if it were to sustain such a goal. One option, for instance, would involve "social engineering" on a vast scale. If some method could be found of so manipulating the child's early enviroment as to produce a radical increase in I.Q., then this treatment might be administered in inverse proportion to genetic endowment, giving more help to those with a genetically low I.Q. and deliberately denying help to those with a genetically high I.Q. While writers like Husen[24] have seriously advanced this argument, the political objections to such a course of

---

[23] Regression to the mean, which can be predicted from genetic theory, is the commonly observed fact that the average or "mean" I.Q. of children in any given social class lies halfway between the parental mean and the overall population mean of 100.

[24] Husen, T., *op. cit.* Husen's argument is that equality of opportunity in the old sense of free access to a relatively undifferentiated school system is not enough. Stress should be laid, in his view, on achieving equality of performance on the part of pupils leaving the system, and for this it would be necessary to give some pupils unequal—that is, preferential—treatment.

action are overwhelming: only an extremely authoritarian regime could prevent its most intelligent parents from offering their children the advantages being given to others. A second option would necessitate "genetic engineering", whether eugenic (controlled breeding) or molecular (physical alteration of particular genes), and the authoritarian implications of this choice are even more frightening than the first. In any case, there are sufficient genetic "accidents" (i.e., highly intelligent children born to parents of below-average I.Q.) to cast serious doubt on the possible benefits of such policies, and it ought to be recorded that intelligence is not the only quality valued by society in calculating the worth of individual citizens.

Mortality

According to the P.E.P. report, *World Population and Resources*,[25] death control should proceed hand-in-hand with birth control. But, because the former generally precedes the latter, and because death control is generally regarded as beneficial while birth control is subject to hostility from large sections of the populace, world population has been accelerating rapidly. In this country, mortality for most age groups is declining steadily, although the death rate has stabilized at around 11.8 per 1000.[26] Drugs introduced in this century (particularly the antibiotics like penicillin) have increased overall expectation of life, but eventually senescence—the rundown of the brain and heart—takes its toll.

The decline in deaths during infancy and early childhood is still proceeding. Since the turn of the century infant mortality (deaths during the first year of life) has fallen from well over 150 per 1000 live births to 18.5 in 1970. These infant deaths are concentrated in the last stages of pregnancy, at birth, and during the next few days; indeed, it is interesting to note that more infants are lost by being stillborn and by dying in the first year of life than children and adults during the next 40 years. These early mortalities are primarily caused by congenital defects, injury at birth, etc., while deaths after the first week are caused by respiratory infections, accidents, alimentary infections, all of which are

[25] *World Population and Resources*, Political and Economic Planning, London, 1955.
[26] 1974 figures. The main causes of death are diseases of the circulation, cancer and respiratory illnesses.

correlated strongly with adverse social factors and environment. Titmuss[27] showed during World War II that the relative disparity in infant mortality between the classes had hardly changed since 1911, while more up-to-date figures for Scotland[28] show the continuing persistence of these disparities. The still-birth rate is two and a half times as high in the families of unskilled workers as in those of professional men; the neonatal death rate (in the first 4 weeks of life) twice as high in the unskilled groups as in the skilled, and the post-neonatal death rate (4 weeks to 1 year) almost six times as high. Similar disparities were shown to exist for the whole of Britain in the Perinatal Mortality Survey carried out in 1958.[29] Among professional people perinatal mortality declined from 74 to 69 per cent of the national average between 1950 and 1958; among semi-skilled workers it was unchanged at 108 per cent, and among unskilled workers it increased from 118 to 128 per cent. While these figures may suggest strongly that the position is worsening for the lower classes, it has to be remembered that there has been a progressive diminution of the proportion of the population belonging to social classes IV and V in the Registrar-General's classification—partly as a result of reclassifying certain occupations, but also partly a result of genuine upward mobility—and this helps to mitigate the disparities slightly.

How can these class differences be explained in view of the free availability of health services and despite the great improvements in nutrition and housing which have taken place over the last decade or so? It has been suggested by Illsley[30] that the poorer reproductive performance of the lower social classes is due to a process of "social selection" of the healthier and more intelligent women into the higher social strata. Morris,[31] on the other hand, has pointed out that the consistent differences in rates of reproductive casualty between particular occupations within the same class may argue against this, for they would imply an almost incredible tidiness in socio-biological relationships. The Perinatal Mortality Survey[32] supports Illsley's view implicitly by showing

[27] Titmuss, R. M., *Birth, Poverty and Wealth*, Hamish Hamilton, 1943.
[28] Quoted in Arie, T., "Class and Disease", *New Society*, 27 January 1966, pp. 8–12.
[29] Butler, N. R. and Bonham, D. G., *Perinatal Mortality*, Livingstone, 1963.
[30] Illsley, R., "Environment and Childbearing", *Proceedings* of the Royal Society of Medicine, **46**, 54 (1953).
[31] Morris, J. N., *Uses of Epidemiology*, Livingstone, 1964.
[32] Butler, N. R. and Bonham, D. G., *op. cit.*

the relationship between a woman's physique and her performance in pregnancy and childbirth: perinatal mortality rises as the mother's stature declines. Moreover, the distribution of tall women (over 65 inches) varies with class, so that 41 per cent of the women in class I are regarded as "tall", while other classes average only 26 per cent. There is also a highly significant degree of self-recruitment within the professional classes and the semi-skilled/unskilled groups, with the result that women with low mortality are retained in the highest social groups and those with high mortality are drawn into the lowest groups. When it comes to shopping for medical care the non-manual classes, typically with their better education and greater knowledge of what is happening, take advantage first of what is going and benefit more from administrative and technical changes in medicine. Finally, it should be noted that surgical, medical and dental facilities are generally superior in the southern half of the British Isles, a fact which may be associated causally with the larger proportion of middle-class people in that area. It would hardly be surprising if many surgeons, doctors and dentists preferred to work in areas where the majority of their patients would be people like themselves (i.e., middle-class); nor would it be amazing if the middle class chose to gravitate to localities where health care was more readily available. The result is a framework of reciprocal causation which tends to perpetuate the very inequalities (in this instance, inequalities of infant mortality) of which society then complains.

It is certainly clear that further reduction of the infant death rate presents social as well as medical problems. Persistent environmental and educational variations are probably a major cause of this dilemma, since there is an inevitable lag between the arrival of increased prosperity and its expression in better health.[33] The authors of *Growing Up in Newcastle-upon-Tyne*[34] admit that many parents still live in unsatisfactory or over-crowded houses and suffer from personal instability or frustration; and although standards may have risen since 1960, they have risen purely in absolute and not in relative terms, with the result that the frustration has not been dissipated. It is precisely these considerations which are coming

[33] See Brown, G., "The Social Causes of Disease", in Tuckett, D., ed., *An Introduction to Medical Sociology*, Tavistock, 1976.
[34] Miller, F. J. W., Court, S. D. M., Walton, W. S. and Knox, E. G., *Growing up in Newcastle-upon-Tyne*, Oxford, 1960.

into greater prominence now that the more serious illnesses are coming under control, that primary poverty has almost disappeared, and that standards of hygiene, nutrition and education are rising.[35] Miller and his colleagues[36] argued that "the health of children and the outcome of disease are closely related to family environment". A "good" environment is specifically defined as including "a sound dwelling of sufficient size, a reasonable income wisely used, and parents who enjoy a satisfying relationship with each other and are sensitive to their children's needs". All these attributes, it will be noted, are at present most easily acquired by middle-class families. If nothing else, they generally have an income sufficient to obtain a satisfactory residence, and an income which tends to remain stable from month to month. This gives the salaried employee an inestimable advantage over his wage-paid counterpart in planning his long-term expenditure.

In childhood, death rates between the classes have narrowed much more than in infancy. Death rates from all causes at 1 to 2 years of age showed an excess in 1930–32 of over 400 per cent between classes V and I; in 1950–51 this had fallen to 63 per cent (the beginning of this improvement is already detectable in the last 3 months of the first year of life). Infectious diseases in childhood are inevitable in all social classes, but the risk of death has been considerably reduced. In the case of rheumatic heart disease, for instance, at one time an area of great discrepancy between the classes, death rates have fallen so near to zero that comparisons are meaningless. Morbidity in childhood as measured by consultation rates[37] shows clear class gradients in respect of certain diseases and conditions. Measles, bronchitis, impetigo and injuries are most common in class V, while whooping cough, asthma, some upper respiratory infections and unexplained febrile illnesses have their greatest

---

[35] If this does not seem noticeably to be the case, compare present standards with the practices reported in the 1843 *Report* of the Children's Employment Commission. In that document, the Nottingham coroner was quoted as saying that "Godfrey's Cordial", a preparation of opium given to infants to keep them quiet, was often administered on the day of birth, with the result that "a great number of infants perish . . . Those who escape with life become pale and sickly children, often half idiotic, and always with a ruined constitution".

[36] Miller, F. J. W., Court, S. D. M., Walton, W. S. and Knox, E. G., *op. cit.*

[37] Logan, W. P. D. and Cushion, A. A., *Morbidity Statistics from General Practice*, H.M.S.O., 1958–62.

incidence in class I. The cohort survey undertaken by Douglas, by contrast, found little social class difference in the proportions of children having the common childhood infections, but poorer children were more likely to be admitted to hospital or to die.[38]

The falling death rate from childhood diseases has only emphasized the number of permanent disabilities and handicaps left by these same conditions. The frequency of deformities like mental deficiency, deafness, defects of vision and so on is higher in homes where the income is either inadequate or irregular or both, where the parents are ignorant of their responsibilities, and where the very multiplicity of children makes it impossible for any single sufferer to be granted enough attention. Such homes belong almost invariably to members of the lower social classes, although their numbers are declining with increasing standards of education and literacy, the dissemination of child-care knowledge through the media of child welfare clinics, periodicals, broadcasting and the press, to say nothing of advances in medical facilities and techniques. The State provides family allowances to help maintain the child; pre-natal and post-natal care are readily available. Far from diminishing the family's responsibilities in this direction, however, the State agencies have supplemented the family's primary concern for the health of its members, so that families if anything are faced with more exacting demands, and have themselves generated higher expectations.

Of course, not all parents conform with this pattern. The National Food Survey,[39] for example, drew attention to the inadequate diets of large poorer families. There is little overt malnutrition as such but considerable evidence of "sub-clinical" deficiency states and unrealized potential for growth. In 1939, a similar situation had been widely publicized when the foster parents of evacuated children had complained of the bad feeding habits of their charges. They would not sit down to eat, did not use cutlery, and preferred to eat white bread, margarine and cheap jam seated on a doorstep, or fish and chips from a newspaper. They demanded pickles, ice-cream, biscuits and sweets, strong tea and beer. They were unaccustomed to green vegetables, soup, puddings and salad. Some said they had never seen their mothers cook, and had no hot meals at home. What became clear—then as now—was that the prime cause

[38] Douglas, J. W. B. and Blomfield, J. M., *Children Under Five*, Allen & Unwin, 1958.
[39] Lambert, R., *Nutrition in Britain 1950–60*, Codicote Press, 1964.

of malnutrition and of poor diet was ignorance even more than poverty, because some of the most wholesome, nutritive foods such as herring, cheese and green vegetables were within the financial reach of all. The contemporary tendency of young mothers to rely upon frozen and tinned foods, and packaged meals, probably has some association with their difficulties in managing household budgets, and remains therefore—together with continued ignorance of what constitutes a healthy diet—one of the root causes of family misery.

Equally the problem of (avoidable) physical ill-health among children has by no means been solved. Vermin—especially pediculosis or lousiness—provides an instructive example. Along with overcrowded conditions in which children tend to stay up or awake until the adults retire, lice, scabies, bedbugs, fleas, and associated skin diseases are deterrents to sleep and hence to rest and good health. Of the poorer child population of 10 large towns in 1940 it was reckoned that 40 per cent had head lice or nits, and that children under 5 were the most infested. In one city two out of every three girls of school age and between 5 and 13 per cent of the women were lousy. Some 23 per cent of the evacuees to East Suffolk were found to be verminous in contrast to 2 per cent of the indigenous children. Although the number of children found to be verminous in 1969 was 194,000 (less than a quarter of the figure in 1926), the significant factor is that infestation nowadays is more than ever a "family disease", occurring mainly in houses without modern facilities and where parents are inadequate. Such family diseases remain hard to deal with, especially where people share the same sheets[40]—indeed, with some conditions there has been an alarming rise in the number of cases, perhaps provoked by the appearance of insecticide-resistant strains among the bacteria themselves. For example, the 38,577 scabious schoolchildren recorded in 1947 had fallen to a mere 2650 10 years later. In 1967, though, the School Health Service treated well over 11,000, and there was a fourfold increase between 1965 and 1969 when the figure reached over 17,000.

With death rates in adult life the class differentials are once more restored, as the following table demonstrates. According to *Occupational*

---

[40] It is relevant to note that various Medical Officers of Health have remarked upon the comparative cleanliness of West Indian immigrants and others from the Commonwealth who still exercise more parental control and community discipline.

TABLE 1.1. The Class Distinctions of Disease

Cause of death	Unskilled	Semi-skilled	Skilled	Managerial	Professional
ALL CAUSES	+43	+3	Average	−19	−24
Tuberculosis	+85	+8	−4	−43	−60
Stomach cancer	+63	+14	+1	−37	−51
Lung cancer	+48	+4	+7	−28	−37
Coronary disease	+12	−4	+6	−5	−2
Bronchitis	+94	+16	−3	−50	−72
Duodenal ulcer	+73	+7	−4	−25	−52

This table gives the increased or decreased risk—in percentage terms—of a man from each of the five main social classes dying from certain causes. The particular work he does is not the main contributory factor as similar differences of risk exist for wives of men in these categories. Diet and lifestyle, however, are major influences.

Mortality 1970–72 (H.M.S.O., 1978), the son of a professional man can expect on average to live more than 5 years longer than the child of an unskilled worker. To put it another way, while one-third of all unskilled workers die before retirement age, just over three-quarters of professional men live to collect their pension. Not only does life expectancy increase as one moves up the social spectrum, but also causes of death themselves are not distributed evenly throughout society. Conditions which predominate among unskilled labourers include the common respiratory infections (influenza, pneumonia, bronchitis), rheumatic heart disease, tuberculosis, syphilis, stomach cancer and (for women) cancer of the cervix. The opposite trend, with highest mortality in the upper social groups, appears in coronary heart disease, leukemia, poliomyelitis, cirrhosis of the liver, benign and malignant hyperplasis of the prostate and (in women) cancer of the breast. Some of these associations are not particularly surprising, such as the fact that urban mortality rates for chronic bronchitis are higher than rural figures. It is interesting, however, that even if air pollution is held constant, there is still an association along class lines: agricultural labourers have a higher certified mortality than farmers.

In particular the high mortality from coronary heart disease within class I has been the subject of considerable study, as more than twice as many men die of coronary heart disease in middle age as from lung cancer. The certified death rate from coronary heart disease has risen from about 20 per 100,000 men in the 55–64 age group in the 1920s to the present level of about 600 per 100,000, though changes in ability to recognize the condition and in fashions of diagnosis must partly account for the trend. Detailed investigation of possible causes suggests that an important factor may be the nature of men's work, which distinguishes the experience not only of the social classes from each other, but also of husbands from wives (and women have a very low incidence of coronary heart disease). It is possible that the social class gradient for mortality through coronary heart disease is largely attributable to the variation in physical activity required by different jobs. Thus the higher a man's social class, the less physically active his work is likely to be. If the Registrar-General's mortality figures are analysed by degree of physical activity in the occupations of the men who died, the social class gradient virtually disappears; in other words, the apparent relationship with social class is masking a much more significant relationship with physical activity.

Old age is a biological term rather than a social category, yet in some ways retirement is a relatively new phenomenon in British society. It is only since the 1946 National Insurance Act that compulsory retirement at the age of 65 has begun to be regarded as the norm for male workers. Many men continue to work after reaching 65, but this kind of provision (where it occurs in organisations as opposed to the self-employed) invariably meets with criticism from younger men whose promotions are accordingly postponed. Currently, the tendency is for the age of retirement to be reduced still further, to 60 or even 55, perhaps with the flexibility of voluntary departures. Such arrangements have proved particularly advantageous in cases of corporate mergers or as means of avoiding large-scale redundancies, but they take very little account of the possible readiness with which the individuals concerned face retirement.

The evidence suggests that this preparedness varies enormously and is not necessarily more prominent in the managerial, executive and professional sectors. One study of 101 retired men[41] showed that 30 per cent regarded retirement as "somewhat unsatisfying" or "very unsatisfying", and that this percentage included an abnormally large proportion of

[41] Beveridge, W. E., "How worthwhile is retirement?", *New Society*, 3 June 1965.

semi-skilled and unskilled workers. Yet retirement can be just as damaging for the executive who has been highly successful, wrapped up in his work, and deriving almost all his social contacts from colleague relationships.[42] When the retired men in the above survey were asked what they missed most of all in no longer being at work, 75 mentioned the companionship of the workplace. Money was stressed by 27; 20 quoted factors connected with the nature of their jobs; and 14 mentioned the satisfaction of leading a regular kind of life. Income was important not only for its own sake but also because it enabled them to satisfy certain social needs and sustain their self-respect. "To have money was to be able to hold their heads high, to remain on an equal footing with their friends, to be independent. To be short of money was to be forced to recognize their dependence on others, to lose their dignity as men."[43] Similar results were observed in a Nuffield Foundation study of 507 men aged between 55 and 70 in the Slough area: "The essential need . . . was for some occupation. The difficulty was that few of them seemed to conceive that an unpaid occupation could yield a satisfaction equal to that of paid employment. Paid employment was to them more than the money involved; it gave them status and made them feel part of the community."[44]

If retired men feel the desire to obtain a paid job, their opportunities for doing so clearly vary according to the occupations they have performed in their working lives. Many skilled men are capable of finding useful and interesting jobs after retirement, but semi-skilled and unskilled categories have more problems because they have less to offer a potential employer. Managerial and professional men are frequently faced with an unacceptable lowering of sights in paid employment that forces them either to embrace the benefits of retirement more wholeheartedly or to find satisfaction in unpaid, voluntary service as, say, a Justice of the Peace or a Commissioner of Inland Revenue. Much depends on the stereotyped belief among employers that older people are too slow (and have worse sickness absence records), though even if this were true it does

---

[42] The Ford Motor Company has an old-established voluntary retirement scheme under which individuals can leave at age 55 with 53 per cent of full pension, up to 93 per cent of full pension at age 64. While more and more employees opt for one of the earlier alternatives, hardly any member of the management or senior staff has done so. See Wilsher, P., "Another Life at 55", *Sunday Times*, 9 January 1966.

[43] Beveridge, W. E., *op. cit.*

[44] *Workers Nearing Retirement*, Nuffield Foundation, 1963.

not necessarily mean that they are inefficient. In practice older workers tend to establish a steady routine so that in the long run their output may well be higher than that of younger men. World War II, when the percentage of employed persons aged over 65 more than doubled, revealed conclusively that the so-called disabilities of old age are largely imaginary. Rowntree's study of the subject, published in 1947, stated that only in very few cases was it found necessary to alter piece-rates or pay older workers lower hourly rates on grounds of their low productivity. If any adjustment on account of age was necessary it usually took the form of lighter work rather than reduced working hours. The Slough survey[45] confirms these observations empirically by showing that only a small proportion of the 507 men in the sample were still employed on production, and some of these had gradually been confined to more limited and specialized operations. At least half of them were engaged on building repairs, floor cleaning and the clearing and disposal of scrap—jobs where their relative slowness would be less crucial to the performance of the enterprise.

Instead of seeking out ways to supply retired people with paid jobs, however, it would perhaps be more productive to examine the problem of making retirement itself a more satisfying experience. To be done properly, this would entail the provision of a transition and adjustment period between the end of work and the beginning of retirement.[46] At the present time, according to Beveridge, "There seems a natural reluctance to face up to the necessity for retirement because it means to some the end of real life. Society has offered them few satisfactions apart from work and, when society proposes suddenly to take away their work and its satisfactions, they can think of little else to live for."[47]

---

[45] *Workers Nearing Retirement, op. cit.*

[46] Some companies already do this. At Michelin's Staffordshire works, everybody is allowed to taper off their work commitments during the final months of their working lives, during which they reduce their attendance to four, three, two and finally only one nominal day per week. Joseph Newsome at Dewsbury uses a particularly interesting variation on this pattern for its management staff whereby every senior man's last 2 years of office are split into four 6-month periods. In the first of these he gets two extra weeks retirement leave in addition to his normal holiday; in the second, 3 weeks; in the third, his successor is formally appointed and his work load is reduced to 4 days; in the final period his successor takes full responsibility and the retiring manager assumes the role of consultant on a 3-day week basis.

[47] Beveridge, W. E., *op. cit.*

How well are old people cared for? A good deal of assistance is now provided by the State or by agencies working under the supervision of local authorities—old people's bungalows and flats, meals-on-wheels, and pensions themselves with supplementary benefits. The provision of these services has led to the familiar charge that families no longer feel responsible for looking after their aged dependants. As a consequence, old people feel neglected and discarded, a feeling which is unmercifully accentuated by their enforced retirement at 65 when they are still reasonably fit and active. That this is a general view about the position of the old in industrial society is shown by the fact that it even appeared in an essay by Talcott Parsons.[48] Parsons compares the typical "conjugal family" of industrialization with the extended kinship systems characteristic of primitive or peasant societies. In the "conjugal family", young adults live with their spouse and dependent children in social units from which the elderly parents are excluded. "This situation", says Parsons, "is in strong contrast to kinship systems in which membership in a kinship unit is continuous throughout the life cycle. There, very frequently, it is the oldest members who are treated with the most respect and have the greatest responsibility and authority. But with us there is no one left to respect them, for them to take responsibility for or have authority over."

While there is some truth in the observations made by Parsons, many of his conclusions have been vitiated so far as Britain is concerned by the research of Jeremy Tunstall into the actual condition of old people.[49] Parsons, for example, argues that the older generation is structurally (as well as psychologically) isolated from married children. Yet Tunstall's figures show that if one looks at widowed old people only—those for whom social isolation is a real threat—47 per cent of widowed old people in Britain live in a household with a child. Of all old people with any children alive, 89 per cent have a child living within 1 hour's journey.

In practice, too, it is essential to define precisely what is meant by the "aloneness" experienced among old people. Tunstall identifies four possible interpretations:

[48] Parsons, T., *Family Socialization and Interaction Process*, Routledge & Kegan Paul, 1956.
[49] Tunstall, J., *Old and Alone*, Routledge & Kegan Paul, 1966.

1. *Living alone,* in accordance with the Census definition of a one-person household;

2. *Social isolation,* based on a scoring system of "social contacts" over a weekly period, to give each person a social contact score;[50]

3. *Loneliness,* a self-ascribed category; and

4. *Anomie,* roughly defined as "a sense of hopelessness".[51]

From Tunstall's sample of 538 old men and women, it was clear that the vast majority of old people in private households live with other people. Only 22 per cent live literally alone, while the size of the group described as "socially isolated" was three-quarters as large. Nineteen per cent of the group were found to be highly anomic and only 9 per cent appeared to experience frequent symptoms of loneliness. Thus if Tunstall's categories of aloneness are taken one by one, four-fifths of old people are not alone. On the other hand, the proportion of old people living alone is almost certainly increasing—partly as a result of personal choice of old people and partly because of an increased supply of housing, including special housing for old people. These one-person households are characteristically composed of childless widows and single women (men are encountered less frequently in one-person households because their life expectancy is less), whereas widows who have had children during marriage are more likely to find security, social contacts and possibly even a home with the families of their offspring.

At one time, the static and even declining numbers of old people in institutions were cited as further evidence of the fact that the modern family is fully prepared to accept its responsibilities in caring for the old. Abel-Smith and Pinker, for instance, have pointed out that "Despite much higher standards of social welfare, much smaller families, and above all a lengthening of life among the "institutionally prone, society was not carrying a larger institutional burden in 1951 than in 1911."[52] Such arguments are currently much less reliable as it is now established

[50] This method was first used by Peter Townsend in Bethnal Green. See Townsend, P., *The Family Life of Old People,* Routledge & Kegan Paul, 1958.

[51] See Srole, L., "Social integration and certain corollaries", *American Sociological Review,* December 1956.

[52] Abel-Smith, B. and Pinker, R., *Changes in the Use of Institutions in England and Wales Between 1911 and 1951,* Paper to the Manchester Statistical Society, 10 February 1960.

social policy to favour domiciliary care rather than institutionalization, with the result that the numbers in institutions have automatically fallen —but for reasons unconnected with family cohesion. Whatever the figures say, however, there is much that remains to be done—in the formal provision of housing equipped to meet the needs of elderly people, in preparation and adjustment for retirement itself—before old age ceases to bear its stigma of decrepitude and negativism, and becomes a phase of positive fulfilment.[53]

The Effects of Immigration

One of the major changes in the British population structure since the 1950s has been the vast influx of immigrants, particularly from the Commonwealth and from Ireland. The 1966 sample Census estimated that up to that time there had been 942,310 Commonwealth immigrants and 879,530 immigrants from Ireland.[54] Since 1966 the rate of inflow to the United Kingdom has fallen drastically, though people from the "new" Commonwealth and Pakistan have formed a higher proportion of the population, rising from 2.6 per cent in mid-1970 to 3.3 per cent in 1975. Immigration only counted for nearly half the increase, while the rest derived from births among immigrant families. In 1970 only 30,000 Commonwealth citizens were admitted to settle in Britain (of whom

---

[53] If it is any comfort, the alleged respect accorded to old people in primitive societies (and endorsed by Talcott Parsons) has little basis in fact. In many such societies old age scarcely exists if it is defined as beginning at 65, but even if one defines the old in a non-literate society as simply the oldest people alive, the picture is still hardly one of universal respect. Simmons has analysed the status of elderly people in 71 primitive societies (Simmons, L., *The Role of the Aged in Primitive Society*, Yale University Press, 1945) and has found a whole spectrum of situations, ranging from complete control and power on the one hand to degradation and even death on the other. One relevant factor is that patterns of life expectancy in primitive societies are similar to those in industrialized nations; thus women live longer. Old women in primitive societies tend to fare badly: they have little prestige, they may become scapegoats and stand accused of witchcraft, or are even killed by young male relatives (in the case of the Labrador Eskimo) if unable to keep up with the group.

[54] The Commonwealth immigrants included 267,850 from the Caribbean, 232,210 from India (including "white" immigrants), 73,150 from Pakistan, 59,190 from Cyprus, 88,510 from Africa (including "white" immigrants) and 155,310 from the "white" Commonwealth. The Irish comprised 674,560 from Southern Ireland, 179,930 from Northern Ireland, and 24,040 for whom place of birth had not been ascertained.

some 23,000 were dependants of Commonwealth citizens already resident in Britain), while in the same year there was a net *emigration* of 75,000 United Kingdom citizens to Commonwealth countries. Mass immigration ended after the Commonwealth Immigrants Act of 1962, but the accompanying table shows how the number of coloured people in the population has continued to increase, primarily as a result of an excess of births over deaths.

As the figures suggest, Britain is now coping with the emergence of second-generation coloured populations whose attitudes to the facilities provided for them by British society may be less obviously compliant than those of their parents. "If first-generation immigrants have been bitter about discrimination, second-generation immigrants may be more bitter. Many may be driven into deviant behaviour of all kinds. At the same time British society will be experiencing technological change at an unprecedented rate, creating new problems of adjustment and new tensions. Colour distinctions will add to these special educational, industrial and social difficulties."[55] It is a mistake to think that the longer the coloured immigrant has been at work in Britain, the more likely he is to have caught up with the indigenous population (in financial and status terms). On the contrary, whereas both first- and second-generation immigrants may be exploited at work and elsewhere, what the second-generation immigrant possesses, which puts his resentment into an enhanced category, is the acute *consciousness* of being exploited, as his reference groups are drawn from the immediate neighbourhood rather than from some obscure and far-distant country of origin. As an indication of the basis for resentment, for instance, it may be sufficient to say that although unemployment increased two and a half times between November 1973 and February 1976, within minority groups it increased more than four times.

Immigrants are not distributed evenly throughout the country. The Irish, for example, form over 1.9 of the total population in Britain, but over two-thirds of the constituencies have less than this proportion; at the other end of the scale, 10 per cent of the constituencies have at least 3.7 per cent each. The concentration of immigrants from the "new" Commonwealth is even greater, focussing particularly on London and the

[55] Social Science Research Council, press release to announce the formation of a Race Relations Research Unit at the University of Bristol, December 1969.

TABLE 1.2. Mid-year Estimates of the Population of New Commonwealth and Pakistani ethnic Origin, Great Britain, 1966–75 (in thousands)

	1966–67	1967–68	1968–69	1969–70	1970–71	1971–72	1972–73	1973–74	1974–75
Population at start of period	1016	1103	1217	1320	1411	1501	1583	1673	1744
Births	+45	+47	+50	+52	+52	+49	+47	+45	+44
Deaths	−3	−3	−4	−4	−4	−4	−5	−5	−5
Natural increase	+42	+44	+46	+48	+48	+45	+42	+40	+39
Migration	+45	+70	+57	+43	+42	+37	+48	+31	+32
Change in year	+87	+114	+103	+91	+90	+82	+90	+71	+71
Population at end of year	1103	1217	1320	1411	1501	1583	1673	1744	1815
% of home population at end of period	2.1	2.3	2.5	2.6	2.8	2.9	3.1	3.2	3.3

Midlands. It is interesting to note (as the following table demonstrates) that in some of these areas a very high proportion of immigrants own their own homes when compared with the indigenous population.

TABLE 1.3. Total households (absolute numbers) and Owner-occupiers (percentages) for four areas with high immigrant population (1971).

	Total households		Owner-occupiers (%)	
	Coloured	Non-coloured	Coloured	Non-coloured
Wolverhampton	5895	81,329	65.7	39.9
Manchester	5861	178,879	48.3	33.0
Bradford	5561	94,446	72.5	54.4
Leicester	5101	90,391	76.5	43.4

Two main patterns of male immigration have been isolated. A male works in Britain in order to send money to his family in another country, eventually returning to that country himself; or he comes first to Britain to establish himself financially, saving enough money to pay for his dependants to join him. Consistent with both of these views is the fact that the number of married men exceeds the number of married women in most immigrant groups (though not in the case of the Irish). Clearly the motives of the immigrant will determine, to a large extent, the success of any moves towards assimilation into British society; in recent years an explicit policy of assimilation seems to have been discarded precisely because of its inadequate appreciation of this fundamental point. Furthermore, assimilative theory seemed to assume that the coloured population was a homogeneous collection of individuals. In practice distinctions have to be drawn not only between different nationalities and ethnic groups, but also within these between castes, classes and occupations, and between individuals, families and types of community group. A study of second-generation Punjabis in Coventry, for example, could discover none who had married an English girl. Many young workers handed over their entire wage packets to their parents, who bought land in India, thus cementing the children's ties with that country. Contrary to what one might expect, too, this survey[56] also found that the better educated Indians were the ones more likely to

[56] Reported in *The Sunday Times*, 11 January 1976.

conform to the traditional way of life. More generally, Rose[57] has shown that the pattern of group formations among British coloureds is changing rapidly and in different directions among West Indians, Indians, Pakistanis and Cypriots, as well as between the first and second generation of immigrants. It is also equally possible, as Banton[58] suggests, that the assimilative readiness of the host society is changing as the immigration perspective becomes less appropriate and is replaced by a racial perspective.

Natural increase is high among most immigrant communities, the reason chiefly being that people who emigrate generally do so during their reproductive years. The adult non-white British are almost all first-generation immigrants: 92 per cent of them entered the country between 1964 and 1976, and not more than 4 per cent were born in Britain. Most of them are aged between 16 and 35, which partly accounts for their large number of child dependants—although another factor is that they have come from countries with higher fertility rates than those in Britain. There has been a slight decline in the birth rate among non-whites since 1970, and their fertility rates may eventually fall into line with the white population as their age-structure begins to match that of the indigenous British and they come to take on prevailing social values. Meanwhile, the bulge in the coloured population is likely to continue. A further contribution to this process is the evening-out of any imbalances between the sexes as more female dependants arrive.[59] Among the Irish, many of whom are Roman Catholic, religious background rather than age is probably a major element in fertility rates. Taking the 1966 birth rate figures for London and Birmingham alone, for instance, the Irish had an average of 2.52 children per family, the West Indians 2.43, the Pakistanis 2.30. At 42 per cent, the Irish had the highest percentage of families with three or more children (compared with 36 per cent of Indian families, 35 per cent for West Indians and 34 per cent for Pakistanis). Overall, Irish fertility exceeded that of the total population by 77 per cent.

There is overwhelming evidence that the coloured population in Britain suffers discrimination on grounds of colour in employment,

---

[57] Rose, E. J. B., *et al.*, *Colour and Citizenship*, Oxford University Press, 1969.
[58] Banton, M., *Race Relations*, Tavistock, 1967.
[59] In 1976, 65 per cent of Pakistani adults in Britain were male.

housing, leisure activities and over the whole range of their social relationships. And, as Halsey[60] has noted, "Differences in power and advantage, whether based on colour or any other socially evaluated attribute, tend to be generalized and to be transmitted between generations. They therefore form systems of social stratification which are highly resistant to change." There is no evidence that the job levels or the incomes of West Indians or Asians living in Britain are rising to produce parity with white employees. Long-established immigrants do not have higher job levels than recent arrivals, so it cannot be argued that those who have been in Britain longer can progress up the job scale. Of course, to some extent this is an inevitable consequence of the unskilled jobs which most coloured immigrants occupy, as there is little promotion from unskilled jobs anyway.

The number of dependants in Asian and West Indian households to every wage-earner (even though extended families of different generations, usual in India and Pakistan, with grandparents, parents and grandchildren living together in the same accommodation, are less common in Britain) means that even if non-white workers were to earn the same as whites (which they do not), they would still be poorer, as their wages would have to be used to support a larger number of people. This disability, if it can be so described, is compounded by the fact that many Asians in particular have a limited command of the English language.[61] As a result, they tend to have the worst jobs and accommodation, located in decayed inner-city areas, where they can feel secure among others like themselves. Culturally, they are enclosed and cut off from the indigenous whites, and can have a viable existence only within their own communities.

A higher proportion of Indian men are at work than is the case in the white population, but that is entirely due to the age structure. Among West Indian women there is a much higher number going out to work than among native whites: something like three-quarters compared with half. This is the case despite the fact that most West Indians are in the child-bearing age group and have young dependent children. Among

---

[60] Halsey, A. H., "Race relations: the lines to think on", *New Society*, 19 March 1970.

[61] About half can speak English reasonably well, but only a third do so fluently. Males show a greater propensity to learn and speak English than females, perhaps because, for males, there is a greater necessity to do so.

Asians, on the other hand, Muslim women are not likely to go out to work because of cultural customs, although they may work at home. Other Asian women go out to work about as often as white women. Patterns of employment, however, show that for both Asians and West Indians job levels are much lower than among whites. West Indians supply very few non-manual workers and almost none in the professions and in management; Asians are predominantly concentrated in semi-skilled and unskilled jobs. Although there are fewer Asians than West Indians doing skilled work in the middle range of jobs, there are far more doing non-manual work. Generally, Asians have lower job levels than West Indians and whites, but a greater number are at each end of the jobs range and fewer than West Indians in the middle. Average incomes are usually lower than whites, and it is only by doing shift work that non-white workers can raise their earnings to the lowest level that white people get. One further fact worth noting is that the proportion of Asians who are self-employed is the same as that for the indigenous population, but the Asians tend principally to be running small shops and restaurants, whereas the white self-employed have a much wider range of jobs, such as law or accountancy.

It has already been noted that many immigrants (especially Asians) are owner-occupiers when compared with the whites. Intolerable private rented accommodation, difficulty in obtaining council houses and the need to have large homes in which to house extended families, were factors which forced Asians into buying old houses in rundown areas. Because West Indians arrived first in Britain, they were able to get on to council housing lists at a time when pressure was less; but both they and Asians typically wait longer for council accommodation than the whites —and when they are rehoused, it is often in inferior buildings, or on poor estates with older houses and located at a greater distance from shops and other facilities. In the private sector, the range of houses available to immigrants is often narrow, and they often find it impossible to obtain mortgages. As a result the non-whites (particularly Asians, once again) buy property informally from friends and relatives, a method which stretches financial resources to the limit. They can afford to buy only the cheapest accommodation, and they cannot afford to pay for improvements. The corollary is that white people tend not to buy housing in black areas, and some may deliberately move if non-whites begin to move in, the result being the emergence of separate, "closed" communities.

Brooks[62] has written a particularly interesting analysis of the problems of adaptation and assimilation for coloured workers in London Transport, and his study to some extent contradicts the general picture of discrimination in employment which is often taken for granted in the context of immigrants. The core of the book consists of detailed reviews of the work situation and relationships between white and coloured workers, crews and passengers, and crews and supervisors, in three departments within London Transport—central buses, the railway operating department and the permanent way department. At the time of the fieldwork (1965–67), the three employed nearly 40,000 operatives and supervisors, of whom some 7000 were coloured immigrants, mostly West Indians. In all three departments, white native workers had voiced their opposition to and resentment of the employment of coloured immigrants, which began in the late 1950s. Opposition had apparently been comparatively muted in permanent way, where status considerations were of less concern, more widespread in railway operating, and perhaps most intense in central buses, although strike action had been threatened only in one or two garages. Colour was the most frequently mentioned reason for objections, followed by fears that wages, conditions and standards would be threatened.

The author emphasizes that it was not so much relative numbers as the rate of build-up of immigrant numbers which was important in conditioning the native response. According to Brooks, there is probably an optimum rate of build-up of coloured immigrants in a work force (i.e., slow rather than fast) varying according to the traditions and culture of the organization, the skills and other attributes of the newcomers, the tasks to be learned and performed, and the technical and social organization for these tasks. While the traditional ethos and status consciousness of most public services would be likely to produce an adverse reaction to the employment of any identifiable group of outsiders (including women on the buses), in many respects London Transport has proved particularly well suited to the absorption of minority groups. Brooks emphasizes the importance of the bureaucratic nature of the larger organization,

[62] Brooks, D., *Race and Labour in London Transport*, Oxford University Press, 1975.

with procedures which tend to be impersonal and thus not to discriminate; the centralized recruitment system; the need for some formal training of recruits; the disciplinary procedure—all these maintained standards and reduced the possibility of arbitrary behaviour. The anti-discriminatory tendency of formal procedures also emerged in the important area of promotion, where the most serious ethnic discrimination is often to be found in industry as a whole. In railway operating in particular, the use of the impersonal seniority criterion as an important mechanism in the career pattern has worked in favour of immigrants. On the buses, on the other hand, the usual promotional step from bus crew to inspector presented problems because of the specific nature of the inspector's job—isolated and potentially conflict-provoking in relations with both public and bus crews. It was not until 1968 that London Transport appointed any West Indian bus inspectors (possibly as a result of the impending extension of the Race Relations Act).

Rose[63] has shown that immigrant children generally have poorer educational performance (with all that this implies for later life chances) than indigenous children. Coloured children, even with a full British schooling, have distributions which are negatively skewed on all measures of school attainment and, what is more, they do worse the more they are concentrated in predominantly working-class districts, as they are. In the Sparkbrook area of Birmingham, for example, 1964 figures revealed that well under a half of the population was English-born, almost a quarter were Irish, and almost a third were from the coloured Commonwealth.[64] Trevor Burgin's study of Huddersfield, *Spring Grove*,[65] about the first school in Britain to contain more than 50 per cent of coloured immigrants, makes a strong case for keeping the proportion of immigrants in any school below half, and preferably below one-third, in order to avoid the ghetto-like effects of the existing situation with its poor prospects for assimilation or even mild adaptation to the norms of British society.

A more detailed, large-sample report on the problems encountered in

[63] Rose, E. J. B., *op. cit.*

[64] Rex, J. and Moore, R., *Race, Community and Conflict*, Oxford University Press (for the Institute of Race Relations), 1967.

[65] Burgin, T. and Edson, P., *Spring Grove*, Oxford University Press (for the Institute of Race Relations), 1967.

multi-racial schools[66] showed that even the official statistics were inadequate on the number of immigrants actually in the schools. As defined in 1972, an immigrant pupil born in the United Kingdom remained an immigrant only until his parents had been in the country for 10 years. A proper count would have added 57,000 to the 1971 provisional total of 271,000 immigrants in schools in England and Wales. For one primary school and nursery with over 600 children, Townsend and Brittan found 200 "definition" but 300 "non-definition" immigrant children. However the term "immigrant" is defined, it appeared that coloured children were likely to be 1 or even 2 years behind their white English contemporaries by the age of 16 or 17—even though twice the proportion of immigrants stayed on at school beyond the minimum leaving age. Townsend and Brittan offer some convincing explanations for this phenomenon. First, more than half of the immigrant pupils had a mother tongue which was not English, and schools did make special arrangements to teach English to such children. But "Many schools end their special arrangements at too early a stage, when competence has been achieved at a conversational level" even though this is not enough to cope with secondary education. Second, it was found that many schools placed children with language difficulties in classes with retarded non-immigrant pupils, with unsurprising results for the standards achieved by the immigrants. Third, the authors singled out West Indians as the immigrant group with which most discipline problems arose—partly because they took advantage of a more relaxed regime in school than the stern disciplinary approach taken at home. Fourth is the fact that home–school relations involving coloured parents tend to be sporadic and ineffective. Many schools reported problems with Asian mothers, most of whom spoke little or no English; and most secondary schools reported that they saw less than one in ten of the Indian and Pakistani parents even once a year.[67]

[66] Townsend, H. E. R. and Brittan, E. M., *Organization in Multiracial Schools*, National Foundation for Educational Research, 1972.

[67] Only a minority of schools have attempted to improve communication links with immigrant parents by, for example, sending out information in languages other than English. One school, according to Townsend and Brittan, had been enterprising enough to advertise school functions at the local Indian cinema.

As to the origins of racial prejudice itself, Leach[68] argues that in any human society in which social stratification develops to produce a privileged ruling class lording it over an underprivileged working class, then the ruling class is likely to develop mating patterns which would have the effect—if consistently followed—of turning the members of that class into an inbred aristocracy, incipiently "a race apart". In practice, such endogamous conventions often have little practical effect, perhaps because too many individuals manage to break the rules. But where such rules exist—that is, wherever there is a convention that the aristocracy should be endogamous—then this constitutes a potential seedbed for racial prejudice. Whether the potential becomes actual depends on further factors which are not fully understood. According to Leach, the probabilities seem to be that if, on account of some recent pattern of immigration (or other historical circumstances such as slavery, colonization, or conquest), any substantial section of the subordinate working-class group is readily distinguishable in appearance from their rulers—either because of customs concerning clothing or because of real physical difference—then that visible subordinate group is likely to become the target of race prejudice on the part of the rest of society. The social effects of the prejudice, which may or may not be fully perceived by those who exercise it, is to inhibit the social mobility of those against whom the prejudice is directed and to ensure that they remain an identifiable group "at the bottom of the stack".

Anatomical difference is a convenient rather than a necessary component of race prejudice. There have been many historical instances in which the focus of hostility was a difference of custom rather than a more conspicuous difference of physique, such as skin colour. But in any situation of race prejudice, the essential idea is always that the subordinate group constitutes "a breed apart". If it so happens that the members of the group in question actually look different physically, then this provides a focus ready made and makes it all the easier to preserve the prejudice. Whether the prejudice eventually dissipates itself through social integration or is perpetuated indefinitely from generation to generation depends on the structure of the social system as a whole rather

[68] Leach, E., in Ebbins, F. J., ed., *Racial Variation in Man*, Institute of Biology and Blackwell Scientific Publications, 1975.

than on the continued existence of any visible stigma; and also on whether the social system seeks deliberately to control, inhibit or even to exploit the existence of prejudice.

Several surveys have suggested that since race prejudice derives from ignorance, then the prejudice could be dispelled by increasing social contacts with members of other races. Other researchers have argued that contact may even increase conflict, particularly between a dominant native group and a substantial and rapidly growing minority. This latter view is supported in some research carried out by Taysir Kawwa[69] among British children living in Islington (with a large immigrant community) and Lowestoft, which at the time had practically no immigrants at all. The results demonstrated clearly that the likelihood of conflict between racial groups is in proportion to two factors: the size of the minority population and the speed of its growth. A subsidiary observation was that the London children were slightly more prejudiced against Cypriots than against black people, a fact which may be explained partly in terms of the cultural and linguistic barriers which exist in the case of Cypriot children.

Yet the existence of race prejudice, and the empirical evidence of inferior treatment and life-chances (which applies to the working class in general and not merely to immigrants), do not by themselves generate social conflict. Goldthorpe[70] has already drawn attention to the surprising paradox of gross inequality coexisting alongside a high degree of political consensus, and perhaps the best explanation for this curious phenomenon has been produced by Runciman.[71] The real determinants of behaviour, according to Runciman, are not actual but rather *relative* deprivation: if people feel themselves to be deprived in some way, it is because they compare themselves unfavourably with some relatively (in their eyes) advantaged group. Runciman is able to show that reference groups, especially among the working class, have been limited in scope to those nearest in the scale of stratification. In other words, a manual

[69] Kawwa, T., *British Journal of Social and Clinical Psychology*, Vol. 7, No. 3, p. 161, 1968.

[70] Goldthorpe, J., "Social inequality and social integration in Britain", *Advancement of Science*, December 1969.

[71] Runciman, W. G., *Relative Deprivation and Social Justice: A Study of Attitudes to Social Inequality in the 20th Century*, Routledge & Kegan Paul, 1966.

worker tends to compare himself with his workmates or neighbours, rather than with the rich. Whether or not the presence of a significant coloured minority could eventually disturb this pattern is not entirely clear. As Halsey[72] points out, very little is known about the motivation of coloured people and in particular the nature of their reference groups, and much that is currently written about the subject tends to be polemical speculation rather than objective analysis.

Nowhere are polemics more evident than in discussion of the eventual proportion of coloured immigrants in the total population of the United Kingdom. Despite emotive talk of a "flood" and a major threat to established cultural patterns, the fact is that on present policies, coloured immigration on any scale will end shortly after 1990. The coloured population will rise from 1.9 millions today to about 3.3 millions by the end of the century, and then remain a roughly constant 6 per cent of the total population. To assert this is, admittedly, to indulge in a forecasting exercise incorporating some scope for error, but on the other hand the forecast is based on reasonably reliable demographic techniques.

The table below, for instance, shows how many immigrants were allowed to settle in Britain in 1976. These figures reveal a picture of immigration at a well-recognized state in a migration cycle, the two components of which are, firstly, the number of immigrants still to come and, secondly, the number of children that will be born to them after they arrive. The migration cycle of the West Indians, now complete, had the customary three stages. In the first, lasting from the mid-1950s to the early 1960s, men came to Britain to find jobs. Most were followed by other members of their families. Stage two was inaugurated with the Government restrictions of the early 1960s, which reduced the number of new workers to a trickle. The families of men already resident in Britain continued to arrive, and the numbers of British-born black babies rose sharply. Stage three began around the end of the 1960s. The number of incoming dependants so fell that, between 1971 and 1976, 5000 more West Indians actually left Britain than arrived. At the same time, the West Indian families settled in Britain dramatically reduced their birth rate. In 1970, 14,100 babies were born to West Indian-born mothers—a rate which implied that the average family would end up with four

72 Halsey, A. H., *op. cit.*

TABLE 1.4. People Allowed to Settle in Britain During 1976

WHITE		
From non-Commonwealth countries excluding Pakistan	19,800	
Had at least one British parent or grandparent; and/or arrived from the old Commonwealth	6300	
Total (potential white immigrants)		26,100
NON-WHITE		
U.K. passport-holders (chiefly East African Asians) and their dependants	11,700	
Husbands or wives of British residents	18,400	
Dependant of British residents	18,500	
Total (potential non-white immigrants)		54,600
Grand Total		80,700

Notes

(1) Another 200 had completed 4 years of approved employment and were permitted to settle.

(2) A further 5800 were exempt from deportation under the "5-year rule", introduced with the 1971 Immigration Act. This provides that a Commonwealth or Pakistan citizen who was living in Britain on 1 January 1973 cannot be deported once he has remained in Britain for 5 years.

(3) The figures for "white" immigration do not include people from Ireland or from other Common Market countries.

(4) The immigration of U.K. passport holders is rationed by a voucher system. The current limit is 5000 voucher-holders a year, plus their dependants—but in practice this limit has not been reached.

children. But by 1976 the number of babies had halved to 7200—implying a completed family size of two children, the same as for indigenous Britons.

Of course, differences in traditional family patterns cannot guarantee that a similar migration cycle will be repeated among Asians, but broadly speaking there is sufficient evidence to indicate that the sequence is occurring in roughly the same way. U.K. passport-holders apart, immigration by new Asian arrivals has virtually ceased, and what is currently taking place is the consolidation of families whose breadwinner is already settled (i.e. the second stage of the migration cycle). In 1976, just 200 people who had arrived initially with short-term work permits were allowed to settle permanently; and only 1735 new permit holders were admitted—a figure which has steadily fallen and continues to do so. Nearly every other immigrant from the "new" Commonwealth and Pakistan was a spouse or dependant of someone already legally settled in Britain.

If all immigration—including wives, dependants and the most compassionate cases—were to cease immediately and totally, the population of "new" Commonwealth and Pakistan origin in Britain would still increase by 800,000 to 2.7 millions by the end of the century. Most of this increase is explained by the age range of the immigrants themselves, which inevitably produces an excess of births over deaths, but some is also attributable to the higher fertility rate among Asian women. As with West Indian women, however, this fertility is falling. If, as is more likely, immigration is not totally ended, then the total non-white population will of course rise higher than the minimum of 2.7 millions. The most reliable estimates suggest that the number of dependants likely to arrive by the end of the century is a little over 300,000;[73] to these must be added the future babies of these families, bringing the total additional population to about 400,000. U.K. passport-holders, chiefly East African Asians, together with their families and future babies, may swell the total by another 150,000 at most, and to this may be added a handful of totally new working immigrants and their dependants admitted for special reasons. The cumulative total, therefore, becomes 3.3 million non-white Britons. In the next century, the growth rate will slow down, with very little net immigration (unless Government policies change), and a family age distribution more like that of white families in the indigenous population. Non-white deaths will start catching up with non-white births. Demographically at least, there will be stability.

[73] In fact the gross figure is higher than 300,000, but this is a net figure taking account of non-white emigration from Britain, now running at around 10,000 a year.

The Family

Wives, submit yourselves unto your husbands, as it is fit in the Lord.
Husbands, love your wives, and be not bitter against them.
Children, obey your parents in all things: for this is well pleasing unto the Lord.
(The Epistle of Paul the Apostle to the Colossians, iii. 18–20)

Love and marriage, love and marriage, go together like a horse and carriage—You can't have
one without the other.

(Popular song)

Introduction

It is only necessary to glance at the immense amount of literature which has been published on the subject of the family in order to obtain an impression of the high esteem in which it is held in our value system. Because familial relationships are so basic, indeed, the terminology of the family is often used in other circumstances to emphasize certain ideal types of relationship. Thus the word "brother" is used in trade unions and religious orders, since it emphasizes the values of equality and solidarity, and the term "family" is itself employed in many senses other than those implied by immediate kinship relationships. The crucial role of the family may help to explain the deeply felt concern over what is alleged to be a family "problem" in modern British society—a topic which has featured prominently in the work of social commentators virtually uninterruptedly since the end of World War II. Evidence of the problem is derived from apparent trends in the birth rate, the abandonment of the aged, the figures for divorce, desertion, crime and illegitimacy, the number of children under the care of local authorities, and the increasing proportion of mothers out at work. All these "facts", and more, have been cited in support of the argument that in modern industrial society

51

the family has been stripped of its proper functions and, unless some drastic action is taken, the family as a social institution will collapse in ruins. The vehemence with which such contentions are advanced is in no way diminished by the fact that similar forecasts about the imminent demise of the family have been advanced regularly since the time of Plato, yet still the family manages somehow to survive.

From careful study of the evidence, sociologists more frequently take an optimistic view. Talcott Parsons has argued, for example, that it is not so much that the family has lost functions as that it has taken on new and more specialized ones.[1] Fletcher concludes that

> If we take . . . the "essential" functions of the family—the satisfaction of the sexual needs of the married couple, the careful upbringing of children, and the provision of a satisfactory home for its members—it is perfectly clear that the modern family—entailing the equal status of wife and husband and their mutual consideration in marriage; the high status of children; and the improved standards of income, housing, household equipment—aims at, and achieves a far more satisfactory and refined provision for these needs than did either the pre-industrial family or the family of early industrial Britain, in which women were inferior and subjected, women and children were frequently exploited within or outside the family, and conditions in the home were so deplorably inadequate.[2]

The main objective of this chapter is to examine the validity of these opinions and to place the family in a meaningful context. Two factors which must be granted special consideration in any discussion of this topic are the changing position of women in society and trends in marriage and divorce, both of which being the subject of later sections.

The Family Today

In non-industrial societies, the family's duties include provision of the necessities of life, care of the old, and education of the young. These duties are not only the concern of the family itself, but also of the whole kinship group. MacIver[3] writes that the pre-industrial family was a "multi-functional" unit, to a large extent self-governing, performing its

[1] Parsons, T. and Bales, R. F., *Family, Socialization and Interaction Process*, Routledge & Kegan Paul, 1956.

[2] Fletcher, R., *The Family and Marriage*, Penguin Books, 1962.

[3] MacIver, R. M. and Page, C. N., *Society*, Macmillan, 1957.

own religious services, responsible for its children's education, and providing an economic basis for the home. He further argues that, with the development of complex industrialization, certain "non-essential" functions have been taken over by specialized agencies operating outside the sphere of the family. Government has been taken over by the State, religion by the Church, education by a publicly sponsored system of schools—and the growth of the factory system means that the family has ceased to be an economic unit. Some writers have taken the view that these developments have stripped the family of those tasks essential to its cohesion, with the result that parents have callously abnegated their responsibilities to the Welfare State. By contrast, authorities like Mac-Iver hold that because the family has been relieved of the burden of its "non-essential" tasks, it may concentrate more completely on the satisfactory accomplishment of its basic functions, for which, too, professional advice and financial assistance are available on a scale hitherto unprecedented. Propositions of this kind are difficult to quantify, but in fact standards of parental care have never been higher, the State has made parents more professionally concerned about such matters as health and education, and social security has done much to remove economic pressures on the family and so preserve its unity.[4] It is perhaps worth examining briefly the current position as regards the basic functions of the family as outlined by Murdock: sexual, economic, reproductive, and educational.[5]

Most of the recent surveys indicate that the sexual function is probably less confined to the family than was the case before World War II, although sexual behaviour is a topic notoriously difficult to investigate. In the United States Kinsey[6] showed the increasing importance of pre-marital and extra-marital sex, though this was coupled with a decline in recourse to prostitutes. Schofield's inquiry into the sexual behaviour of

---

[4] The fact that families in general are not *conscious* of any reduction in economic pressures (especially in a period of rapid inflation) does not alter the validity of this assertion. The pressures undoubtedly continue, but do so within a framework of continuously rising expectations so that they are less concerned with sheer subsistence and survival.

[5] Murdock, G. P., *Social Structure*, Macmillan, 1949.

[6] Kinsey, A. C., Pomeroy, W. B. and Martin, C. E., *Sexual Behaviour in the Human Male*, W. B. Saunders Co. (U.S.A.), 1948; same authors plus Gebhard, P. H., *Sexual Behaviour in the Human Female*, W. B. Saunders Co. (U.S.A.), 1953.

teenagers in Great Britain found that 20 per cent of the boys interviewed and 12 per cent of the girls had experienced sexual intercourse.[7] These figures, however, do not necessarily indicate any large-scale tendencies towards promiscuousness in British society, for Schofield also found that much pre-marital intercourse takes place between partners who intend to get married in any case. Another consideration is that assessment of trends in such a sensitive matter as sexual behaviour is difficult in view of the paucity of information about earlier historical periods. Life in Victorian England certainly seems to have been anything but chaste: Fletcher[8] mentions the younger middle and upper class males who were saving up for a "good" marriage but who were denied sexual access to their intended spouse and who consequently provided prostitutes with a large clientele.

So far as the reproductive function of the family is concerned, there can be little doubt that this has declined in the statistical sense, since families are having fewer children compared with Victorian times. Even children born outside marriage (8.1 per cent of the total of all live births in 1970, though the proportion has risen slightly in subsequent years) tend to be brought up in the environment of the nuclear family: either the mother will keep the child despite the personal hardship involved, or the child will be adopted. Certainly there is no evidence to support the view that an increasing proportion of illegitimate children are cared for in institutions. True, the total number of children in the care of local authorities has risen each year since 1972, but most of the increase is accounted for by children in foster homes and those with parents, guardians, relatives and friends under local authority supervision, reflecting the modern social work emphasis on retaining family connections where possible. In any event it is not clear to what extent illegitimacy can be seen as the product of an urban or an industrial society. The illegitimacy rates in Merionethshire have been persistently higher than the British national average,[9] and rural illegitimacy is not a specifically

[7] Schofield, M., *The Sexual Behaviour of Young People*, Longmans, 1965. Because of the predicted unreliability of the responses, a much more recent study of 16-year-olds deliberately avoided questions about experience of sex. See Fogelman, K., ed., *Britain's Sixteen-Year-Olds*, National Children's Bureau, 1976.

[8] Fletcher, R., *op. cit.*

[9] Emmett, I., *A North Wales Village*, Routledge & Kegan Paul, 1964.

recent development. Recent figures on abortions, too, which can be seen as a deliberate attempt (after contraception has failed) to thwart the reproductive process, show that East Anglia achieved the third highest rate of abortions in 1969 among all the regions in the country.[10]

Figures from Scotland (which, unlike England, publishes regular statistics on the social class of new-born babies) appear to indicate that illegitimate births are mainly concentrated in classes III and IV (the Skilled and Semi-skilled occupational groups), with the lowest proportions among classes I and V (Professional and Unskilled respectively). Yet the reason for such a concentration has more to do with classification than with any variation in moral standards between the mothers concerned. Legitimate babies are classified according to the social class of their fathers, whereas illegitimate babies are normally given the social class of their mothers; and classes III and IV include nearly all the jobs done by young women—typists, sales assistants, textile workers and so on. In practice it is probably more correct to argue that illegitimacy and its related problems are spread fairly evenly among girls from every kind of background. Overall, the falling numbers of children—especially noticeable among working-class families—could well indicate nothing more than a greater concern for the quality of life and the allocation of limited resources within the family: consequently the reproductive function has merely changed its scale rather than its character.

The same cannot be said of the family's economic role, however. Viola Klein[11] has argued that the process of industrialization has affected the family in three significant ways. First, the centre of production has moved from the home to the factory and the family has become an "income unit". Second, the unit of production (the factory, shop or office) normally employs the individual worker rather than the entire family. Third, the process of industrialization ensures a supply of goods and services produced outside the home but consumed within it. The

---

[10] *The Registrar-General's Statistical Review of England and Wales (1969): Supplement on Abortion*, H.M.S.O., 1971. Of the total of 54,819 abortions in 1969, almost half were performed on single women, most of whom in turn had no previous children. Environmental reasons as causes for the abortions were given in a quarter of all cases compared with less than 10 per cent for the previous year. Women in skilled occupations accounted for the highest number of abortions of any occupational group, while professional women remained the lowest.

[11] Klein, V., *Britain's Married Women Workers*, Routledge & Kegan Paul, 1965.

family is still an economic unit, but the focus of its economic behaviour has become consumption rather than production or distribution.

The fourth function of the family identified by Murdock is socialization, a problem which has attracted considerable attention from social psychologists since it is during its formative years that the child acquires the foundations of its future personality, attitude structure, and style of life. In fact the family is only one of the agencies contributing to the socialization process, and in recent years the family has been supplemented or replaced (depending on the point of view adopted) by other social institutions, such as the class structure, ethnic and cultural factors, the mass media, the growth of an industry in parental guidance and advice, to say nothing of the educational system itself. The complex nature of socialization is aptly illustrated by research into educational sociology; on the one hand domestic environment and parental attitudes may enhance and reinforce educational achievement at school by a kind of circular feedback process,[12] while conversely education may merely serve to segregate the working-class boy from his family.[13] Even earlier than formal education, child-rearing in infancy is subject to class variations which must affect subsequent behaviour. Spinley's early study of socialization in a London slum, for example, revealed the inconsistent methods of training employed by working-class parents, admittedly in an atypical area.[14] At an early age, the child was sent out to play in the street, and he quickly became a member of what Dr. Robb[15] has called "a unisexual gang of boys of his own age". There is little evidence to suggest that much has changed since this research was conducted; on the contrary, the child's reliance on his peers for a frame of reference may well have been enhanced by the increasing tendency for mothers to go out to work. It is important to note that the influence of the peer-group, the gang—with its own hierarchical structure and group norms—is directly competitive with that of the home. Working-class children come to regard their homes as places where they do not spend many hours;

[12] Douglas, J. W. B., *The Home and the School*, MacGibbon and Kee, 1966.

[13] Jackson, B. and Marsden, D., *Education and the Working Class*, Routledge & Kegan Paul, 1962.

[14] Spinley, B. M., *The Deprived and the Privileged*, Routledge & Kegan Paul, 1953.

[15] Robb, J. H., *Working-Class Anti-Semite*, Tavistock, 1954.

according to Mays[16] writing of the Liverpool dock area, "over the age of twelve, boys do not spend much time in the home, except when they are sick". This lack of restraint surrounding the working-class child means that he is less able to cope with stress situations. Yet ironically, as Morris[17] points out, he will encounter more of such situations, because he usually has to bring up a family on a limited, possibly irregular income, and money disagreements may be one of the most potent sources of marital discord.[18]

By contrast the middle-class child is normally reared in a more carefully controlled way. His feeds are regulated, his periods of rest and play are subject to a firmer discipline. Play is restricted to the house or garden, and the street play group scarcely exists. Mogey's *Family and Neighbourhood*[19] shows that one of the effects of the housing estate is that parents dislike their children playing in the street in case they pick up undesirable habits or accents. And as Professor Worsley[20] has argued, "The middle-class striver . . . has his 'deferred gratification' pattern well built into his psyche during that brief period between potty and primary school: his life is a career-pattern—and he sees it as such—long before he enters the world of work."

John and Elizabeth Newson[21] have conducted the definitive study of child-rearing methods in Britain, among a large sample in Nottingham, and their observations confirm the crucial significance of social class and occupation in the structure of family relationships. It is clear that what the father does for the children, and what he is expected to do, must be considered in the broader context of his occupation—the adequacy of his pay, degree of physical exhaustion entailed, regularity of work, stability of income and working place. Hours of work are particularly

[16] Mays, J. B., *Growing Up in the City*, Liverpool University Press, 1954.

[17] Morris, T., *The Criminal Area*, Routledge & Kegan Paul, 1957.

[18] There is an unavoidable hint of stereotyping about such generalizations. Nevertheless, the picture of the working class here presented is not particularly new: Seaman's study of the nineteenth century refers to "the generous, feckless, uncompetitive, residually tribal and resolutely pragmatic attitudes of the working men of real life". See Seaman, L. C. B., *Victorian England*, Methuen, 1973.

[19] Mogey, J. M., *Family and Neighbourhood*, Oxford University Press, 1956.

[20] Worsley, P. M., "Authority and the young", *New Society*, 22 July 1965, pp. 10–13.

[21] Newson, J. and Newson, E., *Infant Care in an Urban Community*, Allen & Unwin, 1963.

important in determining not only the amount of time the father spends with the family but also the extent to which he can help in the baby's care. In certain occupations this is especially obvious: miners and factory employees often work in alternating shifts: commercial travellers, long-distance lorry drivers and steeplejacks may spend several days at a time away from home; electricians, railwaymen and doctors may be constantly on call; teachers, shopkeepers and young professional men often work late in the evening. Thus some men have finished with work as soon as they get home, some bring it with them and are therefore only semi-available to their families for much of the time; and some, like small shopkeepers and writers, live with their work and are in and out of the living quarters all day. Working-class fathers are more likely to follow shift-work routines, in which case they are frequently home during "normal" working hours, whereas for most professional and white-collar workers this is a strange and rather uncomfortable experience, often associated with illness, convalescence, or temporary unemployment. Manual workers, too, are usually paid for the number of hours they have clocked in, or else on piece rates based on the precise output, and they tend to feel correspondingly less obligation towards their employers when they wish to take time off for domestic or even purely personal reasons. It is not rare, therefore, for the working-class father to take a week off work when his wife has a baby.

Over the last 25 years the average number of hours actually worked per week by the manual worker has fluctuated gently around the 47 mark, and it is evident that the British worker has preferred to take the benefits of rising prosperity in increased earnings rather than in increased leisure.[22] There is a clear relationship between age and the amount of overtime worked, a peak being reached in the thirties, the age of a married couple with a growing family (77 per cent of workers in this age-group work some overtime, 38 per cent more than 10 hours). Equally, the majority of shiftworkers are unskilled workers with dependent families, and most of those who choose jobs involving shiftwork do so because of the higher earnings (87 per cent of those working regular

[22] Most of the data in this paragraph are derived from *Hours of Work, Overtime and Shiftworking*, Report No. 161 of the National Board for Prices and Incomes, H.M.S.O., 1971.

overtime gave no reason other than pay for doing so). Specifically, 32 per cent of shiftworkers are young marrieds. Shiftworking is undoubtedly seen by these individuals mainly as an alternative to heavy overtime as a means of increasing earnings for the unskilled, as successive waves of Polish, Italian and coloured immigrants have discovered. But, mining apart, it should be pointed out that shiftwork is becoming part of the definition of the job in an increasing number of cases, such as metal manufacture, chemicals, brick, cement and glass, where continuous operation is necessary to avoid heavy penalties in operating costs. Overtime, too, has elements of compulsion or quasi-compulsion about it. Quite apart from the contractual overtime found in transport undertakings and public utilities, in many firms, particularly in construction and engineering, production schedules and manpower levels are planned, and contracts accepted, on the assumption that regular overtime will be worked. Both overtime and shiftwork involve some degree of disruption in sleep patterns and social life,[23] but the patterns of life of the British worker do not seem to change much whatever hours he is working. When it comes to bingo, going to the pub, visiting relatives or watching television, the figures vary very little as between shiftworkers and high and low overtime workers. Fewer shiftworkers attend sporting events and considerably fewer take their wives out once a week—but the proportion who take their wives out less than once a month is evenly divided among all categories.

In terms of family relationships, the working hours experienced by the working-class father, coupled with his attitudes to work, seem to mean that he feels entitled to be a part of the normal domestic scene, while he expects his wife to fit her pattern of living around him. If he has to sleep during the day, for example, it is the wife's job to ensure that there is peace and quiet. By contrast, professional and white-collar workers usually work office hours, which are not only constant and predictable, but also fit fairly closely with school times, the other great pace setters in a mother's day.

The Newsons found that a sense of partnership is often a feature of

---

[23] There is, however, no conclusive medical evidence to support the view that shiftwork or regular overtime are health hazards; any tendency in this direction is probably countered by a degree of self-selection.

domestic family life for young married couples, a point of view echoed by Willmott and Young:[24]

> ... the younger hunsband of today does not consider that the children belong exclusively to his wife's world, or that he can abandon them to her (and her mother) while he takes his comfort in the male atmosphere of the pub. He now shares the responsibility for the number of children as well as for their welfare after they are born. ... The man's earnings may still be his affair, but when it comes to the spending of the money, his part of the wages as well as hers, husband and wife will share the responsibility. ... Not only do fathers, as well as mothers, have more money; they also take a pride in their children's turn-out. Both of them now share in the hopes and plans for their children's future.

Yet there are various degrees of partnership and various patterns of co-operation between husband and wife. Although two husbands may both undertake a wide variety of domestic chores in the home, the roles assigned to them by their wives may still differ considerably. One wife may expect her husband to do these things as a matter of course and complain if he does not; while another may believe that domestic work is her responsibility alone, and that in helping her the husband is merely demonstrating his devotion and kindness. These attitudes seem to be rather independent of social class, but the Newsons have found that as one proceeds down the social scale the sex roles become more sharply defined and more rigidly stereotyped. Perhaps this is partly due to the fact that in many of the socially lower occupations brawn still counts for more than brain: hence the distinction between "men's work" and "women's work" becomes increasingly obvious.

Following Bott's small study in London,[25] sociologists have frequently sought to distinguish between couples according to their "role segregation", that is, according to whether, and if so in what ways and to what extent, they decide and do various things together. But understanding of this phenomenon in British society, and of its effect (if any) on upbringing is rather poor. It seems likely that working-class marriages are more generally segregated than middle-class ones. This certainly fits with Kohn's rather generalized stereotype of the middle-class father being supportive, and thus supplementing the mother; and of the working-class father

---

[24] Young, M. and Willmott, P., *Family and Kinship in East London*, Routledge & Kegan Paul, 1957.
[25] Bott, E., *Family and Social Network*, Tavistock, 1957.

being more absent and more punitive, thus complementing her. At the same time, Gavron's research in Kentish Town,[26] the work by the Newsons in Nottingham, and Toomey's study in Chatham and Rochester,[27] have all found the most involved father to be those in class III, the intermediate group. For Gavron and Toomey it was the manual fathers, for the Newsons the non-manual ones. These couples also tended to be more socially isolated than most, and to have exceptionally high and strongly felt aspirations for their children. Several pieces of work on the lower social classes or on more traditional communities like those of miners have corroborated Kohn's stereotype for those groups. This does not mean, of course, that lower class families are arenas of maternal strain, paternal anger and childish anguish. Except where the father is under severe stress, as in mining or fishing, these families are as happy as others though the children are not "successfully" trained for that middle-class achievement that is measured by most personality and intelligence tests. It is, nevertheless, the case that in these lower-class families the mother acts out the role characteristic of mothers in all classes to an extreme degree: that is to say, the role of the main socializing agent.

Class differences are also prominent in the mother's attitude towards the child-rearing process itself. Many working-class women, according to the Newsons, find the role of "Mam" highly satisfying in and of itself, with her children as a symbol of status in themselves and an extension of the mother's personality. In the working-class household, babies are frequently picked up, petted, shown off to visitors, teased and stimulated in a way that would be looked upon with disfavour by middle-class parents. The convention within the latter group seems to be that babies figure less frequently as a topic of conversation, and children are ignored unless they demand or provoke attention. The Newsons suggest that this may be connected with the fact that many middle-class mothers seem to see the period of infancy not as a time of fulfilment but as an abnormal and in many ways deplorable interlude in an otherwise sane and well-ordered life. Ideally, the middle-class woman has a tasteful and well-run home into which it is possible to invite visitors at any hour. Once babies

[26] Gavron, H., *The Captive Wife: Conflicts of Housebound Mothers*, Penguin Books, 1968.
[27] Toomey, D. M., *Urban Studies*, Vol. 7, No. 3, 1970, p. 259.

arrive, however, the reality frequently includes piles of dirty and mal-
odorous clothes in the kitchen, toys all over the house, and dribble (or
worse) on the living room carpet. Under these conditions she may find it
difficult to reconcile her ideal self-image as mature and sophisticated
with her actual role as a housebound baby-minder, nappy washer and
domestic slave. The resultant state of conflict and frustration may be
shown in a variety of ways. The mother may live nostalgically in the past;
she may see the humorous side of her predicament and tell funny stories
against herself; or she may adopt a tone of mock callousness towards her
children ("You can have mine any time you like" and so on).

The Newsons also investigated the extent to which husbands and
wives were able to go out together once they had young children to look
after. Again there is a clear class relationship. More than twice as many
white-collar and professional couples were able to go out together sometimes (during the baby's first year) when compared with class V couples.
Paid baby sitters were used so little that the ability to afford them did not
seem a very important factor; what may have been more crucial was the
impressionistic evidence that middle-class wives wanted to go out
whereas working-class wives were content with television as their sole
source of entertainment (though the latter "contentment" may have
been little more than a straightforward rationalization from financial
constraints). Working-class parents (fathers in particular) did not trust
their baby sitters and therefore often stayed home on principle while the
children were young.

These observations are particularly interesting in view of the fact that
several sociologists have tried to argue that leisure pursuits are no longer
enjoyed communally within the family and that the provision of leisure
itself is less spontaneous and more dependent on external agencies.
Unfortunately the comfortable cliché of Victorian leisure as one long
musical soirée is very remote from reality. Only a comparatively small
percentage of households could afford a piano and certainly in working-
class homes there were no such things as mutually shared pleasures
among husbands and wives. As Willmott and Young have pointed out in
their study of East London families,[28] working-class housing was
formerly so overcrowded, dirty and uncomfortable that husbands were

[28] Young, M. and Willmott, P., *op. cit.*

glad to get away to the pub. It cost a good deal, measured in glasses of beer, to rent a seat at the pub, so very often the housekeeping allowance had to suffer. As one informant said, "From the home point of view there was no enjoyment at all for the man, so when he did get a bit of money he tended to go round to the pub and spend it there." Today, housing conditions have improved so much that husbands no longer need to escape to the pub, and they are more likely to "fetch a bottle in so that they can watch the telly at the same time". In the 1950s, too, Willmott and Young were able to comment upon the relative novelty of the week-end, "a new term and a new experience for the working man. With it has come the sight of young fathers wheeling prams up Bethnal Green Road on a Saturday morning, taking their little daughters for a row on the lake or playing with their sons on the putting green".

Table 2.1 gives a summary of class differences in baby care as found by

TABLE 2.1. Class Differences in Baby Care Methods

Characteristic	I and II Professional and managerial	III White collar	III Skilled manual	IV Semi-skilled	V Unskilled
Age 21 or less at first birth	24	25	40	46	53
Breast feeding					
At 1 month	60	50	50	51	34
At 3 months	39	34	24	22	12
At 6 months	20	12	11	11	7
Dummy					
At some time	39	53	71	75	74
At 12 months	26	38	55	57	46
Bedtime					
6.30 p.m. or earlier	47	31	29	24	31
8 p.m. or later	7	12	20	23	26
Sleeps in room alone	54	42	20	18	3
Diet inadequate	5	10	13	13	32
Genital play checked	25	50	57	69	93
No smacking	56	38	32	42	35
General smacking	39	53	60	54	58
Frequent tantrums	9	8	14	15	23
Father's participation					
High	57	61	51	55	36
Little or none	19	6	16	18	36

(*Note:* all figures are percentages.)

the Newsons in Nottingham. In nearly all cases this reveals a general trend running right through the occupational groups, with the largest distinctions in behaviour concentrated between middle-class and working-class attitudes. The other main rift, between unskilled workers and the rest, can sometimes be linked with lower material or educational standards, as in the cases of inadequate diet or the baby sharing its parents' room, but this does not always apply. It is tempting to suppose, the Newsons argue, that there is some basic difference—in personality or occupational ethos or both—which makes the labourer so reluctant to help with the baby, and his wife so (comparatively) slow to start potty training, so unsuccessful if she does start, so apt to induce tantrums and so very intolerant of the baby's genital play. The findings for class IV are somewhat anomalous in that they do not always fit in with a well-defined class trend, the reason probably being that class IV is a ragbag of occupations which have very little in common. Some of the occupations included (such as hall porter, bus conductor and ticket collector) are partly clerical and offer secure and respectable, if poorly paid, employment; but the jobs of iron furnacemen and tobacco workers, for example, are far heavier and dirtier and less secure. It seems reasonable to suppose that the semi-clerical jobs in class IV attract men whose attitudes and general way of life have more in common with those of shop and office employees than of manual workers, and this would explain the inconsistent findings within this group.

One of the major questions to which sociologists and psychologists have addressed themselves is the precise impact of child-rearing methods on the subsequent behavioural development of the individual. The most pervasive theory of child development was produced by Bowlby,[29] namely, that every infant needs a continuous relationship with a warm, loving mother-figure (not necessarily the child's natural mother) in order for it to develop into a normal healthy adult. Without such a relationship, according to Bowlby, delinquency, mental instability and other personality disturbances are apt to result. Bowlby's work, as well as discussing the evidence for the effects of maternal deprivation, also considered what could be done to prevent it; he argued that mothers

[29] Bowlby, J., *Child Care and Growth of Love*, Penguin Books. This is a popular version of Bowlby's original treatise, *Maternal Care and Mental Health*, World Health Organization, 1951.

should be encouraged and helped to care for their children, to accompany them in hospital and so forth, and that foster care should be developed. In his day-to-day clinical work with parents and children, Bowlby had been unconvinced by the then prevailing view that babies clung to their mothers because of their need for food. Through ethology and a study of Lorenz's work on imprinting, it gradually became clear that infants become attached to their mothers not because they are fed but because they are endowed by nature to seek proximity to a care-giving adult. For the species to survive it is necessary for individuals to eat, engage in sex and to avoid danger. The drive to keep close to a care-giver is an insurance against danger and as important as the other drives. In subsequent research, Bowlby tackled more fully what happens when young children are separated from their mothers—noting the various stages of protest, despair and detachment—and from which he argues that anger and anxiety result. These reactions provide the basis for many of the fears, phobias and depressions that become mental problems.

Bowlby's ideas have been profoundly influential in affecting, for instance, the guilt of the middle-class working mother, the slow development of nursery schooling in Britain, and the long-held conviction of many social workers that families should be kept together, even in the most appalling conditions. On the more positive side, there is now a far more sympathetic attitude to frequent visiting of young children in hospital by their parents. At the same time, there has been a growing accumulation of evidence to counter Bowlby's flat assertion, in 1951, that "Good mothering is almost useless if delayed until after the age of two and a half years." Thus a study of Aberdeen women[30] discovered that of those from "broken" homes, 44 per cent had lost their father by death before the age of 14, 26 per cent had similarly lost their mother, 15 per cent had experienced the separation, desertion or divorce of their parents, and 15 per cent were illegitimate. All of these categories were more prone to have left school at the minimum age, to have had a manual job before marriage, and to have been under 20 at their first delivery. Those who

[30] By Illsley, R. and Thompson, B. In interpreting these findings, it should be borne in mind that girls are more affected by their family environment than boys, and are affected differently. The results may not, therefore, apply similarly or equally to boys, even in Aberdeen.

had been brought up by a mother and a stepfather had fared particularly badly; those whose fathers had died (and who had not had a stepfather) least so. On the other hand, a break at an early age did not seem to be any more affecting. And psychologically, these women from broken homes seemed emotionally more stable than the control group, and better adjusted to marriage and to pregnancy. They were also at least as knowledgeable about maternity.

Criminological studies of delinquent boys, however, have found that parental separation was even more crucial than parental death. Extrapolating from Illsley and Thompson's findings about the greater adjustment of their women from broken homes, it may be that the delinquent boys from such homes are more delinquent (in the legal sense), precisely because, by comparison with girls, they have been forced to adjust earlier and more wholeheartedly to the culture of dissociation that Downes describes as characteristic of working-class youth. For it is among the working class that parental separation seems more frequent; and it is working-class boys that are most frequently charged by the police. Douglas, too, found that an insecure background, of a kind caused by parental conflict, had a more marked effect than a parent's death.[31]

Whatever this and similar evidence signifies, it is clear that the situation is a good deal more subtle and complex than Bowlby first anticipated. In a recent critique of Bowlby,[32] for example, one author distinguishes between the long- and the short-term effects of different kinds of deprivation on the child. Most studies on the short-term effects of parental separation are based on children admitted to hospital. There seems to be general agreement that most—though not all—children suffer some short-term distress in these circumstances and that this is most pronounced in children aged between 6 months and 4 years. The long-term impact is more difficult to measure. Douglas, in 1975, reported a positive association between early hospitalization and later adolescent delinquency, but the Clarkes argue that early admission to hospital is merely (very often) a symptom of a disadvantaged home, and it is these general disadvantages—which continue throughout childhood—rather than the hospitalization itself that cause later problems in adolescence. In the

[31] See Douglas, J. W. B., *The Home and the School*, MacGibbon & Kee, 1964.
[32] Clarke, A. M. and Clarke, A. D. B., eds., *Early Experieince : Myth and Evidence*, Open Books, 1976.

words of the Clarkes, "early learning will have effects which, if unrepeated, will fade with time. It will not *per se* have any long-term
influence upon adult behaviour other than as an essential link in the
developmental chain". Again, the Clarkes state in the introduction to
their book: "Our main conclusion is that, in man, early learning is
mainly important for its foundational character. By itself, and when
unrepeated over time, it serves as no more than a link in the developmental chain, shaping proximate behaviour less and less powerfully as
age increases."

In attempting to summarize the significance of early experience,
longitudinal research has begun to provide an understanding of the
pattern of human growth. Three quite specific features have emerged,
each with important practical implications for this field. First, the
development of various basic characteristics does not proceed in equal
units per unit of time, i.e., growth does not take place at an even pace.
Second, for most aspects, the period of most rapid growth occurs in the
early years, from conception to the age of 6 years or so, and is then followed by periods of less and less rapid growth with a spurt at puberty;
for some characteristics there is as much quantitative growth in a single
year of a child's life as there is in 8 to 10 years at later stages in his
development. Third, available evidence suggests that environmental
influences have the greatest effect during the most rapid periods of
growth. From this, it follows that the experiences and opportunities
during the early years of life are vital—though not, of course, exclusively
so—to later development. This position is ultimately the one adopted
by the Clarkes (and it is not so very different from the theory originally
advanced by Bowlby):

> It is unclear whether the limits to personal change are the same throughout the
> period of development, or whether, as we rather suspect, they get progressively
> smaller as age increases and as personal characteristics in adolescence and young
> adult life begin to achieve an autonomy and self-perpetuation. This is our so-called
> "wedge" hypothesis, suggesting a greater potential responsiveness during early
> life and childhood at the "thick" end, tailing off to little responsiveness in adulthood,
> the "thin" end of the wedge.

One major ancillary problem, remaining to be resolved, concerns the
extent to which early experiences for the child are reversible and, arising
from this, the optimum period for benevolent intervention in the child's

development in order to improve the chances of normal progress. Bronfenbrenner[33] suggests that there are five main stages of intervention: preparation for parenthood; the period before children arrive; the first 3 years of life, during which the primary objective is to establish an enduring emotional relationship between parent and infant—"the enduring one-to-one relationship, so essential to the development of the young child"; and the next two stages covering the ages 4–6 years and 6–12 years, which see a gradual change, with the parent no longer being the child's principal teacher but rather acting as a supporter of his learning, both in and out of school. There seems little doubt that, if intervention is necessary, then it is preferably undertaken as early as possible, for various reasons. First, it is more likely to be effective, in view of what has been said above about the nature of child development. Second, it is far more economical of resources than the practice of waiting until children show serious behaviour or neurotic difficulties, by which time the early experiences have become too deeply ingrained to be easily eradicated. As Bronfenbrenner himself stresses, the family "is the most effective and economical system for fostering and sustaining the development of the child"; and "initiating appropriate intervention at earlier stages can be expected to yield cumulative gains". The Clarkes conclude, however, that intervention does not mean "half-hearted attempts to 'prop up' families which may be essentially irredeemable . . . the prime question here is where the line should be drawn. At the moment it seems to be too close to sentimentalism and insufficiently in children's best interests". So, in the final analysis, the work of the Clarkes and their associates does not totally undermine, by any means, the pioneering studies of Bowlby; what they have simply sought to do is to place Bowlby's ideas in a more reasoned perspective, so that the reversibility of early experience is stressed rather than the allegedly inevitable connection between childhood deprivation and subsequent emotional or delinquent problems.

The preceding discussion on the basic functions of the family, as defined by Murdock, has been designed to show that although these functions may have altered in scope, any decline has been more than compensated by the increasing professionalism and concern with which

[33] Bronfenbrenner, U., in Clarke, A. M. and Clarke, A. D. B., eds., *op. cit.*

the remaining tasks are performed, to say nothing of the much greater degree of introspection and analysis surrounding the performance of family responsibilities (illustrated by the wide publicity given in the mass media to the publications of researchers like the Clarkes and Bowlby, discussed above). If it is true that the functions of the family have become more specialized, then this merely reflects the changes that have occurred among social institutions more generally. The stress within the family is now upon the effective socialization of the child and the provision of emotional support and stability for the adult members, particularly as this concerns the occupational role of the male. The widespread belief that there has been a serious breakdown in family life does not stand up to critical examination, at least in a definitive report on young people in Britain.[34] "The concept of the 'generation gap' ", says the report, "is part of popular mythology. However, there is little evidence in our findings for its widespread existence. The great majority of both parents and children reported harmonious family relationships." In support of this conclusion the attitude of 16-year-olds to marriage and family life seems highly significant. Only 3 per cent were opposed to marriage altogether. Among the rest, most thought that the best age to marry was between 20 and 25, with two children as the ideal family. In other words, they constituted a remarkably conventional generation of young people not markedly different from the parents.

Another fashionable generalization concerning the family is that it has been reduced to its nuclear essentials in recent years. Crosland[35] has argued that whereas, in Victorian times, the family was regarded as the entire sum of different generations (any photograph of an elaborately posed nineteenth-century group will support this remark), today one thinks of the family as simply the parents and their dependant children. Crosland goes on to attribute this change, at least in part, to the comparatively novel features in our society of occupational mobility and housing developments (suburbs, new housing estates and new towns). Talcott Parsons[36] in the U.S.A. also cites high geographical and occupational mobility as the factors responsible. Support for the generalization itself comes from such studies as Mogey's *Family and*

[34] Fogelman, K., ed., *Britain's Sixteen-Year-Olds*, National Children's Bureau, 1976.
[35] Crosland, C. A. R., *The Future of Socialism*, Cape, 1956.
[36] Parsons, T., *Essays in Sociological Theory Pure and Applied*, Free Press, 1949,

Neighbourhood,[37] which explores the differences between Barton, a new housing estate near Oxford, and the older neighbourhood-centred society of St. Ebbe's. Interviews showed that husband and wife in Barton shared more activities in the household daily routine—families would go for a joint holiday for the first time; more husbands and wives went walking with their children. It appeared that the housing estate encouraged the nuclear family as distinct from the extended family. In the latter, the mother, married daughter and children form one clique, while the husband is expected to spend much of his time with other men in the locality. Homans, too, writes[38] that the extended kinship unit has tended to disappear because it has fewer uses: the nuclear family moves more frequently and relatives are rarely available to fill their traditional functions, such as baby-sitting.

While this emphasis on the nuclear network may be true of some families, however, it is by no means true of all. In the first place demographic research has established that the nuclear family is not a new phenomenon. Laslett[39] concludes that "the English peasantry and the English townsfolk in the seventeenth or eighteenth century lived in nuclear families, independent families, of man, wife and children, sometimes with additions . . . the family in England ten or fifteen generations ago was not so very different from the family in England as it is today". At that time the average family size was four or five, and while the upper social strata had much larger domestic units, the number was increased not as a result of the inclusion of other related adults, but rather the inclusion of domestic servants. Perhaps this evidence lends support to the view that the nuclear family was a necessary precondition for industrialization, and that where this kind of family was absent the development of industrialization was retarded. Among others, Nimkoff[40] has taken this view, and Turner[41] has put the case in more explicit terms:

> Labour migration to the urban industrial areas is positively emancipating the individual from his obligations to his kinship group. Again, if a man wishes to

[37] Mogey, J. M., *op. cit.*
[38] Homans, G. C., *The Human Group*, Harcourt Brace, 1950.
[39] Laslett, P., *The World We Have Lost*, Methuen, 1965.
[40] Nimkoff, M. F., ed., *Comparative Family Systems*, Houghton Mifflin, 1965.
[41] Turner, V. W., *Schism and Continuity in an African Society*, Manchester University Press, 1957.

accumulate capital to set up as a petty trader or tailor, or to acquire a higher standard of living for himself, and his elementary family, he must break away from his circle of village kin towards whom he has traditional obligations. Everywhere, we see the spectacle of corporate groups of kin disintegrating and the emergence of smaller residential units based on the elementary family.

Class differences probably account for some significant variations from the current nuclear family norm. It seems likely that while there may have been a shift towards the nuclear family becoming coterminous with the domestic unit, this need not be an *isolated* nuclear family and need not imply any significant reduction in interactional and recognized ties even if they are spread over a wider area. In the 1950s, Willmott and Young[42] discovered in the East End of London that "the extended family is still very much a reality" and they speak of "a living extended family which includes within it three and even four generations". In a more recent study of Swansea, Rosser and Harris[43] found that although the extended family endures, it is more physically dispersed than formerly. Moreover, the internal diversification brought about by occupational and social mobility and by the revolution in status, attitudes and interests of women has tended to reduce the cohesion of the extended kinship unit and give greater emphasis to the relationships of marriage and the "elementary" family. But since the extended family has the functions of providing aid and social identification to its members, and since the ownership of cars and telephones assists communication, it remains strong.

Some of Townsend's work[44] has reinforced the Bethnal Green observations concerning the greater number of generations participating in the extended family. His 1962 research into a probability sample of 2500 persons in Britain revealed that 22 per cent of the elderly population had great-grandchildren. The existence on a substantial scale of families with four generations still alive is, as Townsend says, a relatively new phenomenon in the history of human societies, and has arisen fundamentally from the combined consequences of increased longevity

[42] Young, M. and Willmott, P., *op. cit.*

[43] Rosser, C. and Harris, C., *The Family and Social Change*, Routledge & Kegan Paul, 1965.

[44] Townsend, P., "The four generation family", *New Society*, 7 July 1966. See also Shanas, E., Townsend, P., Wedderburn, D., Friis, H., Milhøj, P. and Stehouwer, J., *Older People in Three Industrial Societies*, Atherton, 1967.

and earlier marriages. At one time the extended family consisted of one surviving grandparent at the apex of a structure with large numbers of children and other relatives spread out below. Nowadays there may be two, three or all four grandparents alive and often a great-grandparent too. The kinship network has changed and this has had important effects on the ways in which the network is broken into geographically proximate groupings and households. Specifically, according to Townsend, "The relations between ascendant and descendant kin and affinal kin have been strengthened as compared with those with collateral kin: parents and children and in-laws count more, cousins, aunts and uncles less." In general there is more stability and continuity at the centre of the family, and consequently less need to integrate numbers of middle-aged and elderly spinsters. With fewer "denuded" immediate families (those in which at least one member is missing because of death), a model type of extended family is beginning to replace a wide variety of families and households ranging from isolated individuals at one extreme to kinship tribes at the other.

Some evidence indicates the importance of class in establishing family structure. Young and Willmott, in writing of a middle-class London suburb, indicated that there was less emphasis on kinship than in Bethnal Green, and more emphasis on friendship.[45] On the other hand, one of the most important conclusions from *The Family and Social Change*[46] was that there were small differences between middle-class and working-class families; to give one small example, 44 per cent of middle-class married women had seen their mothers within the 24 hours prior to the survey, compared with 56 per cent of working-class women. These figures lend support to the view that, in the extended family, the mother retains a central position. In Bethnal Green, ties were so strong between mother, daughter and grandchildren that prospective husbands had to learn two roles: that of son-in-law as well as that of husband. Speaking of the slight positive tendency for women to set up home near their relatives, Mays[47] says that "a mile can be thought of as a wide separation" in the Liverpool dockland.

[45] Young, M. and Willmott, P., *Family and Class in a London Suburb*, Routledge & Kegan Paul, 1960.
[46] Rosser, C. and Harris, C., *op. cit.*
[47] Mays, J. B., *Growing Up in the City*, Liverpool University Press, 1954.

Nevertheless there are significant regional differences in social norms which overlay the structure imposed by class, and this may help to explain the somewhat atypical results obtained in Swansea. Gorer concludes that "People in the working class outside the southern counties of England do tend to live near their kinsfolk; it is the people of the south, especially the middle class . . . who are most often separated from their kith and kin and therefore dependent on friends and neighbours for help and companionship."[48] Equally, Fletcher argues that

> in localities (urban and rural alike) in which a strong community life and spirit has continued—as in Bethnal Green, in the villages of the Forest of Dean, in small mining towns—the inter-relationships and the degree of mutual aid between the family and wider kindred may still continue to be of importance. In the larger conurbations, in suburbs, in growing dormitory areas, and in New Towns, however, the distance between the individual family and its wider kindred is likely to be much more marked.[49]

The Emancipation of Women

In the nineteenth century the effect of marriage was that "all the wife's personal chattels became the absolute property of the husband, while the husband could dispose of the wife's leasehold property during his life and enjoyed for his own benefit her freehold estate during her life . . . the married woman, both physically and economically, was very much in the position of a chattel of her husband".[50] These sentiments are echoed by McGregor:[51] "Outside the family, married women had the same legal status as children and lunatics; within it they were their husband's inferiors. By marriage they moved from dependence on fathers or male relatives to dependence on husbands." A recent study of lower income families within the Victorian middle class,[52] for instance—the kind of families with only one general servant—finds no evidence of that paraphernalia of gentility, of the enervating leisure and

[48] Gorer, G., *Exploring English Character*, Cresset Press, 1955.

[49] Fletcher, R., *op. cit.*

[50] Graveson, R. H. and Crane, F. R., eds., *A Century of Family Law, 1857–1957*, Sweet & Maxwell, 1957.

[51] McGregor, O. R., *Divorce in England*, Heinemann, 1957.

[52] Branca, P., *Silent Sisterhood: Middle Class Women in the Victorian Home*, Croom Helm, 1975.

the elaborate dinner parties which form the staple of most books on the Victorian middle-class home. Instead, the typical picture is of a hard-working woman, exhausted by physical toil and the demands of her children, living on a tight budget in unhealthy conditions, but with new aspirations most of which she found herself unable to fulfil.

Undoubtedly the achievement of political equality for women in the early twentieth century has been accompanied by a considerable measure of effective social equality. Women now have recognized rights with regard to the ownership of property; educational opportunity; entry to many occupations.[53] They now enter marriage on a completely voluntary basis and on an equal footing with their male partners. While in many respects this has been a laudable development, it has brought new problems in its train. For example, whereas the husband in Victorian families automatically made the decisions and had complete control, today the refusal to accept this practice has caused some vagueness over what should be the individual responsibilities of husband and wife. Young and Willmott, in their survey of Bethnal Green,[54] found that 32 of the 45 husbands in the marriage sample gave some assistance with the housework; 29 had done the washing-up at least once in the week previous to the interview. The authors note that Booth and Rowntree, in their surveys of London and York respectively, made half a century earlier, do not mention washing-up, probably because in 1900 there was no question about who did it. At the same time, there continues to be widespread acceptance of the idea that the wife/mother must carry the primary responsibility for the family, however co-operative husbands may be. Thus, for example, two books about work for wives in middle life[55] scarcely touch on the possibility that the husband's domestic role is any more than one of encouragement or an occasional

---

[53] These rights have been reinforced by legislation on discrimination and equal pay, even if the precise impact of the law has not been so positive as was originally intended. Moreover, there remains a deeply ingrained pattern of sex stereotyping so far as occupational choice is concerned. In other countries, such as Sweden and the U.S.S.R., where women perform occupational roles hitherto regarded as the prerogative of the male, this has probably come about as a direct consequence of the desperate scarcity of labour which has forced employers to discard their traditional prejudices.

[54] Young, M. and Willmott, P., *op. cit.*

[55] Labovitch, P. and Simon, R., *Late Start: Careers for Wives*, Cornmarket, revised edition, 1969; Musgrave, B. and Wheeler-Bennett, J., eds., *Women at Work*, Peter Owen, 1972.

helping hand with the washing up. Perhaps such values, deeply en-
trenched, help to account for the likelihood of emotional and physical
overload, and possibly guilt and self-doubt, for the woman in "dual-
career" families of the type studied by the Rapoports.[56]

On the wife's part, there is a growing demand for leisure, particularly
at week-ends; and although this may seem trivial, it is symptomatic of
social change and is often a source of conflict. As Reisman[57] noted in
The Lonely Crowd: "The current divorce rate is, in part, an index of the
new demands made upon marriage for sociability and leisure by sensitive middle-class couples—these demands . . . include the expectation
that each partner grow and develop at approximately the same rate."
The fact that such difficulties can be resolved, albeit painfully, is illustrated by the following narrative by an Irish woman of 40, married to an
Irish building construction worker, with two young daughters at school:

> I started in hotel work, but when I got married I certainly didn't think I'd have
> to work. Now I go out cleaning, which means I have some money of my own. But
> really I've never realized until now how much I've put up with in the past. He
> used to shout at me and order me about, demanding his dinner and never shifting
> out of his chair, saying Sunday was his day of rest. Now I've told him I'm not going
> to have it any longer, Sunday is my day of rest too, and just standing up for myself
> has made a difference. He has his night out playing darts. I have my night out with
> the mother's group at the church. The other night he went to the pub by himself,
> and said when he came home he didn't like it without me! It's a real change.[58]

In a real sense, the physical health of wives has been related to the
improved status of women. Concern for the welfare of expectant mother
has turned child-bearing into a normal, healthy function instead of a
painful, burdensome disease. Today, moreover, the typical pattern is
for pregnancies to be concentrated into the first 10 years of marriage
and for them to take place at planned intervals. Titmuss,[59] for instance,
has estimated that in the 1890s the average "working-class mother
spent about 15 years in a state of pregnancy and in nursing a baby for
the first year of its life"; this 15 years has now dropped to 4. The increased leisure for women resulting from their fewer confinements and

[56] Rapoport, R. and Rapoport, R., *Dual Career Families*, Penguin Books, 1971.
[57] Reisman, D., *The Lonely Crowd*, Yale University Press, 1950.
[58] Quoted in Raven, S., "Anyone for open marriage?", *Sunday Times*, 28 January 1973.
[59] Titmuss, R. M., *Problems of Social Policy*, Allen & Unwin, 1950.

also from their adoption of various labour-saving devices in the home has given them far more time and opportunity to take up some extra-familial pursuit, in the form of a kind of leisure which covers a broader horizon than the home itself (e.g., voluntary service) or paid employment. Without such outlets, Myrdal and Klein[60] argue, the contemporary housewife would suffer from social isolation: not only because she feels obliged to remain in the home to look after the children, but also because (in the middle class) she has internalized certain values of privacy and "keeping oneself to oneself". Her solitude makes her feel that life is passing her by and she resents the fact that her husband is virtually her only contact with the outside world.

This situation provides another potential source of conflict within the family. Myrdal and Klein further quote from Reisman's *The Lonely Crowd*:

> The housewife, although producing a social work-product, does not find her work explicitly defined . . . in the national census or in people's minds. And since her work is not defined as work, she is exhausted at the end of the day without feeling any right to be.

Such views are echoed and expanded in a recent wide-ranging study of housework,[61] in which Oakley demonstrates that there is no universal division of labour by sex, nor a nurturing instinct attaching exclusively to women which would make housewifery part of the natural order. On the contrary, housework on its present scale is peculiar to modern industrialized countries, where women spend large and undiminishing amounts of their time in child and husband-servicing activities which embody the most frustrating aspects of industrial labour —fragmentation, isolation, repetitiveness, lack of creativity, and pace. Surveys purporting to show a growing involvement of men in housework, according to Oakley, have misunderstood and misrepresented the marginal, infrequent and spasmodic involvement of some men in some of the less unpleasant work and in the more rewarding bits of child-care. Although, on the whole, women of all social classes tend to unite in disliking some or most housework tasks, middle-class women

[60] Myrdal, A. and Klein, V., *Women's Two Roles: Home and Work*, Routledge & Kegan Paul, 1956.
[61] Oakley, A., *The Sociology of Housework*, Martin Robertson, 1975.

are more likely to reject the idea that they are "housewives". Nevertheless, housewifery is virtually inescapable, in Oakley's view, for its values are inculcated in childhood as an integral part of becoming a woman, wife and mother, in fact of becoming "feminine". Indeed, the housewife may grow somewhat obsessional because to create and externalize seemingly fixed domestic standards for herself is the only way, albeit self-defeating, in which she can reward herself for tasks which carry no other reward.[62]

So it seems possible that the improved physical health of married women has been bought—because of the inability of housework to keep pace with the rising aspirations of women—at the expense of reduced mental health. For the United States (and there is no reason to suppose that the situation is any different in Britain), Bernard[63] has forcefully argued that marriage as currently practised is, contrary to popular opinion, good for men but bad for women. American married men over 30 suffer conspicuously less depression, severe neurotic symptoms, phobic tendencies and passivity than single men. Between the ages of 45 and 64 they suffer less from chronic illness; they commit suicide half as often. They suffer less from symptoms like nervous breakdown, insomnia, headaches and palpitations. On the other hand, the statistical portrait of American married women is quite different. Their physical health, as measured by absence of chronic ailments and restricted activity, is as good as that of their husbands, and better in old age, but "they suffer from greater mental health hazards and present a far worse clinical picture". They experience frequent psychological distress symptoms, and are more likely than married men to commit suicide. Even more striking is the superior mental health (except in the menopausal decade) of single women over married women. In Bernard's view, the psychological difficulties of married women have their origin in the gender-typing of childhood, reinforced by the tendency of males to bolster up their "authority" by marrying women who, though normally from the same social background, are slightly younger, slightly less

---

[62] Oakley rejects the idea that housewives should be recognized by payment, on the grounds that this would merely reinforce the gender-typing of housework. On the other hand, it is arguable that payment would at least offer an increase of status that would make housework more acceptable to men.

[63] Bernard, J., *The Future of Marriage*, Souvenir Press, 1973.

well educated and in slightly less "good" jobs. If the husband values her work as a wife and mother, that helps her to maintain her psychic equilibrium (and not to feel too deeply her reduced status in the world outside)—but plenty of husbands do not explicty recognize the contribution of their wives inside the home. Even those who do, thinking of their partners principally as housewives, cannot take seriously their ventures in other directions. Yet wives who work outside the home tend to have far better health than those who work inside it only. They may be neurotic, but are less likely to be psychotic, and are less likely to complain of pains and ailments, and are far less subject to symptoms of psychological distress.

There are now over 8 million working women in Britain, comprising 40 per cent of the total labour force.[64] It is somewhat surprising to find that the level of female employment has been fairly constant over the decades, albeit at a somewhat lower level than in France. Yet such consistency conceals major changes in the type of work undertaken by women and also in the status of the women themselves. For example, the percentage of married women in the female labour force has increased from 16 per cent in 1931 to nearly 64 per cent today. Among married women aged between 25 and 34, two-thirds are in gainful employment of some kind. In the group aged between 35 and 44, the proportion is three-quarters, dropping to slightly more than two-thirds in the 45–54 group. Even among women in their early twenties—the group in which one might expect to find the greatest number of mothers with really young children—wives make up more than a third of those at work. Mothers have increasingly wanted to work, partly as a consequence of the poverty of families with children relative to the childless, but also because of women's desire for new social and economic roles and relations. The proportion of employed mothers has now risen

[64] The proportion of women of working age actually in full-time employment varies from 10 to 70 per cent in other countries. The group of countries with the lowest proportion of women at work includes Latin America, South Africa, Spain, Portugal, the Netherlands and the predominantly Mohammedan states in Africa and Asia. Apart from the Eastern European countries, those with the highest rates of female employment are Finland, Denmark, Turkey, Austria, Thailand and Japan. These differences are not merely a reflection of variations in living standards; they are also the product of the relative status enjoyed by men and women under varying cultural, political, economic and religious systems. In Britain the current figure is about 54 per cent.

to over one-third, and it has been estimated that 2.5 million children under the age of 11, including 820,000 pre-school children, have working mothers. This rise has occurred in spite of employment, child-care and social security policies geared to a conception of the male bread-winner based full-time at work, with the mother's work subordinated to child-care responsibilities in the home.

What sort of work do women undertake? One thing is clear: at least in terms of paid jobs, women are doing less and less housework. Well over a third of women workers were in domestic service in 1891, a peak year for servants; in the nineteenth century the line between the working classes and the rest of society was indicated by servant keeping. The cult of gentility demanded that the wife of any man aspiring to that status could not clean her own floors, cook her own meals or take care of her own children, and the result was a vast proliferation of one and two-servant households. The role of these female servants was summarized by W. R. Greg in *The National Review* in 1869.[65] They were seen as discharging a most important and indispensable function in social life: "In a word, they fulfil both essentials of a woman's being; they are supported by, and they administer to men."

Even in 1931 a quarter of the total number of women at work were chars or maids. Now less than 10 per cent do this sort of work—in hotels, canteens or homes. Domestic service has thus been replaced by work in manufacturing industry, distributive trades and services of all kinds, including insurance, banking, transport, catering and laundries. Some of these tertiary industries are, indeed, predominantly female (such as hairdressing, nursing and other services ancillary to medicine), and Lockwood[66] speaks of the "white-blouse brigade", that one-third of all employed women who act as clerks, typists and shop assistants. Although women are principally engaged in non-manual jobs, there are also some manufacturing industries which rely on large quantities of female labour. Examples include clothing and textiles, or the manufacture of electrical, radio and electronic equipment, in which women are able to use to advantage their greater manual dexterity. With some

[65] Quoted in Horn, P., *The Rise and Fall of the Victorian Servant*, Gill & Macmillan and St. Martin's Press, 1975.

[66] Lockwood, D., *The Black-Coated Worker*, Allen & Unwin, 1958.

large industries, such as those connected with food, the proportion of women employed may be as high as 40 per cent. In engineering, on the other hand, women comprise no more than a quarter of the total, and most of these are concentrated—not surprisingly, perhaps—in light engineering. Women tend to congregate in particular branches of industry, like clothing and toy manufacture, because these are occupations which have traditionally been performed by women. When the Industrial Revolution took these processes out of the home and into the factory, women have been willing to follow the trend. It is worth noting, too, the correlation between the growth of the social services and the participation of women. This correlation is twofold: while the social services require large numbers of skilled workers and have to a large extent recruited women for this purpose, it is also true to say that women, both politically and professionally, have had their fair share of responsibility in calling forth these services.

Undoubtedly one of the most potent factors encouraging companies to take on women immediately after World War II was the general situation of labour scarcity existing in most sectors of industry at that time. The exigencies first of reconstruction and then of rearmament, plus the tendency of young people to undertake longer periods of further education, plus the increase in the number of old people in the population, produced a gap in the supply of labour relative to the demand, which women were called upon to fill. Once virtually all the unmarried women had been employed, moreover, any further increases could only come from married women. Their return to work was made possible, as has already been suggested, by the smaller size of the family and by the practice of concentrating procreation and child-rearing in the first 10 to 15 years of marriage. Yet in the wider perspective, the range of job opportunities open to men are often quite different from those available to women, so much so that in many cases there are virtually two separate labour markets, one marked "male" and the other "female". Over two-thirds of all gainfully employed women are concentrated in slightly more than 20 types of work, including clerical activities, retail distribution, nursing, cleaning, and primary school teaching. Broken down still further, the figures reveal that women hold jobs of relatively low status and responsibility. Among women in manufacturing industry, too, most are classified as unskilled and only a very small number have attained supervisory positions. A recent report[67] has highlighted the situation by listing the proportion of women in certain professional bodies. Among those with the lowest are the Institution of Electrical Engineers with 0.1 per cent women out of over 30,000 members; the Institution of Mechanical Engineers with 0.1 per cent women out of nearly 74,000 members; and the Institute of Building with no women among its 21,000 members. Women constitute 6.4 per cent of the Bar Council, 3.2 per cent of the Law Society, 17.8 per cent of the British Medical Association, 13.1 per cent of the British Dental Association, and 4.2 per cent of the Royal Institute of British Architects. The subject areas in which women achieved the largest numerical increases (for attendance at vocational courses in colleges of further and higher education), in the 5 years up to 1973–74 were hairdressing, law, art, industrial design and librarianship—and the report says that "Little comfort can be derived from the increase of 0.1 per cent on the numbers of women students on engineering courses."

All this means that, so far as many jobs are concerned, men and women are essentially non-competing groups. It has thus been possible, despite the apparent paradox, to describe Britain as suffering from a persistent shortage of labour while simultaneously female job seekers have remained unemployed. An automatic market adjustment has not been possible because the labour shortages have occurred primarily in certain skilled occupations and highly qualified positions. Since these shortages are growing steadily more acute, however, the goal of greater social and vocational equality for women has attracted increasing attention and there has been mounting pressure for the recruitment of women into occupations traditionally the preserve of the male sex. These pressures received some recognition in 1970 with the introduction of legislation to enforce the establishment of equal pay for both men and women if similar work is being undertaken, and with subsequent legislation to counter discrimination in recruitment and selection procedures. Although, as a result, the wage rates of women have risen one-third faster than men's, female workers have still not deprived themselves of one of the major features that renders them attractive to cost-conscious companies, namely, their relative cheapness. In April

[67] *The Vocational Education of Women*, London and Home Counties Regional Advisory Council for Technological Education, 1976.

1976 the average weekly pay for full-time women was £46 compared with £72 for men, and 43 per cent of women against 5 per cent of men earned less than £40 per week. Also industry has developed several skilful techniques for evading legal obligations towards female employees so that differentials based on sex can continue to be justified.[68]

Women tend to confine themselves to relatively unskilled jobs, not necessarily because they lack ability but because they are less interested in self-advancement. A recent study of women at work, for example, revealed that only 57 per cent of working wives would accept promotion involving more responsibility, compared with 81 per cent of men.[69] They regard industry as a man's world and they enter it simply as a means to an end; perhaps for this reason they are difficult to organize in large numbers. Feeling themselves a temporary part of the workforce, women seldom rock the boat: perhaps because so much energy goes in juggling the conflicting and heavy demands of home against job, women tend to see work problems individually rather than collectively. Very few will join a trade union, and those who do will almost invariably be passive members. They develop little sense of comradeship and "belongingness" in the firm, and no interest at all in such matters as joint consultation. On the other hand, women possess a greater sense of loyalty towards their employers—arising from a sense of gratitude which is itself dependent on a feeling that they are lucky to be working at all—and will obey orders more readily than equivalent male employees. They like routine and are frightened of change, possessing what has been called an "innate conservatism"; yet this may be an advantage to a company which requires them to do simple repetitive tasks, for which women are admirably suited. It has to be recognized that women will more readily tolerate this type of work because, typically, they do not stay in the job for life (they usually work until or just after marriage, and return to the labour force when their main child-rearing period is over), and their limited time horizons make it

[68] These include making sure that men and women do different jobs so that, although equal pay theoretically prevails, the wages for "female" jobs are so low that males do not in practice apply. Large extra payments or special bonuses for long service with the firm, especially unbroken service, inevitably mean that men will earn more than women for the same job, as very few women (apart from lifelong spinsters) can claim such seniority.

[69] Walters, M., "Women at work", *Sunday Times*, 27 February 1977.

easier for them to tolerate adverse conditions or uninspiring work routines. Moreover, married women in particular are seldom the sole or major bread-winners in the household. As a result, they can be conscious of the fact that if they leave their paid employment—either voluntarily or because of enforced redundancy—the consequences are not so drastic as if their husbands lose their jobs. And it is likely that this awareness, of the relatively small penalties for leaving the job, paradoxically makes the job itself more tolerable than it would be if the job-holder felt that it had, perforce, to be endured indefinitely.

It has already been argued that women perform well at routine tasks, and from this observation one might derive the plausible (yet illogical) inference that women workers actively prefer repetitive jobs incorporating a short job-cycle. Nonetheless a growing body of research has indicated that while female employees may not be explicitly dissatisfied with routine work, they are more likely to be positively satisfied (and therefore more highly motivated) if the work is felt to be "interesting, varied, providing a sense of achievement and challenge and, very importantly, as making good use of abilities".[70] In the Walters survey,[71] men responded predictably when asked what things were most important on the job: they stressed their role as breadwinners who expected or hoped to work continuously. Some 60 per cent (as opposed to 33 per cent of women) mentioned a secure job with a steady income. For men —but not for women—high wages and promotion prospects were as important as working conditions or job interest. Women put far more stress on jobs that fitted in with their domestic schedules, by providing such benefits as flexible hours. Though nearly half the sample of working wives wanted to be within easy travelling distance of their jobs, only a quarter of the men mentioned this advantage.

The most obvious reason prompting women to seek employment, particularly married women, is the desire for more money. Half of the sample of working wives, in the Walters study, declared that if they stopped working the family would have to do without luxuries. Of course, the term may be deceptive: luxuries may mean not holidays or

[70] Wild, R., Hill, A. B. and Ridgeway, C. C., "Job Satisfaction and labour turnover amongst women workers", *Journal of Management Studies*, Vol. 7, No. 1, February 1970, pp. 78–86.
[71] Walters, M., *op. cit.*

cars but things like children's clothes. Working-class families would be more likely to take a severe drop in living standards if the wives stayed at home, and more than a quarter of the wives questioned said that their wages were an essential part of the family budget. Oddly enough, however, three-quarters said they would work even if they did not need the money: they would get bored if stuck at home, they would need outside interests, and they enjoyed meeting people. Non-working wives liked the freedom of being at home, but almost half were prepared to admit its darker side—the isolation, depression, and feeling of being trapped. Most psychological studies of motivation have echoed this impression that money is not necessarily the predominant causal factor in prompting women to seek employment; it is equally plausible to argue that mothers go out to work in order to achieve the social companionship they lose once their children are all at school. Certainly women more than men are apt to resist any disturbance to their informal social groups in the work situation. Nonetheless the money is part of the reward from working, and the way in which the wages are spent indicates that the woman generally works neither to meet basic economic needs nor to provide personal pleasures for herself. In the majority of cases, wives go out to work principally to provide "extras" for the family and for the house. In addition, many women enjoy the independence derived from spending their own money, though in nearly every case they stress the vital importance of the children's welfare. Such motives and feelings are relatively classless in their impact, given the fact that under modern economic conditions it is virtually impossible to establish a home on the basis of the husband's income alone.

Something has already been said on the question of housekeeping allowances, a phase which is not quite yet an anachronism despite the prevalence of joint bank accounts. It appears that, for most wives, the housekeeping allowance does not fluctuate from week to week, except for those whose husbands' earnings vary (such as window-cleaners), and even here there is a tendency for the allowance to be stabilized. Indeed, the pressures towards stabilization—derived from the wife's preferences, the hire-purchase instalments and mortgage repayments or rent—have been translated generally into demands for stability in wage-earners' incomes rather than the retention of bonus systems whose weekly payments can fluctuate so irregularly and markedly that family budgeting becomes impossible.[72] If the man gets a rise, it is customary for the wife to receive only a proportionate increase. The weekly amount of the housekeeping money is almost invariably based only on the husband's regular wage, excluding overtime and bonus earnings, but with the growing egalitarianism in marriage, it is becoming very rare to find marriages where either partner has sole, undisputed control over the family finances. Typically, such matters are now the mutual concern of husband and wife.

It is clear that part of the alleged conflict between motherhood and a career is artificial since there is little evidence to support the beliefs of the pessimists that the employment of wives contributes to delinquency and neglect among their children. The Bermondsey report[73] showed that children of working mothers, far from suffering ill-effects, did *better* in the 11-plus examination, became independent and "grown-up" more quickly, were every bit as healthy, and were more regular attenders at school than those with "housewife" mothers. Of course, such generalizations can be interpreted in more than one way: if children with working mothers are more regular attenders at school, the cause may simply lie in the fact that there is nobody at home to look after them if they are mildly ill, therefore they are more likely to be forced to go to school. At the same time, Jephcott is firm in believing that the children themselves are not unhappy about their mothers going out to work: "They often enjoy their improved status: it feels grown-up to have the key, the run of the home and the chance to boss the young ones about."

With regard to the arrangements made for the care of pre-school children by mothers at work, several studies have shown that conditions have markedly improved since the 1843 Children's Employment Commission,[74] referring to domestic workers, stated that "married women, having no time to attend to their families, or even to suckle their offspring, freely administer opium in some form or other to their infants, in order to prevent their cries interfering with the protracted

[72] See Bolle de Bal, M., 'The psycho-sociology of wage incentives", *British Journal of Industrial Relations*, Vol. 7, No. 3, November 1969, pp. 385–98.

[73] Jephcott, P., Seear, N. and Smith, J., *Married Women Working*, Allen & Unwin, 1962.

[74] Quoted in Fletcher, R., *op. cit.*

labour by which they strive to obtain a miserable subsistence". Writing
of the work done by females in the coal mines, Dr. Pinchbeck[75] remarks: "The tragedy was that the 'savage rudeness' of the upbringing
of girls in the pits was not counteracted by any system of education.
Introduced into the pit in early childhood before any correct ideas of
conduct could be formed, they gradually grew accustomed to obscene
language, vice, and debauchery." Today, it is not only true that children are valued more (even though their economic value is zero) but
also arrangements for their proper care are easier to make. Whereas in
the nineteenth century it was not exceptional for a mother who had just
had a baby to return to work after about 4 weeks, in modern times the
relieving of economic pressures has reduced to negligible proportions
the number of women at work with children under 1 year old. Furthermore, mothers may choose between a wide variety of available facilities: day nurseries, nursery schools (operated by the local authority,
private enterprise, or by factories themselves), neighbours, child-
minders, mothers or mothers-in-law. Most of the evidence supports the
conclusion that in working-class communities Granny is the favoured
alternative because she can give the child personal attention and love,
whereas the nursery can only give professional expertise. Conditions
favour the proper care of children in other respects, too: families are
smaller in the sense that they each have fewer children, which means
that each child can obtain more consideration and attention; greater
longevity means a larger supply of Grannies. Finally, the eagerness with
which factories seek women employees is reflected in their willingness
to make special arrangements, either by setting up nurseries of their
own, or by operating specially timed shifts to cater for mothers with
young children.

On the other hand, the National Opinion Poll quota sample study[76]
reveals a much less optimistic picture. First of all, women with children
under 5 tend not to work. Four out of 10 of the non-working wives in
the sample had pre-school children as compared with 1 in 10 of the
workers. More than half of the stay-at-homes had stopped work because
of the birth of a child, and the same proportion expected to work again.

[75] Pinchbeck, I., *Women Workers and the Industrial Revolution, 1750–1850*, Routledge &
Kegan Paul, 1930.
[76] Walters, M., *op. cit.*

Nurseries, public or private, were used only by a tiny minority—and no one used a work creche—reflecting nothing but the almost complete absence of adequate child care.[77] The traditional solution for working mothers—grandmothers and other relatives—does not work as much as it theoretically might: women are isolated by the break-up of old tight-knit neighbourhoods, and perhaps older women who have worked for much of their lives feel less inclined to look after grandchildren. Only a tiny proportion of well-off women can buy themselves out of the problem of child-care by acquiring the services of nannies, au pairs, or cleaners; 9 out of 10 working wives have no outside help of any kind.

Still, the improved status of women undoubtedly means that if they no longer wish to be confined to a role of child-bearing and domesticity, they can choose to go out to work and pursue whatever aims and interests they may have. But from other points of view the change has not been a radical one. Only a minority of married women permanently combine employment with their lives as wives and mothers. Work is regarded as something secondary, something the wife can legitimately undertake when the children have become older. For instance, a finding[78] among highly-educated women showed that girls who have high aspirations both at school and again 8 years after taking their degrees have notably lower ambitions while they are actually at university. It is as if they cannot visualize their own lives until they know whom they are going to marry; in other words, they accept the likelihood that they will accommodate their lives to the career-patterns of their husbands. This fact means that girls face an extra difficulty when deciding on a career. Young men are able to have "continuous" lives: they may not necessarily know where they are going, but the fact of marriage does not normally throw a smokescreen across a long-term view of their future. By contrast, the career curves of the vast majority of married women are likely to have a downward loop or even a clean break at the time when a mother has young children to look after. Given the present

[77] Tizard has argued that the paucity of day-care services is a consequence of the ideologically-founded belief that young children require continuous mothering. See Fonda, N. and Moss, P., eds., *Mothers in Employment*, Brunel University Management Programme, 1977.

[78] Fogarty, M., Rapoport, R. and Rapoport, R., *Sex, Career and Family*, P.E.P. and Allen & Unwin, 1971. See also, Pahl, R. and Pahl, J., *Managers and Their Wives*, Penguin Books.

age of marriage and of child-bearing, this is likely to be during a woman's late twenties and early thirties, just the time when the man has completed his training and is moving into substantial management or professional responsibility. The handicap of "discontinuous" work experience is not felt exclusively among middle-class or highly educated women, either. No jobs have hours which are flexible enough to cope with school holidays or emergencies. In Walters survey, 16 per cent of working mothers said that they had to stop work during school holidays, and if children succumbed to ailments as common as mumps or measles, 11 per cent would have to quit work altogether while 36 per cent would try to take unpaid leave. In these circumstances, it is scarcely surprising that women regard their jobs as peripheral to their "real" responsibilities, and themselves as peripheral to the work force.

Thus the "natural" order of things is still that the man provides and the woman is supported. Inevitably this leads to role conflict. According to the traditional norms, women should be weaker than men, require protection, be passive, patient, self-sacrificing and sensitive—in other words, they should possess qualities quite inappropriate for the more important positions in industrial, commercial or public life. Women may win esteem by being women, but at the same time this reduces their chances of competing for the jobs that offer social prestige on a wider basis. The Swedish sociologist Edmund Dahlstrom has described the situation as follows: "The dilemma of women thus consists of a choice between appearing effective and unfeminine, or feminine and ineffective." That this dilemma is real is illustrated by the way in which the mass media publicize women in public life or senior managerial positions by stressing their "femininity". It is relevant to note in this context that American studies of role conflict among female college students have shown that many girls act out an unintelligent role in order to win prestige among their (predominantly male) friends.[79]

Yet, despite their continuing and severe problems at work, a subtle

[79] The persistence of role stereotypes may well explain why women find it so difficult to rise to high positions in industrial and commercial organizations. Even in cases where equal pay has been in existence for several years, very few women have risen above the lower grades. Local government has perhaps been an exception to this rule, principally because of the uncompetitive rates of pay which have reduced the proportion of suitable male job applicants and thus created the impression that women enjoy equality of

change has taken place in how women see themselves. Working wives seem gradually to be losing their sense of being merely housewives doing a job. More and more, they regard themselves as working women who run homes. Views on this vary significantly according to class. Only one-third of wives with manual jobs see themselves as working women; they may well find housework a relief from a job that is even more tedious and repetitive. Among middle-class women, more highly educated, better paid and more likely to be in intrinsically rewarding jobs, the proportion rises to 6 out of 10. While there is this growing readiness to question what was formerly taken for granted, very few women have completely reconciled their two roles, and there is little evidence of the much-heralded shift to "symmetrical families" where the roles are less rigidly divided and men take a full part in domestic work.[80]

Marriage and Divorce

Christianity, based on the doctrines of St. Paul, has always stressed the indissolubility of marriage, and its loathing of adultery is incorporated in the Ten Commandments. There were several loopholes in the regulations against divorce in the medieval period and it was not until the Council of Trent (1545) that divorce was finally abolished. The Roman Catholic Church, however, has always provided one way out in the form of a Decree of Nullity, whereby a marriage may be declared null and void after an inquiry by an ecclesiastical court. Although this is not exactly equivalent to a divorce, it is more frequently used than is generally imagined. The Sacred Roman Rota, the final court of appeal, deals now with about 200 cases a year, granting nullity to about half of them. The Church of England is far more tolerant, even allowing individual clergy, if they wish, to perform a marriage for a

---

[80] Young, M. and Willmott, P., *The Symmetrical Family*, Routledge & Kegan Paul, 1973.

---

opportunity in this sector. Fogarty and his colleagues suggest several ways in which organizations could (and should) facilitate the career opportunities of women, e.g., a guaranteed right to return to work after maternity (a basic form of this right is now guaranteed by legislation) and a willingness to promote women at later ages than would be usual for men. See Fogarty, M., *et al.*, *op. cit.*

divorced person with a spouse still living. Few actually do, but the fact remains that the permission is there.

So far as civil divorce is concerned, this was obtainable only by private Act of Parliament until 1857, when the Divorce Court was established; even thereafter divorce was effectively confined to the wealthy. In 1925 a first attempt was made to give assistance to poorer people requiring a divorce, and this achievement was consolidated by the Legal Aid Act of 1949. All through its complex history, the law of divorce has consistently penalized the poor, but the changes made in 1949 and the more liberal regulations for legal aid introduced in subsequent years have certainly resulted in significantly more equality before the law.

Until very recently, divorce procedure was based rigidly on the principle of the matrimonial offence. In order to secure a divorce, it had to be shown that a "guilty" spouse had committed a matrimonial offence (in practice, adultery, desertion, or cruelty) against an "innocent" spouse. If the husband was the "guilty" partner, he had to support his ex-wife: if the wife were guilty, she had to support herself. Unfortunately, the concept of the matrimonial offence excluded the most straightforward reason why marriages break down: because the partners can no longer get on with each other. What little evidence there is suggests that couples do not seek divorces because one of the spouses commits a matrimonial offence, but simply because they cannot make their marriages work. Gradual realization of this fact has led to the Divorce Reform Act, 1969, which embodied a radically different approach based on the assumption that the sole grounds for divorce is the irretrievable breakdown of marriage. Adultery, desertion and cruelty are still retained as evidence of marital breakdown, but these have been supplemented by two additional grounds for divorce:

1. the parties to the marriage have lived apart for a continuous period of at least 2 years immediately preceding the presentation of the divorce petition and the respondent consents to a decree being granted; or

2. the parties to the marriage have lived apart for a continuous period of at least 5 years immediately preceding the presentation of the petition.

While these innovations may give the impression that divorce has become easier to obtain, other aspects of the legislation may well have the contrary effect. Firstly, the Act lays considerable emphasis on reconciliation.[81] Secondly, in cases where the petitioner for the divorce is claiming that the partners have lived apart for 5 years or more, the respondent may oppose the grant of a decree nisi on the ground that the dissolution of the marriage would result in grave financial or other hardship to him or her.[82] Underpinning this is the Matrimonial Proceedings and Property Act, 1970, which makes provision for the protection of wives and children on a more satisfactory basis than ever previously existed. Yet however elaborate the statutory provision for dividing the family assets on breakdown, the effect could well be serious in the first instance for the standard of living of both parties, particularly for the majority of the population on average incomes. Thirdly, although the Divorce Reform Act specifies irretrievable breakdown as the sole ground for divorce, three of the possible five justifications still retain the concept of the matrimonial offence. Nor is it sufficient as before merely to prove the offence. In an adultery case, for example, the petitioner must also affirm that he finds it intolerable to live with the respondent, satisfy the court that the marriage has irretrievably broken down and that reconciliation has been considered. Again, in instances of desertion, simple desertion is not enough; the court must be satisfied that the marriage has irretrievably broken down. None of these safeguards, however, satisfies the opponents of any move to liberalize the existing legal provisions for divorce, who maintain that the increasing number of divorce petitions must eventually erode the social institution of the family. It is to the consideration of these beliefs that we must now turn.

It is logical to assume that if people were taking marriage more lightly and divorce more easily, then the divorce rate for recent marriages would rise. In fact, well over half of all divorces occur among couples whose marriages have lasted for more than 10 years, and more

---

[81] Divorce Reform Act, 1969, section 3 (1): solicitors acting for a petitioner for divorce are required to certify whether they have discussed with the petitioner the possibility of a reconciliation and given him the names and addresses of persons qualified to help effect a reconciliation between parties to a marriage who have become estranged.

[82] Divorce Reform Act, 1969, section 4 (1).

than a fifth of the marriages that ended in 1975 had lasted more than 20 years. On the other hand, the statistics do show a gradual and significant increase in the early breakdown of marriage, and attitude surveys reveal a relaxation of attitudes towards pre-marital sexual relationships and trial cohabitation before marriage. Most people who obtain a divorce do so in their late twenties, and the commonest duration of a marriage ending in divorce is 4 years. The number of couples divorcing while they still had children under 16 rose by 8 per cent in 1975, compared with 1974, whereas those without children rose by only 4 per cent. The continued rise in divorces for marriages where the partners are in their early twenties is perhaps not surprising given that such couples often spend their first years of married life in conditions of extreme stress, staying with relatives or in the search for acceptable housing. Moreover, almost three out of five of Britain's teenage brides today are pregnant at marriage, and it is well established that the shot-gun wedding is more likely to end in breakdown. As Musgrove[83] remarks, "The surprising thing is not that some youthful marriages break down, but that so many survive in an atmosphere of disapproval and disparagement. . . . The trend to more youthful marriage should be accepted and aided instead of deplored."

No one can deny that there has been an increase in the number of divorces since the beginning of this century. The number of decrees absolute increased from 3668 in 1931 to 24,396 in 1961 and 45,036 in 1968, or from 0.4 to 2.1 and 3.6 per 1000 of the married population. In 1969 divorces exceeded 50,000 for the first time; in 1971 there were 119,000; and in 1974, 131,000. Decrees made absolute in 1975 numbered 120,500, which suggests that the trend has settled down after erratic movements when the Divorce Reform Act came into force in 1971. Table 2.2 shows some of the changes in the total number of divorces and how this has been spread over various age-groups and marriage durations.

Predicting figures of this kind, the Royal Commission on Marriage and Divorce,[84] 20 years ago, concluded that "matrimony is not so secure now as it was a hundred or even fifty years ago. . . . There is a

[83] Musgrove, F., *Youth and the Social Order*, Routledge & Kegan Paul, 1964.
[84] Royal Commission on Marriage and Divorce, *Report* (Cmd. 9678), H.M.S.O., 1956.

TABLE 2.2. Divorces in England and Wales, 1964–73

Year of divorce	Age of wife at marriage	% distribution of divorces by duration of marriage				Divorces (000s)
		Under 5 years	5–9 years	10–14 years	15+ years	
1964	All ages	11	33	20	36	34.8
	Under 20	14	38	19	29	11.8
	20–24	9	30	21	40	16.3
1970	All ages	14	33	21	32	58.2
	Under 20	16	40	20	24	23.4
	20–24	13	29	22	36	26.0
1972	All ages	13	28	18	41	119.0
	Under 20	14	36	20	30	44.5
	20–24	12	25	18	45	53.6
1973	All ages	15	29	19	37	106.0
	Under 20	17	34	21	28	40.4
	20–24	14	27	18	41	48.0

tendency to take the duties and responsibilities of marriage less seriously than formerly ... its growth is insidious and endangers the whole stability of marriage". Some support for the Royal Commission's view can be drawn from the rising proportion of marriages likely to end in divorce. In 1975 Sir George Baker, President of the Family Division of the High Court, declared that the divorce figures were approaching Californian proportions, with one divorce for 3.74 marriages.[85] Yet, looking at the situation in another way, and using the words of O. R. McGregor, it would seem that we have entered the age of universal marriage. More than 12 million marriages are intact in Britain today; and more than 90 per cent of women aged 40 to 44 are married. Although the institution of marriage is being gradually transformed, there is no evidence that it is dying out, despite a slight decline in the number of marriages from 386,800 in 1974 to 380,600 in 1975. It is no longer fashionable to predict that marriage, in any recognizable form, is about to give way to radically new forms of sexual relationships. Marriage has never been more popular, even if it has never been more risky. The divorced appear to be as keen on marriage as the rest, so

[85] In fact, in parts of California the divorce to marriage ratio has reached one to one, so Britain is still some way behind.

even one bad experience does not affect its appeal. Of 486, 000 marriages in 1972, 120,000 (just over a quarter) were second marriages for one or both of the partners. Some were widows or widowers, but a high proportion were divorcees returning to the fray. Statistically they stand a higher chance of success, and that appears to be at least in part due to age. In general, chances of a successful marriage increase with the age of the partners at the time of their wedding. By 1975, about one in six of those marrying were divorced and half of those married someone who was also divorced. The combination of two divorced people remarrying has recently been increasing by about 7 per cent a year.

Yet even the divorce trends themselves have to be interpreted with great caution. As the Law Commission[86] has pointed out, an increased number of divorces is alarming only if it indicates an increase in the number of broken homes, and not merely that a larger proportion of broken homes is leading to divorce. Even an increase in the number of broken homes might indicate merely that there were more marriages subject to the risk of breakdown. McGregor has argued[87] that "there is no evidence that a higher proportion of marriages break up today than fifty years ago, although there has been a massive increase in *de jure* dissolutions of marriages already broken *de facto*". In the past there may well have been many more broken marriages which were concealed because of the financial inability of the partners to enter into divorce proceedings, to say nothing of the social stigma attached to divorced persons in the early years of this century. The introduction of legal aid, coupled with changing moral outlooks on the subject, has made divorce generally available to the masses. Indeed, recent investigations have shown that a manual worker (or his wife) is now statistically as likely as his employer (or his wife) to petition for divorce, although it is relevant to note that there is a marked social difference in the speed with which marriages break down. Nearly twice as many divorcing couples in class V (unskilled) ended their marriages within 5 years, according to *Separated Spouses*,[88] as did those in classes I and II.

[86] Law Commission, *Reform of the Grounds of Divorced: The Field of Choice* (Cmnd. 3123) H.M.S.O., 1966.

[87] McGregor, O. R., *op. cit.*

[88] McGregor, O. R., Blom-Cooper, L. and Gibson, C., *Separated Spouses*, Duckworth, 1971.

As the duration of marriage shortens, so the proportion of lower social class husbands increases.

In 1900 only the well-off could afford access to the High Court, with its power to remedy matrimonial difficulties by dissolving marriages. The majority (and this accounts for more than 90 per cent of the marriage breakdowns in that period) had to be content with proceedings in magistrates courts, which were granted power in 1878 to award separation orders. These orders enabled poor women to live separately from their husbands, but preserved the marriage bonds intact; in addition, wives could also obtain maintenance orders against their husbands, a privilege denied husbands in relation to their wives. At the turn of the century, about 7500 maintenance orders were being granted annually to married women while today the figure is about 15,000 a year. However, it is not known how many maintenance orders have been rescinded *de facto* by the return of a wife to her husband or *de jure* by application to the court. The figures must therefore be interpreted with caution and allowance made for the unknown proportion of "dead" orders. What is striking is the extent to which the class character of this magistrates court procedure has been sustained. *Separated Spouses*, a survey of 544 men and women who had applied for separation orders, showed that the overwhelming majority were drawn from the lowest stratum of the working class. Half the spouses coming before the magistrates courts do not go on to obtain a divorce; they remain, according to the authors of *Separated Spouses*, "in a matrimonial limbo of being legally married but socially unmarried". Moreover, it is this group which presents the most serious difficulties in terms of financial support with husbands on average or below-average incomes struggling to sustain two families; and separation rather than divorce or widowhood is the greatest cause of the one-parent family, a highly exposed and vulnerable unit in society, whose prevalence emphasizes the precariousness of modern marriage. Magistrates generally commit some 3500 men to prison every year for "wilful refusal or culpable neglect" to pay maintenance. The authors of *Separated Spouses* regard this as a practice which "damages the law, degrades marriage and perpetuates the criminal atmosphere of magistrates' matrimonial jurisdiction".

It is clear that while there has been an absolute increase in the number of divorces, it is manifestly wrong to speak of a continuing increase.

On the contrary, the rise can always be associated with particular events, such as the Poor Persons' Procedure Act of 1925, the Matrimonial Causes Act of 1937 (which extended the justification for divorce to cover such situations as mental cruelty), and the Legal Aid Act of 1949. Rowntree and Carrier,[89] too, point out that the main increases in the divorce rate have always occurred immediately after periods of war: 1919 and 1947 respectively mark the peaks for the years after World Wars I and II. Since about 1952 the incidence of divorce has remained fairly steady apart from a steep rise in 1960–64 which can be attributed to the liberalization of legal aid which took place in 1959 and 1960, and a further steep rise following the Divorce Reform Act of 1969. What are the potential causes of divorce? Some have already been mentioned, including the fact that divorce, like education, has now been made available to all sections of society. As the last paragraph indicates, many of this century's increases in the divorce statistics can be traced almost directly to the periodic introduction of new avenues of escape from an unsuccessful marriage. The effects of war were most important in this respect, and in the years immediately after both major wars in this century there were special facilities for servicemen and their wives to obtain divorces. Long periods of separation for married couples during wartime imposed a great strain on women in particular and this easily accounts for the astronomical divorce figures in 1947 (more than 60,000 decrees absolute compared with an average annual rate for 1946–50 of 38,900 per year). Apart from that, the age of universal marriage inevitably increases the risk that some unions will break down. If, as is now the case, 95 per cent of the population will eventually get married, and if 1 in 12 of the population is homosexual, for that reason alone some marriages must be at risk. It may well be, too, that the very popularity of marriage creates its own momentum, encouraging some marital relationships in which one partner has no special vocation for marriage itself.

The crucial factors behind many contemporary marriage failures are complex and difficult to unravel. One significant element is undoubtedly the egalitarianism which characterizes the relationship between

---

[89] Rowntree, G. and Carrier, N., "The resort to divorce in England and Wales, 1858–1957", *Population Studies*, Vol. 11, No. 3, March 1958.

married partners today by contrast with the patriarchal authoritarian-
ism accepted as the normal pattern in the nineteenth century. Perhaps
the greatest strain on contemporary marriage is the changing expectation of women. One marriage guidance expert, for instance, has described the incidence of divorce as the clash of gears as people move
from one level of expectation to another, where the quality of individual experience and the degree of emotional satisfaction become the
prime factors in measuring personal success or failure. There has been
a noticeable move away from rigid, closed and predetermined patterns
of husband–wife relationship towards looser, open, more pragmatic life
styles. The older model, usually based on a couple's own parents'
behaviour, involves a high degree of role conditioning and economic
and emotional dependence by the wife on the husband, who may in
turn feel that he needs a dependant wife. The most typical marriage
breakdowns begin to occur, it seems, when the wife becomes conscious
of a sense of repression, itself a corollary of dependence, and often
associated with the first pregnancy when the wife finds her inevitably
more housebound role a threat to her autonomy as a person.

Another basic element in many divorces is paradoxically the fact that
marriages are lasting longer. As the Law Commission[90] has pointed out,

> Since we tend to marry younger and live longer, the average duration of marriage
> has doubled since the nineteenth century, and marriages are at risk for twice as
> long as they were. . . . Half the married life of the wife is spent after she has finished
> bearing and rearing children. Thanks to family planning and the mechanization
> of the household, wives can take jobs in conditions of full employment and become
> independent of the financial support of their husbands.

What this means, ultimately, is that marriages which in 1900 terminated in the cemetery now survive to be terminated in the divorce
courts.

Some of the so-called threats to the unity of the family are more
hypothetical. Several writers have referred to the growth of the factory
system, which has made the individual wage-earner the economic unit
of society, rather than the family group. Yet was it really desirable that
all members of the family should be forced, from the earliest age, to
labour at home in the most depressing, insanitary and overcrowded

---

[90] Law Commission, *op. cit.*

conditions? In the words of one commissioner quoted in the Hand-Loom Weavers *Report* of 1840,[91] "domestic happiness is not promoted but impaired by all the members of a family muddling together and jostling each other constantly in the same room". Much the same argument could be advanced to counter the oft-repeated canard that improved contraceptive techniques have affected the biological basis of family life by removing any direct link between sexual intercourse and child-bearing and rearing. Although sexual incompatibility may be responsible for some marital breakdowns, the search for and attainment of a successful partnership in this field is, for most people, a bond uniting man and wife even closer together. And the use of the contraceptive pill means that sexual relations can take place without the inhibiting fear of continuous and debilitating pregnancies leading (as in the nineteenth century) to premature death.

Conclusion

From the material in this chapter it must now be clear that, far from being in moral, physical and functional decline, the family today is simply undergoing a process of change whereby it is being adjusted to meet the needs of a highly complex industrial society. The fact that so much literature is devoted to the family surely indicates that its importance is being recognized as never before. The emancipation of women, shorter working hours and increased opportunities for leisure, social welfare, new attitudes to children and family planning—all these factors, and more, have turned the modern family into an institution vastly different from its Victorian forebears. But while, as Hobsbawm[92] has recently shown, the nineteenth-century family (especially in the middle class) was patriarchal rather than egalitarian and based on personal dependence rather than the cash nexus, the family then shared one basic feature with the family today: its object, in part, was to offer a haven of peace and security in a world of uncertainty outside.

The major secular trend has involved a continuous rise in the standards demanded of marriage. The need for companionship is today a

[91] Quoted in Fletcher, R., *op. cit.*
[92] Hobsbawm, E. J., *The Age of Capital 1848–1875*, Weidenfeld & Nicolson, 1975.

requirement accepted by the family members; there is more introspection about personal relationships and compatibility. Because people are more articulate about and conscious of their marital affairs, they are more willing to take their problems—at an earlier stage, when there is a better chance of saving the situation—to agencies like the National Marriage Guidance Council (in 1974, 35,000 people used the service). Where couples find their problems insoluble, however, it is not surprising that they should turn to divorce. Seen in this light, current divorce rates do not mean that there are more unhappy marriages but that more couples than ever before are willing *publicly* to terminate their marriages instead of allowing the *de facto* break to remain hidden. This in turn has been accompanied by a more realistic and objective system of law for coping with marital breakdown. As put by the Law Commission,[93] the aim of a good divorce law should be, first, to buttress the stability of marriage; and second, when a marriage has irretrievably broken down, to enable the "empty, legal shell" to be destroyed with the maximum fairness and the minimum bitterness, distress and humiliation. "If the marriage is dead, the object of the law should be to afford it a decent burial." McGregor[94] also stresses that "all marriages which have ceased to exist in social reality should be legally interred".

Despite all the statistical evidence, and despite the vast amount of work which remains before the British system of family law becomes genuinely effective, there is no real justification for believing that the proportion of marriages which break down has increased during this century. In Fletcher's words, "the picture of marriage in modern Britain is, surely, a picture of considerable health, considerable stability, and an enlarged degree of opportunity and happiness".[95]

[93] Law Commission, *op. cit.*
[94] In McGregor, O. R., Blom-Cooper, L. and Gibson, C., *op. cit.*
[95] Fletcher, R., *op. cit.*

CHAPTER 3

Social Class in Modern Britain

I was brought up in the middle class or upper middle class—I never know quite what I am. But you don't say "won't" and you write thank-you letters when you've been to stay with someone.

(The Sunday Telegraph)

Mr. Justice Lawton said at Sheffield Assizes yesterday: "A bit of wife-thumping on a Saturday night may not amount to cruelty in some parts of England, but a bit of thumping in Cheltenham may be cruelty. The social background counts."

(Daily Sketch)

Introduction: The Existence of Classes

There can be little doubt that stratification of British society by social class represents a meaningful and realistic analysis. Evidence for the pervasive conditioning effects of social class can be derived from virtually every aspect of the individual's behaviour as he proceeds through the major crises of life: birth, marriage and death.[1] If nothing else, the concept of class provides a convenient method of classifying and differentiating various types of attitude and social action prevalent in society (such as voting intentions and practices), without necessarily implying evaluative notions of superiority or inferiority. However, class variations are virtually indistinguishable from status differentiation, where status is defined as "the social evaluation of the individual—the degree of honour which society confers on him".[2] Whereas class involves a series of differences dependent upon skin-colour, income, position, age, sex, intelligence and so on, social stratification is based on the *meaning* which society gives to these objective differences. Max Weber stresses

[1] For an account of the significance of class at the two extremes of life, see Jones, J., "Social class and the under-fives", *New Society*, 22 December 1966, and Gorer, G., *Death, Grief and Mourning*, Cresset Press, 1965.

[2] Cotgrove, S. F., *The Science of Society*, Allen & Unwin, 1967.

101

this point when he insists that status differentiation is analytically distinct from economically determined differences in class situation. By themselves, income and property do not guarantee high status (though they help a good deal).

Position in the status hierarchy is dependent on a whole range of factors, including income, occupation, accent, style of life, place of residence, leisure pursuits, clothes, educational attainment, attitudes and relationships with others. To belong to a given status group does not mean that the individual must conform with the class norms in all these respects; it is the combined effect which is important. Where there is a high degree of congruence between an individual's rankings on the major criteria of status, this indicates a high degree of status consistency (or status crystallization). Status inconsistency, on the other hand, occurs if there is an irregular profile to the various status rankings—as in cases where an individual is highly qualified educationally but belongs to an ethnic group or occupation with relatively low status. Because individual status profiles are seldom completely flat (as distinct from irregular), it is inevitable that the British class structure contains many complexities and contradictions.

The most objective method of allocating social class is a strict occupational classification. For analysing Census material, the Registrar-General publishes a list of occupations with some 20,000 entries which have been allocated to socio-economic groups and to social classes in five categories. The categories, and some illustrative occupations within each, are listed below.

Class I (Professional)
   Accountants, architects, chemists, clergymen, doctors, lawyers, surveyors, university teachers, judges, metallurgists.

Class II (Intermediate)
   Teachers, Cabinet Ministers, journalists, managers in industry, pilots, publicans, farmers, chiropodists, nurses, MPs.

Class III (Skilled)
   Below-ground miners, electricians, carpenters, printing workers, shorthand typists, railway engine drivers, salesmen, shop assistants, waiters, bus drivers, butchers, upholsterers.

Class IV (Semi-skilled)
   Above-ground miners, electrical assembly workers, machine tool
   operators, bricklayers, street vendors, barmaids, bus conductors,
   postmen, fishermen, telephone operators.

Class V (Unskilled)
   Labourers, ticket collectors, stevedores, window-cleaners, mes-
   sengers, lorry drivers' mates.

While this is useful and acceptable for a number of purposes, it does
create problems. Firstly, there is no unanimity over the number of
social classes into which the population should be divided. Glass[3] used
a tripartite structure in his study of social mobility in Britain; the
British Institute of Public Opinion[4] has favoured four; while others have
opted for six or even seven groups. But secondly, even if there were
uniformity on this point, occupational categories would still be open to
the objection that the scale-fixing is completely arbitrary and that each
occupation itself (such as "salesman", which could mean anything
from a specialist in exporting pharmaceuticals to a door-to-door vendor
of encyclopaedias) may incorporate a wide range of class identifications.
The Registrar-General's system puts all military personnel from
privates to generals in the same socio-economic group; and Cabinet
Ministers are placed in Class II, beneath professional men and in the
same category as MPs. In any event, as Collison[5] admits, "social class
is not determined entirely by occupation".

   Some of the problems generated by the vagueness with which terms
like "middle class" and "working class" are employed are illustrated
by a recent study of social change in Bath during the nineteenth century,
which also throws light on the way in which our present class system has
come into being.[6] According to Neale, the usual three classes have to be
expanded by a division of the working class into the non-deferential,

[3] Glass, D. V., ed., *Social Mobility in Britain*, Routledge & Kegan Paul, 1954.
[4] In a survey of the relationship between social status and political attitudes, quoted in Eysenck, H. J., *Sense and Nonsense in Psychology*, Penguin Books, 1957.
[5] Collison, P., *The Cutteslowe Walls: A Study in Social Class*, Faber, 1966.
[6] Neale, R. S., *Class and Ideology in the Nineteenth Century*, Routledge & Kegan Paul, 1972.

collectivist proletarians and the deferential, dependent remainder. He also introduces a new "middling class" which was non-deferential, aspiring to higher status and sufficiently well off, but only just, to see the way ahead lying in individual effort rather than collective action. This middling class in Bath included "compositors as well as doctors, artisans as well as small producers, self-employed shop-keepers as well as bigger and more successful retailers." The economic crisis facing the middling class in the 1830s was that the number of available jobs was not expanding as fast as the number of eligible applicants, and this made the use of influence in the distribution of the jobs that were available an intolerable evil—generating the pressures that were ultimately to be translated into tangible form by the Northcote-Trevelyan reforms of the Civil Service in the 1850s. As to whether Neale's five classes were enough, Neale himself points out that even servants were divided by Webster's *Encyclopaedia of Domestic Economy* into 22 categories. But at the heart of the argument is the sharp distinction drawn, following Dahrendorf, between social stratification, based on objective criteria such as income, and social class based on conflict between those with legitimate authority and those without. Neale argues that class consciousness and class conflict are most intense when authority relationships in several parts of a man's life coincide. He illustrates this when he says that "a young journeyman shoemaker with ambitions to set up on his own, who was also a Baptist or a Primitive Methodist, living in a low rental house in a parish administered by a Church of England controlled vestry, in a city ruled by a closed corporation, legislated against by the combination laws and other governments decrees, in conflict with his employer over piece rates, and looked down upon by his neighbours as well as by his employer's customers, was likely to be seething with barely suppressed hostility to all authority". (It does not require much imagination to see the second-generation coloured immigrant as the twentieth-century equivalent of that journeyman.) At the same time, it is dangerous to be tied down conceptually to a fixed number of classes, such as five, because of the likelihood that they will come to be seen as ladder-like strata. Many of the grievances of the journeyman just mentioned were remedied in the 1830s and 1840s; the professions escaped from the middling class into some kind of middle-class stability; the artisans became identified with the proletariat. Thus one essential component of the class system is its continuous fluidity and flexibility in the face of political, economic and occupational dynamics.

One recent study has attempted to isolate the significance commonly attached to the differing components of class, including occupation.[7] In 1963 over 2000 English adults were interviewed and three-quarters of them were re-interviewed in 1964. Of these, 96 per cent classified themselves as either middle or working class: 29 per cent middle and 67 per cent working. Only 1 per cent saw themselves as upper class, 1 per cent as lower-middle and 1 per cent as upper-working, while a further 1 per cent used other categories. As part of an investigation of what lay behind these self-classifications, subjects were also asked what kinds of people they felt belonged to the various classes. Occupation proved the main discriminating factor, the middle-class man being seen, not surprisingly, as a non-manual white-collar, skilled, professional or self-employed person. At the same time education, income, breeding and consumption patterns were also seen as distinguishing between classes. The authors, on the basis of these subjective identifications on the part of their subjects, propose a sevenfold measure of class as follows:

Class I	Higher managerial or professional
Class II	Lower managerial or administrative
Class III	Skilled or supervisory non-manual
Class IV	Lower non-manual
Class V	Skilled manual
Class VI	Unskilled manual
Class VII	Residual, including State pensioners

In most respects this is identical with the class model frequently employed by market research organizations, which has six categories (A-B-C1-C2-D-E, the C grades being non-manual and manual derivatives, respectively, from the Registrar-General's Class III). The proposed hierarchy has taken the market research group C1 and subdivided it into two separate layers: skilled or supervisory non-manual workers (class III) and other non-manual workers (class IV). Certainly

[7] Kahan, M., Butler, D. and Stokes, D., *British Journal of Sociology*, Vol. 17, No. 2, 1966, p. 122.

these two groups differ markedly in their habits. At the time of the study, 20 per cent of class III read *The Times*, *Guardian* or *Daily Telegraph* as against 5 per cent of class IV; there was also a marked decrease in Conservative support between the two groups.

The remainder of this chapter will be devoted largely to a discussion of the major determinants of social class, their relevance to the British pattern of social stratification, and the changes currently taking place in establishing their role and relative significance. At the extremes of the class structure, attitudes and ways of life seem to remain relatively fixed, reflecting the rigidity of the structure itself and the lack of mobility in either direction. In the more fluid middle ranges, where most social movement takes place, the situation is different. Economic and social changes characteristic of an advanced industrial society are forcing individuals into new conceptions of their social worlds and new appraisals of their values and interests. At the same time, it is sobering to be told that "In spite of changes in our society, the realities of life for people in different social classes have remained pretty constant."[8]

Income and Wealth

It is impossible to discuss economic inequality without becoming involved with questions of values, yet most of the work on economic differentials in Britain has been less concerned with explanation than with defending an ideological position by appeal to what the statistics show, or even worse, what they would show if only they were more "reliable". Certainly it is true that statistics on the distribution of wealth are inadequate. The official estimates prepared by the Inland Revenue since 1960, by the so-called estate duty method, have been criticised on six counts. They are incomplete since, by and large, they exclude people below the estate duty exemption level; the method of estimation of aggregates from the sample of estates belonging to people dying in a particular year by means of the application of 'mortality multipliers' is subject to error; wealth, as declared for estate duty purposes, may be understated; there are alternative bases for the valuation of wealth; there are different views about what should be included

[8] Reid, I., *Social Class Differences in Britain*, Open Books, 1976.

in the definition of wealth (for example, whether or not rights to occupational or state pensions should be attributed to individuals); and finally, the Inland Revenue distribution describes the wealth of individuals, not of married couples or of families, which might be a more realistic unit for analysis. Now while this is a daunting list of criticisms, it does not justify the fatalism involved in avoiding the issues altogether, and Atkinson[9] has recently provided a variety of alternative measures of the concentration of wealth-holding in Britain, adjusting for the likely effect of the problems listed above.

Undoubtedly alternative ways of defining wealth have different social meanings, and the whole discussion itself is riddled with implications for social policy. [For instance, some wealthy people today feel themselves to be threatened, especially in the face of rapid inflation and what they perceive as a general climate of envy. Whether the threat is real or not, they advance the argument that income differentials must be maintained and widened in order to provide incentives for the creation of wealth and to retain people with scarce but valuable abilities in this country, against the pull of emigration.] They also contend that the private accumulation of wealth is essential to encourage productive investment. From Atkinson's work it is possible to extract the view that existing income differentials between a top manager and a labourer may be affected more by custom and accepted values, or by the formal structure of large organizations, than by market forces of supply and demand. But relatively little is known about the possible economic effects of limiting earnings differentials in a country like Britain to, say, 5:1. At the moment, there is no general agreement in society about the weight to be attached to inequality, or the role of economic inequality in economic motivation; and this absence of consensus is perhaps one of the major reasons why every social group feels justified in pursuing its own claims irrespective of the consequences.

[If income alone is used as a major criterion of class, recipients are graded according to the size of their income irrespective of how it has been earned.] Those within the lower ranges are said to constitute the working class.] This holds good to a certain extent, but income alone is

[9] Atkinson, A. B., *The Economics of Inequality*, Oxford University Press, 1975.

not a satisfactory principle for establishing class if only because, as we have seen already and as Lockwood[10] describes, the question of occupational prestige interferes with simple economic rankings. Manual work is generally considered as imparting lower status than non-manual work, yet many occupations within the skilled manual range carry higher earnings than, say, lesser clerical jobs. These status differences in favour of non-manual work are a product of the nineteenth century, when mere literacy was a much more powerful economic asset than it is now, coupled with the more favourable working conditions (and proximity to authority) enjoyed by white-collar employees. Another factor reducing still further the utility of income as a class determinant is that fluctuations in earnings may not be correlated with changes in social status: when a member of class II (such as a schoolteacher) retires, his income may be drastically reduced but his social status remains substantially unimpaired. The way in which incomes are paid is yet another consideration; it is significant that the proportion of the national income paid in salaries has risen from 12 per cent in 1911 to well over half today.

The incidence of graded taxation and death duties has reduced inequalities in the distribution of wealth, with the result that a growing number of families, including many headed by manual workers, now come into the middle income brackets. The income gap between the middle and working classes has been reduced significantly since World War II, and the differentials have been narrowed even more markedly in more recent years. Average gross earnings rose rapidly between April 1970 and April 1975, but the earnings of manual workers rose faster than for non-manual workers; women's earnings rose faster than men's; and younger workers' earnings rose faster than those of older workers. Differentials between the highest and lowest paid in both manual and non-manual jobs declined. The disposable income of all households went up by 97 per cent between 1970 and 1975, while prices rose by 84 per cent.[11] Families composed of two adults and two

[10] Lockwood, D., *The Black-Coated Worker*, Allen & Unwin, 1958.

[11] Inflation climbed to unprecedented levels in 1975, before slackening somewhat in 1976. But while the proportion of tax on average earnings increased, gross earnings rose fast enough for take-home pay to be higher in 1975 than 5 years earlier even after taking account of inflation.

children had disposable incomes 99 per cent higher in 1975 than 5 years earlier, while for single pensioners, disposable incomes rose by 117 per cent. The incomes of the unemployed and the sick, however, did not keep pace with inflation in the same period except on the dates that their benefits actually went up. At the other end of the occupational scale, Table 3.1 demonstrates how professional, managerial and equivalent categories saw their earnings fall behind inflation between 1970 and 1974—and how, in the same period, manual workers more than kept pace.

TABLE 3.1. Average Earnings for Selected Occupations Between 1970 and 1974 (compared with a cost of living rise of 58.9 per cent in the same period)

Occupational category	1970 £	1974 £	% increase before tax
Managing directors	8100	11043	36.3
Senior army colonel	5256	6946	32.1
Company secretaries	4690	6596	40.6
Family doctors	4800	6147	28.0
Chief accountants	3800	5590	47.1
Works managers	3776	5399	42.9
Personnel managers	3448	5265	52.7
NHS dentists	4308	5650	31.1
Sales managers	3999	5680	42.0
Average of all male manual workers	1388	2761	98.9

It is developments like these which have been crucial to the concept of the so-called "affluent society" and the myth that in Britain everyone is becoming middle class. And not only has the income gap between the middle and working classes been reduced significantly since World War II: even more striking is the degree of standardization within the working class itself, as the wages of unskilled and semi-skilled workers approximate more closely to those of skilled employees.

Yet while the trend is currently towards egalitarianism, wide inequalities have remained, seemingly unaltered in the last decade, between those at the top and bottom of the class structure. These inequalities are most easily described in terms of income and the ownership of property. The Inland Revenue unadjusted estimates showed the top 1 per cent of wealth holders owning 24.2 per cent of wealth in 1968. According to Atkinson,[12] estimates of the ownership of the top 5 per cent range between 37 per cent (with state pension rights included) to 57.9 per cent (without allowing for missing wealth or including state pension rights) but "marrying up" individuals on the extreme assumption that the wealthiest females are paired with the wealthiest males.[13] In fact this is not such an unrealistic or extreme assumption at all. In discussing the causes of inequality, Meade[14] emphasizes the role of "good fortune and good luck", particularly when it means being born into a circle of wealth. The wealthy have a pronounced tendency to associate with, marry and leave wealth to their own kind—a tendency reinforced by any tendency of the "able" (defined in this context as the ruthless, intelligent and money-loving) to associate with their own kind.

What are the facts about the distribution of incomes? Earnings from labour take the form of wages and salaries, and earnings from investment are classified as rent, interest and profits. Some analysis of the national income may be attempted on this basis; the 1954 figures showed that wages and salaries together make up about two-thirds of all income, with self-employed and investment incomes obtaining 11 per cent each, but the figures cannot be calculated very precisely. Official statistics are notoriously misleading on the question of whether in fact there has been a trend towards equality of incomes since 1938. Several years ago Professor Titmuss[15] demonstrated how individuals with high incomes may minimize their tax liabilities by manipulating their spending power; thus the continuation of tax relief for mortgage interest mainly benefits those with higher incomes as the allowances are

[12] Atkinson, A. B., *op. cit.*

[13] If we are concerned with the distribution of the capital needed to place a deposit on a house for owner-occupation, or with the ability to plan expenditure over time, then the definition of wealth which confines itself to easily marketable assets is the most appropriate and the valuation of state pension rights becomes largely irrelevant. But even on the most inclusive definition, the concentration of wealth in this country is considerable.

[14] Meade, J. E., *The Just Economy: Vol. 4 of Principles of Political Economy*, Allen & Unwin, 1976.

[15] Titmuss, R. M., *Income Distribution and Social Change*, Allen & Unwin, 1961.

worth more to people on higher rates of tax. A detailed study of the former Ministry of Labour's family expenditure surveys of 1953–54 and 1960[16] concluded that "On the whole the data we have presented contradicts the commonly held view that a trend towards greater equality has accompanied the trend towards greater affluence." Closely argued support for the same hypothesis can be derived from a statistical analysis of the years 1938, 1949, 1954 and 1957 by Lydall,[17] and Nicholson's similar investigations for 1953, 1957 and 1959.[18] In both cases the authors establish that inequality in pre-tax incomes was increasing in the 1950s, but that this situation was being modified to some extent by income tax and direct welfare benefits which performed the function of redistributing income from the relatively rich to the relatively poor. Nonetheless Nicholson in particular is interesting because of his suggestion that income inequality was being reduced just as effectively in 1937 through the same devices, and that the total benefits from the social services since World War II have done little more than keep in line with the rise in national income.

The figures for the 1970s do indicate some slight evidence of a levelling process affecting both income and wealth. Between 1972–73 and 1973–74, the bottom 20 per cent increased their earnings from 5.8 to 6.2 per cent before tax, and from 6.8 to 7.4 per cent after tax; whereas the share of the top 20 per cent declined from 42.7 to 42.4 per cent before tax.[19] Taking out the incomes earned over only part of the year by school-leavers reduces inequalities further since their inclusion inflates the apparent weight of low incomes. Adding back deductions for tax and subtracting school-leavers, the balance is still in the direction of greater equality. On this basis, the share of income taken by the bottom 20 per cent in 1973–74 rises from 6.2 to 7.0 per cent, while the top 20 per cent falls from 42.4 to 41.8 per cent. A similar pattern is revealed in the distribution of wealth, which starts with more concentration than income. Between 1973 and 1974 the share of marketable wealth owned by the top 1 per cent had contracted from 28 per cent of

[16] Abel-Smith, B. and Townsend, P., *The Poor and the Poorest*, Bell, 1965.

[17] Lydall, H. F., *Journal of the Royal Statistical Society*, Series A, Part 1, 1959.

[18] Nicholson, J. L., quoted in *The Economist*, 26 February 1966, p. 814.

[19] Royal Commission on the Distribution of Income and Wealth, *Report No. 3*, H.M.S.O., 1976.

the total to 25 per cent; and the share of the top 5 per cent had fallen from 50.5 to 47.4 per cent.[20] Counting entitlements to pensions as wealth radically alters the picture. The top 1 per cent then owns 13.8 per cent of the nation's wealth, the top 5 per cent owns 30 per cent and the top 10 per cent owns 41.1 per cent. Most of this change comes from including state pensions since nearly two-thirds of the population have no rights in occupational pension schemes.

At the lowest end of the economic continuum, it is clear that poverty in Britain is not as comfortably solid as it was in the days of Dickens or Mayhew. By and large, the conditions found by Booth exist no longer.

> The houses, about 40 in number, contained cellars, parlours, and first, second, and third floors, mostly two rooms on a floor, and few of the 200 families who lived there occupied more than one room. . . . Not a room would be free from vermin and in many life at night was unbearable. Several occupants have said that in hot weather they don't go to bed, but sit in their clothes in the least infested part of the room.

Poverty of this order is now the exception, but for that very reason the problem has taken on far more complex dimensions. "You have to use the word poverty politically," according to Marsden,[21] "but with a small p, because the way you define it is purely a political judgment. You're saying what you think is an unacceptable quality of life below which no member of society ought to fall. You're measuring, or trying to, what standard of living people expect, and drawing a line is a political judgment." As such, the line is necessarily arbitrary. "Another criterion for poverty that you might think about is whether people actually feel poor. The expectations of individuals can be high or low in relation to any line that might be drawn." For instance, there is much subjectivity even in defining a minimum diet for nutrition purposes,[22]

---

[20] The fall in the share of the top 1 per cent largely reflects the slump in stock market prices during the period in question. It follows that any revival in share prices would have the effect of restoring (or even enhancing) differentials.

[21] Marsden, D., quoted in Mansell, C., "Britain's second nation", *Management Today*, April 1975.

[22] During the 1920s and 1930s there was a great deal of discussion on this subject, generally connected with attempted reductions in the rates of unemployed benefits. In August 1931, the unemployed officially numbered 2.7 million. Unemployed benefit stood at 17 shillings (85p) a week for an adult male, 9 shillings (45p) for his dependent wife and 2 shillings (10p) for each child. Ramsay Macdonald stated quite categorically

let alone a minimum standard of living in an advanced and complex industrial society.

Several sociologists argue that it is not possible to select a single yardstick but that poverty should be defined in terms of income inequality. Abel-Smith and Townsend,[23] therefore, say "The approach which we have adopted follows from the principle that the minimum level of living regarded as acceptable by a society increases with rising national prosperity"; this view is echoed in the assertion that "People are poverty stricken when their income, even if adequate for survival, falls markedly behind that of the community."[24] Using criteria derived from this assumption, Abel-Smith and Townsend show that in 1953–54 some 4 million persons (7.9 per cent of the population of the United Kingdom) were not living at a higher standard than 140 per cent of the basic National Assistance scales. In 1960 the analogous figure was 7.5 million persons, or 14 per cent of the population. In November 1972, the estimated number of people with incomes below supplementary benefit levels was 1.8 million, representing 1.2 million families. Those with incomes at or not more than 10 per cent above supplementary benefit entitlement constituted a further 660,000 families. Both these statistics exclude those actually in receipt of supplementary benefit; if these are added—4.1 million people—then the total comes to 6 million people or about 4 million families.

Although many poor people are in households headed by a man in full-time employment, the immediate causes of poverty seem to be associated with old age and large families. A small poverty study in Bethnal Green[25] has shown that 30 per cent of the population, even on a conservative estimate, were poor; mainly solitary elderly women and mothers bringing up children alone. Actual receipt of supplementary benefits and rate rebates among those eligible, however, was a mere

[23] Abel-Smith, B. and Townsend, P., *op. cit.*
[24] *Sunday Times*, 8 March 1964.
[25] Young, M., ed., *Poverty Report 1974*, Maurice Temple Smith, 1974.

that "Unemployment benefit is not a living wage; it was never meant to be that." And for those who could not get unemployment benefit and had no private resources, the only recourse was to local Poor Law Authorities, administering relief partly out of rates, on a means-tested basis. For a fascinating though polemical account of the period, see Orwell, G., *The Road to Wigan Pier*, Gollancz, 1937 (Penguin Books, 1962).

5 per cent. Yet curiously, one of the most bizarre elements connected with the continuing problem of poverty is the incidence of income tax. In the past it has generally not been necessary to pay much attention to this factor because only a minority of employees have been subject to significant levels of taxation. Under rapid wage inflation, however, successively lower-paid groups of wage earners have moved into the tax-paying range so that the average manual worker with two children who paid no income tax in 1950, paid a fifth of his income to the tax-man in 1970. Furthermore, the rules have been altered so that the rate of taxation is now harsher when the worker first enters the tax net. Thus in about 1967 the average wage-earner became liable for the full rate of tax for the first time outside wartime and any further increases in earnings that were negotiated for him were cut back accordingly.[26] The effects have been severe. For instance, between the autumn of 1968 and the spring of 1971, the father of two children with median earnings saw his gross money income rise by 24.8 per cent; after inflation is accounted for this became a gross real rise of 3.1 per cent and, net of taxes, a rise of only 1.6 per cent. The effects upon the distribution of income have been strongly inegalitarian. Over the 1960s, net real income tended to grow more slowly the larger the size of family, and this tendency has not been reversed by the effects of prices and incomes policies in the 1970s. Trinder and Atkinson write that with inflation, "the low level of the tax threshold, the failure to increase family allowances, and the faster increase in the price of necessities all meant that the advantage to the low-paid worker was eaten away . . . households with children have on the whole tended to fare worse".[27] It cannot even be claimed that governments have spent their tax income in a more egalitarian way; the wage-earners' benefits from education and other services have tended relatively to diminish.

Another aspect of the distribution of incomes is the extent to which

[26] See Jackson, D., Turner, H. A. and Wilkinson, F., *Do Trade Unions Cause Inflation?*, Cambridge University Press, 1972. It is important to note that, in working out the complex consequences of these developments, the authors' calculations are on the conservative side. They take no account of the many means-tested benefits (there are over 40 of them) such as rent rebates, free school meals and free dental care, to which a worker may lose entitlement by gaining a wage increase and which mean that such an increase may cause a decrease in net disposable income.

[27] In Young, M., ed., *op. cit.*

particular occupational groupings have changed their relative positions in the earnings hierarchy, particularly so far as manual workers are concerned. In 1960 the six highest paid blue-collared industrial groups were (in order) vehicle manufacturers, printers, iron and steel workers, employees in the publishing and book-binding industry, air transport, and cement. More recently print workers have taken the lead, followed by vehicle builders, air, transport, oil refinery operatives (who have moved up from nowhere), cement, and publishing and bookbinding. At the bottom end of the scale agricultural workers remain the lowest paid of all manual workers, followed by local government employees. It is often said that under a free system of collective bargaining, the strong (i.e., highly unionized) groups get rich at the expense of the industrially weak. The figures suggest, in fact, that supply and demand (as well as established traditions) are equally powerful factors in determining levels of reward. By and large over recent years it has been the workers in the public and private supply service industries who have accumulated the greatest percentage increases in earnings. These service industries, moreover, are not only gaining ground financially but are employing a larger percentage of the labour force.

Financially (as well as in other ways), manual workers still experience several disadvantages in their treatment both at and away from work, when compared with typical non-manual categories. Wedderburn has found that between 80 and 90 per cent of non-manual workers were paid for periods when they were off work on compassionate grounds, as against only 29 per cent of manual employees. Even when manual employees are included in a sick-pay scheme, they are frequently less favoured than non-manual workers in the same scheme. On average 91 per cent of a non-manual worker's pay is accounted for by basic pay as compared with 68 per cent for unskilled workers, who have a higher proportion of overtime and bonus payments. Sick-pay, however, is normally related to basic wages. There are similar tendencies with occupational pension schemes. Between 1967 and 1971, the number of workers covered by occupational pension schemes fell from 62 to 58 per cent. The number of non-manual workers covered rose from 85 to 87 per cent, whereas the number of manual male workers covered fell from 64 to 56 per cent. And among female manual workers, the proportion fell from 21 to 18 per cent.

Apart from income, society is also stratified on the basis of wealth and property, taking the form of investment in stocks and shares, building societies, insurance companies, local authorities, land, buildings and business premises. Income derived from sources such as these is classified as "unearned" for the purposes of the Inland Revenue, and as incomes become very large, so the proportion of unearned income tends to rise at a disproportionately rapid rate. If we apply the criterion of "Total Net Worth"—liquid assets, securities, property, private businesses, loans, motor-cars—we find that in 1954 one-third of the population had a Total Net Worth of zero, and over half had less than £100.[28] The Inland Revenue estimated in 1964 that two-thirds of the British population had no wealth worth reckoning at all, whereas 80 per cent of personal wealth, including property, was owned by some 5 million individuals (9 per cent of the population). But Table 3.2 shows that, although wealth continues to be distributed unequally, the degree of inequality has declined quite rapidly in recent years. Part A of the

TABLE 3.2. Percentages of Wealth for Individuals in Great Britain
Aged Over 24

	Year	Top 1%	Next 4%	Next 5%	Rest
A.	*Inland Revenue Basis*				
	1911–13	69	18	5	8
	1924–30	62	22	6	9
	1936–38	56	23	9	12
	1954	43	28	8	21
	1960	42	33	8	17
	1965	32	26	13	29
	1973	23	24	16	37
B.	*"Corrected" Basis (Excluding State Pension)*				
	1965	29	25	13	33
	1973	19	19	14	48
C.	*"Corrected" Basis (Including State Pension)*				
	1965	22	19	11	48
	1973	14	16	11	59

[28] Crosland, C. A. R., *The Future of Socialism*, Cape, 1956.

Table presents figures which are broadly comparable, showing the percentage of total wealth held by the top slices of the population over 24 years of age. In 1973 the top 1 per cent (some 340,000 individuals) owned 23 per cent of total personal wealth, and on average each of these had a net worth of about £105,000 each. At the very top came about 34,000 people (or 0.1 per cent of the total), owning an average of £300,000 each; the next 4 per cent slice owned an average of £30,000 each, followed by the next 5 per cent with £15,000 each. Although the data are based on estate duty returns and are therefore subject to the limitations already discussed, Day argues[29] that they "accurately reflect the position of individuals who are alive and are hardly biased at all by the widespread avoidance of estate duty through gifts made well in advance of death". Nonetheless, Day does admit that there are some shortcomings of estate duty statistics which do cause some error in the figures. Before 1969, when the law was changed, they failed adequately to pick up wealth held in discretionary trusts, which probably led to an under-estimation of the share owned by the rich. On balance, however, the figures tend to exaggerate the share owned by the wealthy, primarily because estate duty does not fall upon small estates.

Part B of Table 3.2 makes corrections for some of the most important omissions. One of these is the Inland Revenue's serious under-valuation (in Day's view) of household goods and other consumer durables; Day's own figures are based on the Household Expenditure Survey and on reasonable rates of depreciation of items such as furniture and clothes. This kind of adjustment considerably increases the share of wealth held by the less well-to-do. Whether the assessment of wealth should include state pension rights is a problem yet to be resolved,[30] but as parts B and

[29] Day, A., "The nation's wealth/who owns it", *The Observer*, 20 January 1974. If an elderly person makes a gift to his middle-aged son, or even his young grandson, the wealth still appears in the Inland Revenue figures because some middle-aged and young people do die. In the total picture (summarized in Tables 3.2 and 3.3), suitable mortality tables have been used to estimate the wealth of the overwhelming majority of young and middle-aged people who do not die.

[30] The argument for including state pension rights is that the prospect of a state pension means that an individual has less need to put other savings aside for his old age. On the other hand, the wealth represented by state pension rights is not marketable in the sense that it cannot be sold, unlike practically all the other components of wealth in the Inland Revenue data.

C of Table 3.2 demonstrate, it makes little practical difference to the assertion that the distribution of wealth has been getting more equal.

Some part of the reason for this phenomenon lies in the impact of estate duty, but so far as the major wealth-owners are concerned, inheritance remains a very powerful explanation of their continued holdings. More plausible explanations of the increasing equality of wealth distribution are suggested by the analysis of the pattern of wealth holding of different slices of the population shown in Table 3.3. Up to the

TABLE 3.3. Wealth holdings (for September 1973) for the top 20 per cent of the population, excluding all Pension Rights

Nature of wealth holding	Top 0.1% £	Next 0.9% £	Next 4% £	Next 5% £	Next 10% £
Cash and bank deposits	15,000	5000	2000	1000	500
Savings certificates etc.	3000	1000	1000	500	250
At building societies etc.	8000	8000	3000	1500	500
Government securities	6000	3000	500	—	—
Insurance policies	11,000	3000	3000	2000	1500
Shares and unit trusts	138,000	32,000	4500	500	—
Household goods	8000	3000	2000	1500	1250
Other personal estate	21,000	7000	2500	1000	500
Claims against personal estate	−13,000	−3000	−1000	−500	−250
Houses	22,000	16,000	12,000	7000	6000
Other real property	84,000	7000	2000	500	250
Mortgage liabilities etc.	−3000	−1000	−500	−500	−500
Total net wealth	300,000	80,000	30,000	15,000	10,000

Note: The figures do not necessarily add to the totals quoted because of rounding to avoid spurious accuracy.

level of those with an average net wealth of about £30,000 in 1973, about half or more of the total wealth consisted of the value of houses (almost all owner-occupied) and household goods. Thus the increased equality of wealth distribution can largely be attributed to the spread of owner-occupation and to the rapid rises in house prices over the

1960s and 1970s, while share prices have risen much more slowly than the rate of inflation. On the other hand, the top 1 per cent, with 40 per cent or more of their wealth in shares, have suffered from the very slow long-term rise of share prices. In 1976, *The Times*[31] showed that share prices had fallen by more than 40 per cent from the previous peak in 1972, while in the same period average earnings had risen by about 80 per cent. Taking the original ratio between share values and average earnings as 100:100, the relationship in 1976 stood at about 60:180, a huge shift in favour of the wage-earner. Despite increased affluence, the wealth of the poorest half of the population lies mainly with income flow rather than with capital accumulation. And if the wealth of the richest 5 per cent was taken to rest mainly in capital, and assuming the decline in the value of other capital assets held mainly by the rich to have been similar to the decline in the stock market, then the wealth of the richest twentieth of the population had depreciated by three times relative to that of the poorest half.

Two notes of caution have to be sounded with this kind of analysis. First, none of the figures quoted in Day's tables make any allowance for potential liability to capital gains tax. If this were to be included—as it should be—it would probably reduce the net wealth of the top 1 per cent substantially, but have practically no effect on the remaining categories. Second, a slump in stock market prices does not diminish a stockholder's proportionate share of the productive power represented by his holding. It can be argued that it is a "paper" change which would disappear as share prices rise—but if share prices were to remain depressed (perhaps because of a government decision to continue controls over profits and dividends), then there would be a permanent increase in the net worth of the company sector. That is, the gap between the total share values of all companies and their real asset values (their buildings, machinery, and so on) would increase. A permanent fall in share prices relative to other asset values would mean that the rich had suffered a permanent loss in their share of the economic power resting in the means of production, as well as a loss of purchasing power relative to the increased cost of labour.

Further evidence concerning the egalitarian tendencies in personal

[31] Hodgkinson, N., "Richest twentieth getting poorer", *The Times*, 21 October 1976.

wealth distribution has been produced recently by Rothman.[32] In Table 3.4, he has divided the total wealth of the personal (as opposed to the public) sector at the end of three representative years by the total personal disposable income or savings for that year. The result can be considered as showing how many years' income or saving an average man starting from scratch would require to accumulate an average

TABLE 3.4. The Number of Years Disposable Income
and Savings Required to Accumulate Average Wealth

| Year | Number of years required in terms of: | |
	Personal disposable income	Savings
1959	4.3	87
1966	4.2	47
1973–74	5.3	52

amount of wealth. It can be seen from the table that to an average man "average wealth" would have meant about $4\frac{1}{4}$ years of disposable income in 1959 and 1966, but by 1974 it would have meant more than 5 years. Again, with prosperity, the proportion of income that people were able to save had increased. As a result, by 1966, even disregarding interest, it was possible to accumulate average wealth out of a lifetime's savings. Since then asset values have risen faster than savings so that the prospect of achieving average wealth by this means has become more remote.

Income and wealth are often associated with two other factors: relationship to the means of production and security of employment. Together, these constitute the Marxian approach to class. When Marx wrote, they were probably quite effective criteria for establishing and isolating the working class in particular, for this social group was characterized by small, inadequate incomes and the necessity for selling its labour to those who owned the means of production. Today, by contrast, the job security of manual workers has been considerably enhanced as a result of pressure by trade unions and subsequent legislation, though it is arguable that the practical effect of such legislation is in some ways counter-productive if it forces employers to be much

[32] Rothman, J., *The Wealth of the United Kingdom*, Sandelson & Co., 1974.

more economical in their recruitment policies on the grounds that redundancies and dismissals (should they become necessary) are so difficult and expensive to achieve.[33] In a condition of advanced capitalism, relationship to the means of production becomes a meaningless criterion of class as the vast majority of the work force make their living by selling their labour. This majority includes, for example, the professions, who are certainly not members of the proletariat so far as their subjective perceptions are concerned (though they may be proletarians in a doctrinaire Marxist sense).

Nonetheless, Max Weber has argued emphatically that " 'property' and 'lack of property' are the basic categories of all class situations". Weber realized that propertylessness does not necessarily imply that unity of class interests which Marx hoped to find, since the propertyless classes differ widely as regards their life chances. With this in mind, Weber[34] modified Marx's rigid dogma by suggesting that "only persons who are completely unskilled, without property and dependent on employment without regular occupation, are in a strictly identical class position". The middle classes have never been strictly proletarian in terms of income, job security and occupational mobility. The incomes associated with non-manual jobs were originally a reward for scarcity but are now retained as a status differential. In any case, income is not the only consideration in establishing the worth of an occupation. Relative immunity from the ups and downs of the trade cycle has always been the non-manual worker's prerogative, although it has been discovered recently that if a white-collar employee does become redundant, he experiences greater problems in finding another comparable job than the manual worker. Finally, the non-manual worker has a better chance of rising to managerial and supervisory posts, perhaps because of his closer relationship with those already in authority and also because his behavioural norms are more compatible with those of management.

---

[33] Paradoxically, the result may be, as some economists predict, a continuously maintained high level of unemployment in a so-called "full employment" economy.

[34] Weber, M., *Essays in Sociology*, Routledge & Kegan Paul, 1958. See also Bendix, R., *Max Weber: An Intellectual Portrait*, Heinemann, 1960; Weber, M. (trans. A. Henderson and T. Parsons), *Theory of Social and Economic Organization*, Oxford University Press, 1947.

Occupation

Occupation is the most popular and frequently used determinant of class. It is considered the best criterion because it is highly correlated with size of income, it helps shape the way of life and it is firmly associated with social prestige. True, to know an individual's social class is to know little about the person, but class, defined in the most uncontroversial way as social difference related to occupation, is still a hugely important general guide to disparities of educational provision, hours worked, income earned and property owned. Yet the practical difficulties involved in ranking occupations are enormous, as criticisms of the Registrar-General's scheme have already implied. Class I, for example, ignores wealth and property ownership because it is based solely on occupation, with the result that the extremely wealthy are lost to view amongst thousands of "directors" and the like. Class II suffers from the fact that it incorporates large numbers of minor administrative, professional and managerial occupations, as well as farmers, shop-keepers and small employers. It thus mixes up groups which belong to quite different social classes: some members of the "old" middle classes and others of the "new" middle classes, in the terminology of C. Wright Mills[35]—the one-man shopkeeper contrasted with the departmental manager in a large company. These typical anomalies, which are repeated to a greater or lesser degree in the other three classes, are compounded because the classifications involve the *ranking* of the occupations according to prestige, power, level of earnings, skill, and other criteria.

In 1950 Hall and Caradog Jones reported the first English study of occupational prestige. The question under review was whether the general public ranked occupations in a sequence similar to the Registrar-General's standard classification. In the event no significant variations were found, although some major changes in judgment had been made by the time a similar study was carried out by National Opinion Polls in 1974. Asked to list 12 manual occupations, the sample of 2021 gave a ranking of: underground miner, ambulance driver, maintenance craftsman, heavy goods vehicle driver, farm worker, bricklayer, docker, car worker, dustman, railway guard, bus conductor,

[35] Mills, C. W., *The Power Elite*, Oxford University Press, 1956.

and factory cleaner. Predictably, the status given to jobs bears little relation to actual earnings; in 1950, for example, the old crafts, like fitter, carpenter and bricklayer retained a better status than unskilled but high-paying jobs like that of docker (who was then rated as 29th out of a list of 30, just ahead of road-sweeper). The 1974 ranking suggested a relatively new esteem accorded to jobs in social service (the ambulance driver, rated second, was still one of the lowest paid in the whole group), though Young and Willmott's inquiry into Bethnal Green revealed what was then a significant deviant group which graded occupations according to their usefulness in social terms, manual workers generally being ranked above non-manual workers (specifically, dustmen being valued more than the Medical Officer of Health). Willmott's subsequent investigation of Dagenham[36] discovered that when people were asked what social class they thought they belonged to, as distinct from the class to which they had been assigned according to their, or their husband's jobs, a deviant minority appeared to rate occupations in rather unconventional ways or else regarded occupation as insignificant in structuring social position. The proportion of people with manual jobs describing themselves as middle class at Dagenham was 13 per cent, but it is very significant to note that this figure is lower than in other districts where a similar question has been put. In Greenwich the proportion was 23 per cent; in Hertford, 31 per cent; in Woodford, 34 per cent. Willmott concludes, not unreasonably, that the higher the proportion of manual workers in the area, the lower the proportion who assign themselves to the middle class.

The Woodford study[37] showed the same process at work in a heavily middle-class environment. Nearly half (48 per cent) of the 355 manual workers in the general sample considered themselves middle class. Identification with the middle class was nearly as common among unskilled and semi-skilled workers in the general sample, as among skilled employees. Of the 257 skilled workers, 49 per cent said they were

[36] Willmott, P., *The Evolution of a Community*, Routledge & Kegan Paul, 1963. Willmott himself admits that questions like "To which social class do you think you belong?" are not especially meaningful. No doubt if one could question whales, half of them would say they were fish.

[37] Young, M. and Willmott, P., *Family and Class in a London Suburb*, Routledge & Kegan Paul, 1960.

middle class (either upper, middle or lower middle); of the 98 semi-skilled and unskilled, the equivalent proportion was 43 per cent. Apparently Woodford was not unusual in having manual workers who put themselves into the middle class, but it does have an unusually high proportion who do so. According to the authors, "The rule seems to be that the more the middle class predominates in a district the more working-class people identify themselves with it." However, the drawback in accepting these subjective attempts at stratification lies in the difficulty of proving that the concepts of working class and middle class mean the same thing to different people. The middle-class deviants who assign themselves to the working class may think of the middle classes as reserved specifically for the professions and the working classes as composed of all those who are paid wages.

Occupation as a determinant of social grading, then, is only successful up to a point. Status ambiguity occurs especially among those occupations where the size of the income has not kept up with the prestige usually accorded to the job. Lockwood[38] has shown how at one time the mass of clerical workers had been better off in income terms than the majority of manual workers. Today this is no longer true. It has yet to be established whether the old occupational prestige formerly associated with white-collar work can hold out against lower relative incomes, loss of the monopoly of literacy and declining responsibilities. It is relevant to note, moreover, that although manual workers are more likely to allocate high prestige to manual jobs, they also tend to be enthusiastic that their children should obtain the best education possible. Presumably this is because they view education as a means to an end—the end being the "better" job, for which educational qualifications are essential. Such jobs are almost invariably non-manual.

Yet in establishing the validity of this point much depends on the degree of social diversity in the community. As Willmott remarks of Dagenham, "there is no doubt in my mind that education at Dagenham suffers from the estate's social uniformity. Schools in mixed class districts benefit from the enthusiasm and stimulus of middle-class parents and their children, who help to create an atmosphere which can be stimulating, though it can also produce strains for the gifted children

---

[38] Lockwood, D., *op. cit.*

from working-class homes". Among people interviewed in the Dagenham marriage sample there was some support for the view that most parents were not educationally ambitious for their children. One informant may be quoted as being typical of the majority: "I've never really thought about it. I've always taken it for granted he'll leave school at 15 unless he turns out brilliant and goes to College." Other parents laid great stress on the pursuit of "happiness" as though this was inconsistent with educational achievement.

All this raises the question of the extent to which mobility between the classes is a characteristic of British society. In broad terms, something like a third of the population moves upwards, if one compares the job they do with the one their father did, and a further third moves down, in each generation. These proportions remain remarkably constant for industrial countries such as Britain, the United States, West Germany, France and Sweden, despite their widely different cultural and historical frameworks. This mobility index, however, has to be qualified in various ways. First, people change their social class, not solely by altering their jobs, but by changing their status in other ways. Thus Illsley and his colleagues[39] found that 46 per cent of Aberdeen women with professional and managerial class origins married skilled-worker husbands, and 40 per cent of the wives of professionals and managers had fathers who were skilled workers.

Another consideration is, as Glass and his colleagues[40] have found, that the rates of intergenerational occupational mobility have been remarkably stable during the present century as far as men are concerned. On the other hand, it seems likely that the number of occupational positions which could facilitate upward mobility is on the increase. During the last two decades, those industries which have been growing most rapidly not only have the highest proportions of white-collar workers, but also show the greatest relative increase in their ratios of non-manual employees. Census figures indicate unequivocally that more people are classed as professional and managerial, fewer as skilled and unskilled manual workers. And such categories still reveal, as we have suggested already, significant differences in attitudes and

[39] Quoted in Lipset, S. M. and Bendix, R., *Social Mobility in Industrial Society*, Heinemann, 1959.
[40] Glass, D. V., ed., *Social Mobility in Britain*, Routledge & Kegan Paul, 1954.

lifestyles. Manual workers work an average 7 hours more than white-collar workers each week; the sons of manual workers have consistently lower educational ambitions and attainments. Three out of five professional and managerial households own their home or pay a mortgage; the fourth is in furnished private accommodation. By contrast, three out of five semi-skilled manual households are tenants either of a local authority or in unfurnished private rooms; the fourth is a house owner or mortgagee.

Much of the mobility taking place in British society is of a relatively short-range kind. Most mobility represents either a change in status within manual employment itself (which may not perhaps be regarded as social mobility at all) or between manual and lower non-manual work. Most people may intuitively recognize this, for their social aspirations (if they have any at all) do not usually aim very far. Skilled workers typically aspire to further education for their offspring, but their ambitions are consonant with their own industrial experience: they aim at technological studies rather than specifically university entrance. It may be significant in this context to note that social mobility has become increasingly institutionalized through the educational system, and while this may have produced increased opportunities for inter-generational mobility through education, the chances of *intra*-generational mobility through work are declining. As Lockwood[41] has put it, "To enter a factory job with a secondary modern education is to take a job that is more and more a life sentence."

Individual responses to the facts of occupational mobility may vary a good deal. One common reaction is to deny the desire for upward movement altogether. Sykes,[42] in his Scottish survey of manual workers for whom promotion chances were virtually non-existent, found that they frequently expressed hostile attitudes towards advancement on the grounds that it would cause them social problems at home and at work. It is not clear whether this represents a genuine deeply-founded judgment or whether it is a rationalization of and adjustment to the situation in which these employees found themselves. Willmott, too, in his

---

[41] Lockwood, D., "Can we cope with social change?", *New Society*, 28 November 1963.
[42] Sykes, A. J. M., *Sociological Review*, Vol. 13, No. 3, 1965, p. 297.

investigation of adolescent boys in Bethnal Green,[43] discovered evidence of similar "status-assenting" reactions to the social system. On the whole the boys were conscious of their working-class background; they knew that to get on in life they had to become middle class. This in turn meant not only earning more money but, more important, adopting different standards of behaviour and attitudes (say, towards spending and saving), dropping a Cockney accent and "talking posh". Only about 20 per cent, in fact, intended to accept this alternative; some 70 per cent[44] were content to adhere to the aspirations and values of their working-class fathers and remain in a manual occupation.

These problems are examined in particular depth by Goldthorpe and his colleagues[45] in their research into the validity of the "embourgeoisement" thesis. According to this view, the working class is gradually being eliminated as more manual occupations disappear and are replaced by increasing numbers of white-collar jobs, and as the working class itself reaches a level of affluence commonly enjoyed by middle-class employees. Some evidence undoubtedly supports these hypotheses. The work-force employed in traditional extractive and heavy manufacturing industries has declined, while consumer-goods industries, transportation and service occupations have grown in significance. Geographical mobility, for long an accepted feature of managerial and professional employees' existence, has now spread to the manual worker: he seeks better jobs in the Midlands and the South-east, or moves from city-centre slums to suburban housing estates. It is thus feasible that many workers would experience the stress of being isolated from the primary ties and solidarities of their stable communities, with a consequent loss or weakening of family and neighbourhood relationships. As a substitute for these relationships, the affluent worker may

[43] Willmott, P., *Adolescent Boys of East London*, Routledge & Kegan Paul, 1966.

[44] The remaining 10 per cent are what Willmott describes as rebels. They reject both the working-class standards of the local community and the middle-class norms of the "status-dissenting" population; they hate their school and do not get on with their parents. It is in this group that, according to Willmott, serious delinquency could be expected to flourish.

[45] Goldthorpe, J. H., Lockwood, D., Bechhofer, F. and Platt, J., *The Affluent Worker: Industrial Attitudes and Behaviour*, Cambridge University Press, 1968; also, same authors, "The affluent worker and the thesis of embourgeoisement", *Sociology*, Vol. 1, No. 1, pp. 11–31, 1967.

turn his attention inwards by becoming home-centred, dominated by an emphasis on consumer durables and family consumption.

In practice there is little or no evidence to support these readily advanced hypotheseses. Young and Willmott's work in Bethnal Green confirms that upward social mobility does not impair family contacts, and this work is reinforced by Litwak's work in the United States.[46] Holding constant the factor of geographical distance, Litwak found that there was no great difference between mobile and non-mobile persons in visiting and maintaining contact with their extended families; and this held true even when extreme upward and downward mobility was considered. He also found that upwardly mobile individuals were no less identified with their extended family than the non-mobile groups. In explaining these observations, Litwak points to the fact that people achieve status not only by associating with others of equal or higher social position, but also by receiving deference from others. The extended family plays an important status-gratifying role for the upwardly mobile. Providing that family visits can be isolated from the visits of friends who are status equals (a condition more likely to be realized in large urban centres than in small rural communities) the upwardly mobile individual can obtain status both by associating with his peers and by gaining deference from his family.

Goldthorpe and his associates attack the "embourgeoisement" thesis more crucially by questioning the reality of upward mobility in this context. They examine the evidence under three main headings: economic, normative, and relational. Firstly, the economic evidence is not impressive. When gross incomes over total working lives are compared, as distinct from weekly wages, the apparent levelling-up between manual and non-manual employees is not so apparent: pensions, prospects for promotion, sustained earnings, job security, loans and other "perks" are continued sources of inequality. In 1975, the Confederation of British Industry[47] showed that a typical university graduate could wait until he was 35 before his cumulative post-tax earnings began to exceed

[46] Litwak, E., "Occupational mobility and extended family cohesion", *American Sociological Review*, February 1960.

[47] In calculations submitted to the Royal Commission on the Distribution of Incomes and Wealth. The figures were based on the lifetime incomes patterns of a manager and a skilled fitter, with the latter reaching a basic salary of £55 a week at the age of 20 and maintaining that figure until retirement age. The "higher earner" receives a student

those of a skilled worker leaving school at 16. By the end of his life, however, the cumulative post-tax earnings of the graduate would be double those of the skilled worker. In parentheses, it might be added that there is continual debate over the economic returns accruing to the individual from prolonged exposure to higher education, and there is little British evidence on the subject. Taubman and Wales,[48] using evidence from the United States, claim that "except for those with graduate training, there is no evidence of an interaction between ability and education in determining earnings". Broadly, however, they agree that the private rate of return to higher education in the United States is of the order of 10 per cent for a first degree and less for most kinds of higher degree.[49]

Secondly, in normative terms, there is little research evidence to support the view that the working class is losing its traditional attitudes and values and acquiring those of the middle class. Thirdly, relational patterns have undergone little change: middle-class groups can scarcely be said to have relaxed their exclusiveness and begun to admit manual workers to social equality.

These conclusions were validated by a detailed study of car-workers in Luton, who might have been expected to have moved furthest along the "embourgoisement" scale: highly affluent (compared with most other manual workers), geographically mobile, and usually younger. Yet their loyalty to class organizations such as trade unions and the Labour Party had not been affected by their affluence. Their attitudes towards their work were strictly instrumental; in other words, they were not interested in work as an end in itself but merely as a means to achieving ends that lay outside the work situation—in this case, high wages and opportunities for overtime.[50] Perhaps this affected their

[48] Taubman, P. and Wales, T., in Juster, T., ed., *Education, Income and Human Behaviour*, McGraw-Hill, 1975.

[49] Taubman, P. and Wales, T., *Higher Education and Earnings: College as an Investment and a Screening Device*, McGraw-Hill, 1975.

[50] Goldthorpe, J. H., "Attitudes and behaviour of car assembly workers: a deviant case and a theoretical critique", *British Journal of Sociology*, Vol. 17, No. 3, 1966.

grant until graduating, then a salary rising from £2100 a year on graduation to £10,000 a year from the age of 46 to retirement. Like Goldthorpe, the C.B.I. emphasizes that when comparing earnings it is important to examine the incomes of individuals over their lifetimes rather than in one particular year.

commitment to the Labour Party and the trade union, since by contrast with the traditional solidarity of the working class the collectivism of the Luton car-workers was much more instrumental. They saw the union as a means to an end, a way of getting better incomes through collective bargaining and industrial action, rather than part of the "communal" solidarity of the older mining towns. Equally, the purchase of consumer durables did not make them middle class. As Goldthorpe expresses it, "a washing machine is a washing machine is a washing machine"; it is a machine for washing clothes, not an admission ticket to the middle class. In practically all the major areas of life—life-chances, consumption patterns, attitudes and values—the Luton car-workers could not be identified with the middle class.

Middle-class reaction to the concept of "embourgeoisement" also deserves attention. In Woodford, Young and Willmott found that the middle classes were most anxious to preserve their separate identity and to resist the encroachments—real or imagined—of the working class. It was generally felt that higher wages did not necessarily make the workers *socially* more acceptable than before. Indeed, they were often looked down on more than ever. Two conventional stereotypes were frequently quoted. One was that the British workman does not really work (this was supported by a company director who remarked: "The working class is wrongly named because they don't work at all, judging by what happens in our firm"); the other that the working class do not know how to spend all their extra money. In practice the latter statement is little more than a euphemism for the more explicit statement that the working class have a different scale of values than the middle class, so far as expenditure is concerned. The working classes in Woodford were certainly not encouraged to spend their extra money at the local clubs, some of which controlled their membership lists by imposing exorbitant fees, while others used recommendation methods to maintain the exclusiveness of the organization.

While the concept of "embourgeoisement" has now been revealed as something of an illusion, it is nonetheless true that many individuals marginal to the middle class experience the desire to identify themselves with the higher status group. They seek to "bourgeoisify" themselves by limitations on family size, placing high value on education, and by emphasizing respectability. This process has been exceptionally notable in the case of the new clerical strata whose ambitions exceed even those of professional and executive parents.[51] On the other hand, industrial-ization, the economics of mass production, and the community have approached a common norm containing more elements of the old middle-class style than of the working-class manner.

C. Wright Mills once described the new middle classes as proletarian, by the Marxian definition of no longer owning the means of production, yet bourgeois by virtue of their work situation, their evaluation of their own status, and their life chances in the new society. They are the tech-nocrats and bureaucrats of the modern gigantic corporation. In the decline of the small businessman in contemporary America, Mills found evidence to support the Marxist thesis that capital is becoming concen-trated in fewer hands. However, the new middle classes still adhere to the ideology of the old middle classes, namely, that anyone can get to the top. These arguments have only a limited relevance to the British class situation, but their general importance is clear: it is no longer practicable to define class differences purely in terms of property, income, wealth, or even occupation. As in the United States, so in Britain it is questionable whether ownership carries any significance in the running of industry compared with the power exercised by managers and directors[52] particularly when ownership is scattered over many thousands of shareholders.[53]

Even the relatively straightforward criterion of occupational differ-ences can be perceived in three different ways: work-situation, market-situation and status-situation. Whereas at one time clerks were distri-buted over large numbers of small offices, today they work in much larger units and, moreover, their numbers have increased markedly. In 1911 only 19 per cent of the labour force was in white-collar em-ployment; by 1971 this had increased to 48 per cent. Promotion has become more dependent on educational qualifications and the increased recruitment of graduates and "management trainees" has imposed

---

[51] Martin, F. M., "An inquiry into parents' preferences in secondary education", in Glass, D. V., ed., *op. cit.*

[52] See Nichols, T., *Ownership, Control and Ideology*, Allen & Unwin, 1969.

[53] Of course, there are exceptions in the form of exceptionally wealthy individuals (such as Sir James Goldsmith) and also in the shape of investing institutions like banks and insurance companies.

limits on the advancement opportunities available to clerks. In the past clerks were drawn from the middle class and their personal contact with their employers at work reinforced their tendency to emulate the life-style of their employers as well as giving them a certain amount of "reflected" status. Today clerical recruits often originate from the off-spring of manual workers, and clerical jobs themselves do not hold their former advantages of security and pay in such high degree. White-collar workers at the lower levels, therefore, often experience significant status dissonance, and this is reflected in the "proletarianization" of their attitudes (through union militancy and radical politics) developing, paradoxically, alongside the retention of middle-class beliefs, values and aspirations. Thus Price and Bain [54] have found that in 1974 36 per cent of all union members were white collar employees, compared with only 26 per cent 10 years earlier—and, incidentally, the female proportion of total union membership had reached 27 per cent in 1974. [55]

Style of Life

Some authorities consider that style of life is the ultimate factor in deciding social class. According to this approach, classes can be distinguished by, say, characteristic spending habits, leisure pursuits, voting behaviour, religious affiliations, and so forth, Thus the working class is held to spend more on food and less on conspicuous consumption, such as clothes and furnishing, cars and refrigerators. Saving is condemned as anti-social and indicative of the saver's "black-leg" attempts to climb out of his ordained social group. It is only accepted when it is specifically for holidays, getting married, clothes, or Christmas presents. [56] Yet these class-oriented patterns of consumption are not

[54] Price, R. and Bain, G. S., "Union Growth revisited: 1948–1974 in perspective", *British Journal of Industrial Relations*, Vol. 14, No. 3, November 1976, pp. 339–55.

[55] For further reading on the connections between social class and occupation, see Weir, D., ed., *Men and Work in Modern Britain*, Fontana, 1974.

[56] This short-run, almost hedonistic approach to saving has been connected causally with the cyclical fluctuations regularly observed for industrial disputes. Strikes tend to occur less frequently in the late autumn (when people are saving for Christmas) and in the early summer (preparation for annual holidays). Conversely, strikes are concentrated in the immediate post-Christmas period and the early autumn, when a short period of financial stringency is relatively less onerous.

so rigid as one might at first accept. In Woodford, it was true that hire purchase (with, more recently, the credit card)—which permits greater expenditure on conspicuous consumption without interfering with the anti-saving ideology—did tend to blur class distinctions. Those members of the working class, who claimed to belong to the middle class, judged themselves on what they bought rather than how they earned their money. Certainly there was the rivalry over possessions and status symbols which seem to be an essential concomitant of class aspirations. One labourer's wife said: "We get a new Hoover, so she's got to have one. Another neighbour's got a new studio couch, so she's got one and she's still paying for it."

Willmott noted much the same behavioural pattern in Dagenham, but with significant differences. Of the 50 couples in his marriage sample, only 13 voiced any complaints about Dagenham in terms of consumption competitiveness or status-striving. As one respondent said, "There are some who talk about their houses more than others. You hear them talking about their fridges and washing machines and that. The boastful type, we call them—the type who say, 'I'm better than you.' " The majority of such instances, however, occurred among people who had moved to Dagenham within the previous 5 years or so and felt that their homes were being judged by their neighbours on their success or failure in meeting Dagenham's standards. Others included respondents who had lower incomes and larger families, and sometimes resentment was directed at those fortunate families with more than one wage-earner. Yet the overwhelming impression from the marriage sample was that the improvement in material standards was generating very little tension or anxiety. "These things like washing machines have become necessities for working-class people. It's not a matter of copying other people. It's everybody wants them when they can get them." The process by which one family followed another's example was regarded as more the result of friendly endorsement than of rivalry—"People sort of prompt each other", as one woman put it. "Someone will get a new washing machine and they'll show it to you and say how good it is and how much of a help to them. It's not envy or anything, it's just recommendation. And if you don't get the same thing, they often share it with you." Although, as Willmott freely admits, these respondents may be misleading themselves over what is really happening, he does conclude that "many people on the estate seem to see their fellows not as adversaries but as allies in a general advance . . . competition between neighbours certainly seems less keen, anxiety over possessions less sharp, at Dagenham than elsewhere; in the private suburb of Woodford, for example."[57] It seems probable that the extreme social homogeneity of Dagenham is a powerful contributor to this difference.

The position is complicated by changing patterns of consumption since World War II. The greater prosperity of the working class during that war was mainly devoted to more beer, cigarettes and cinemas. In the 1950s the emphasis had changed to food, housing, fuel and light, household goods, private motoring and foreign travel, while housing, expenditure abroad and motoring predominated in the 1960s. The proportion of family income spent on food has fallen steadily in the past decade. In 1971 almost $22\frac{1}{2}$p in every pound of household spending went on food; in 1975 the figure was little more than 21p. People have been cutting down particularly on the consumption of meat and bacon, especially on weekdays, and have compensated by increased purchases of snack foods like "instant" soups, crisps and biscuits—and alcohol.

Ways of spending leisure are also thought of as a means of differentiating between social classes. Gambling, drinking, and sports of all kinds were once considered the traditional pursuits of the working class, but they cannot be seen as having a monopoly in these outlets. Recent years, moreover, have seen a considerable democratization of leisure. Formerly there was a marked difference in the amount and type of leisure between the upper and middle classes and the working class, where the latter group in particular could be characterized by the lack of social amenities available for its use. After 1850 parks, playing fields and libraries began to be supplied; working hours were shortened; paid holidays became the norm; railways brought transport to the masses. The great recreational media of today—motoring, T.V., the cinema and the press—are enjoyed by all social classes. While this is true, it remains equally valid to argue that in many respects the democratization of leisure has been more apparent than real. Class distinctions can still be founded on, say, the kind of programmes watched on T.V., the

[57] Willmott, P., *The Evolution of a Community*, Routledge & Kegan Paul, 1963.

form taken by gambling (football pools, the betting shop, or the casino), the type of drink preferred, and so forth.

In many cases, too, the democratization of leisure has not increased the extent of social mixing between the classes but has rather created a kind of social apartheid: the provision of separate and (allegedly) equal facilities. A good illustration of this process is Pahl's study[58] of a commuter village in Hertfordshire described as "Dormersdell". To resolve the latent conflict between the indigenous population and the newcomers (most of whom were located in an area of woodland about a mile from the village centre), two social systems had come into existence. Even the Women's Institute had two groups, one in the daytime for "commuters' widows" and the other in the evening for the village.

> The Badminton Club is also entirely run for and by young middle-class men and women. However, this is no great loss to the working-class villagers: the younger ones monopolize the Youth Club and the Football Club and have good representation in the Cricket Club; the old age pensioners go to the Greensleeves Club . . . and a few older middle-class people in fact enjoy to go and serve tea or act as treasurer without the indignity of becoming a member.

These differences were accentuated by other divisions within the village, based partly on the breakdown of the traditional rural hierarchy and its replacement by a more polarized two-class system. The traditional villagers felt resentful because they had lost the reflected status of the gentry for whom they once worked, and partly because they were now lumped together with what they felt to be the less respectable working class. The non-traditional villagers resented the apparent privileges of the segregated middle class, and the middle class in turn were hostile towards the apparent lack of enterprise and stubbornness displayed by the villagers. Consequently there was little evidence in "Dormersdell" that the working class aspired to the leisure pursuits of the middle class. Somewhat similar (but not identical) observations have been made in a more recent account of Ringmer in Sussex,[59] which had grown organically up to the 1960s but then experienced an influx of newcomers which caused the population to rise from 2000 to 3500. Integration

[58] Pahl, R. E., "The two-class village", *New Society*, 27 February 1974, pp. 7–9.
[59] Ambrose, P., *The Quiet Revolution: Social Change in a Sussex Village 1871–1971*, Sussex University Press, 1974.

between the new arrivals and the older inhabitants is represented by an index made up of numbers of relationships within the village, the number of people known, friends, club membership and so on. This indicated that the newcomers were as involved in village life as the "natives" and that there was "no evidence of the spiralists who contribute nothing to village life". Yet social distinctions were still apparent in the different types of housing (and associated differences in life styles): Ambrose quotes, with approval, the perceptive view of a resident that "expensive houses and cheap houses are never built in the same area, therefore social divisions are created".

For some people it is the general pattern of family life, the resulting personality formation and inculcation of a common ideology which characterizes each social class. In talking about the working-class family, however, considerable difficulty is encountered. So many case studies from different areas have been made that the result is to a certain extent confusing, showing that the working class is scarcely a homogeneous group. Thus *Coal Is Our Life*[60] speaks of a family system in which "husband and wife live separate, and in a sense, secret lives" whereas the Bethnal Green research revealed "a living extended family which includes within it three, and even four generations" where husbands generally play an equal part. Nonetheless, there are certain basic characteristics. The family is primarily a functional unit, the home is a place in which to eat and sleep and spend one's leisure if one so wishes. Industrialization has destroyed the home as a unit of production and the family now concentrates on alternative social functions, such as reproduction and the early socialization of children. None of this is exclusively relevant to any particular social group and cannot therefore be cited as a class determinant.

More significant is the fact that in the working classes there appears to be a greater segregation of the sexes: in work, in leisure, in the ideology as to the position of the sexes and in the division of the wage-packet. A man's work is his own concern, while a woman's domain is the house. From an early age, the males move outside the family to a unisexual play-group in the streets. Girls, on the other hand, are expected to have little initiative; their education is often considered a

[60] Dennis, N., Henriques, F. and Slaughter, C., *Coal Is Our Life*, Eyre & Spottiswoode, 1956.

waste of time and their primary concern is getting a husband. Such stereotyped patterns are breaking down, with husbands becoming more interested in certain matters—the home, child-rearing, and so on —that were once the exclusive concern of the wife. But what is relevant here is that these attitudes and practices have been, and still are, significantly different among the various social strata, and also that the attitudes are themselves the consequence of a socialization process which begins in infancy. The foundations of sex role identity are well laid by the age of 4. By the time he is 7 the child is "intensely committed to moulding his behaviour in concordance with cultural standards appropriate to his biological sex, and he shows uneasiness, anxiety and even anger when he is in danger of behaving in ways regarded as characteristic of the opposite sex".[61] For example, one study of the sex role concepts of 50 8- and 11-year-old girls showed a very sophisticated and even precocious awareness of occupational sex differences. Activities related to child care, care of the interior of the house and of clothes and food, were assigned to women. Manipulation of the physical environment, machines, transportation, the structure of the house, and most kinds of occupation were assigned to men.[62] Working-class children are more aware of the social pattern of sex differences in behaviour than middle-class children, and this is especially true of girls. As Oakley[63] has argued:

> In later childhood, middle-class girls are not quite so restricted in their definitions of what women should do. . . . For working-class girls, the domestic group of female activities tends to be more rigidly fixed at the centre of their universe. They are much more likely to claim a preference for *all* the traditional female domestic activities (cleaning, tidying, looking after children, washing up) than middle-class girls are.

Education increases these class differences because it is only higher or further education and training which enable women to pursue career-type occupations. The early school-leaver is virtually doomed to a job (rather than a career in the genuine sense of the term) in tradi-

[61] Hartley, R. E., "A developmental view of female sex-role identification", in Biddle, B. J. and Thomas, E. J., eds., *Role Theory,* John Wiley, 1966.

[62] Hartley, R. E. and Klein, A., "Sex-role concepts of elementary school age girls", *Journal of Marriage and the Family,* Vol. 21, 1959, pp. 49–64.

[63] Oakley, A., "Sisters, Unite", *New Society,* 11 March 1971, pp. 390–3.

tional female occupations: unskilled factory labour, clerical work, retail selling and domestic work. The conditioning towards one of these eventual outcomes—job or career—begins even prior to school itself, in the preparation the child receives before going to school. Jean Jones[64] found that middle-class mothers were far more likely to prepare their children directly—by taking them along to the school beforehand, by teaching them various skills, or simply by telling them about school and allaying their anxieties. More important, the orientation of these preparatory acts differed between classes. Working-class mothers were more prone to stress the advisability of remaining passive ("When you go to school, you shut up and do what teacher says") compared with a more active role implied by middle-class parents: "You will meet new friends, there are lots of things to do and learn, lots of nice games to play." The frequency of reading and library membership also favoured the middle class. Only 9 per cent of the working-class mothers in the survey belonged to a library, compared with 75 per cent in the middle-class group. Regular reading to children was an activity among 71 per cent of the middle-class mothers but only 19 per cent in the case of the working class. Middle-class mothers were more inclined to stress the developmental and educational value of reading, rather than its value in keeping the child amused or "quiet". Similar class-based contrasts were elicited in many other similar areas, such as the selection and use of toys, parental relationships with teachers, and encouragement of the child's school performance.

Some fairly recent surveys support the assumption that the working-class family is dominated by the father in his role as wage-earner. Mays[65] states of Liverpool households that "The home is in certain important respect male-dominated. The husband and father *qua* wage-earner is the economic master who decides how much of the income will go to housekeeping and how much he will keep for his own personal use." Willmott and Young admit that, while such authoritarian relationships may have been disappearing in Bethnal Green, the old habits still lingered (perhaps inevitably in a community where young couples tended to live close to their parents). If wives were present when the interviewer asked how much the husbands earned, the latter often

[64] Jones, J., "Social class and the under-fives", *New Society*, 22 December 1966.
[65] Mays, J. B., *Growing Up in the City*, Liverpool University Press, 1954.

became visibly embarrassed or gave a suspiciously round figure. Toomey[66] revealed some significant variations of practice *within* the working class in his study of 180 manual households in the Medway towns. The groups came from five different types of area: post-war council estates (about 41 per cent of the sample), pre-war council estates (12 per cent), "traditional" private and letting property (20 per cent and 11 per cent) and more recently built private estates (16 per cent). When wives were asked if they knew what their husbands earned, only 30 per cent of the pre-war estate residents could reply in the affirmative, contrasted with 60 per cent or more in the other categories. According to Toomey, it is by no means clear why "old-fashioned" attitudes should persist more strongly in the pre-war estates, since the inhabitants of these estates could not be differentiated on grounds of age or income.

Another interesting aspect of Toomey's inquiry is that spouses from all categories visited their mothers at least once a week. The proportions varied little according to type of housing, from 37 per cent in the case of home owners (more of whom lived at a distance from their kin than other groups) to 46 per cent of the pre-war estate residents. The Bethnal Green studies, as we have already seen, equally stress the significance of the extended family: the devoted relationship between daughter and mother means that in old age the elderly are not deserted. Townsend[67] has reported that studies of the social background of the elderly in institutions show how surviving children are the greatest single safeguard for independence in old age. The extended family is not without its disadvantages, however, particularly if it means that "Where the daughter marries she often elects to live within easy calling distance of her own home, and a mile can be thought of as a wide separation."[68] Husbands may resent the wife's attachment to her family of origin and may therefore turn for consolation outside the home.

In many studies the husband is shown as a rather solitary figure standing on the edge of the circle of affection and family activity which surrounds the mother. An inquiry into Manchester dock workers[69] has

[66] Toomey, D. M., *Urban Studies*, Vol. 7, No. 3, 1970, p. 259.
[67] Townsend, P., *The Family Life of Old People*, Routledge & Kegan Paul, 1958.
[68] Mays, J. B., *op. cit.*
[69] *The Dock Worker*, Liverpool University Press, 1954.

suggested that changing work patterns supply a partial explanation for this phenomenon. Before dock work was regularized, the husband was in the home much more. "The children saw a lot of their father" and he "developed a great interest in and high regard for family life". With the introduction of more systematic working hours, dock workers are "no longer able to keep in close touch with what is happening at home . . . and find it more difficult to maintain their traditional authority in the family". Yet such an account seems to describe little more than a highly atypical subculture, in view of the fact that most of the documented trends concerning male involvement in family matters have been in precisely the opposite direction.

Such cases indeed illustrate the dilemma that many of the studies of working-class (and, by implication, middle-class) committee may focus unrepresentatively on anachronistic arrangements not truly typical of the statistically normal family. Elizabeth Bott[70] for example, has analysed the "traditional" manual worker's family structure in terms of its "close-knit" relationships, based on a social network where individuals see people who also see each other so that many links are built up between the members of the network. Such "close-knit" networks are associated with a sharp and rigid division of labour within the family—where, for example, men reject any concern with domestic matters. This contrasts with "loose-knit" relationships where few of the people whom an individual knows have any knowledge of, or relationship with, each other. Here one finds, according to Bott, a much less rigid separation of the spouses' roles in the household and much more co-operation in domestic affairs. From the class point of view there is some evidence that working-class units, under economic pressure forcing mobility of labour, are becoming less "close-knit" and therefore less dependent on the extended family.

Further attempts to differentiate the classes may be made by using certain objective criteria connected with the family, such as population data. The infant mortality rate differs as much between classes as it did before 1914, if not more so, although there has been a heavy fall in absolute death rates for all classes. Also, the working class tends to have larger families than the middle classes, but the discrepancy is not large

[70] Bott, E., *Family and Social Network*, Tavistock, 1957.

and is useless as a means of identifying social position. The democratization of the family has removed entirely some sources of distinctive
behaviour based on class—divorce is now freely available to all income
groups, for example—and in other cases the nature of the class separation has become more subtle and difficult to discern. We are left, for
instance, with such relatively minor phenomena as the first names
allocated to children. For 1975, *The Times* reported that the most popular names included James, Thomas, Nicholas, Sarah, Emma and
Alexandra, and that most of these names had appeared in the "top ten"
for many successive years. The working class, however, appears to be
more susceptible to fashion, opting for short periods to choose such
names as Darren, Garry, Michelle, Lynne, Karen, and the like.

The provision of secondary education for all under the 1944 Education Act has removed one of the most effective determinants of class,
namely, the type and duration of education received. Prior to 1944,
only a select minority received secondary education and the working
class was heavily under-represented. The vast majority had to be content with an inadequate period of elementary tuition in poorly equipped
schools. Since the 1944 Act, however, the education process itself has
become the chief agent of social selection. With the abolition of fees
and a standardized selection system, there is now little means of distinguishing the social classes according to the type of education received, although the working class as a whole is still marginally under-
represented. A greater number of children of skilled workers stay on at
school beyond the minimum school-leaving age, although little difference has been made to the educational chances of children of semi-
skilled and unskilled workers. Many working-class children, furthermore, are penalized by the fact that they are members of large families,
since it appears that constant social intercourse with siblings is of less
value, educationally, than the close relationships inevitably created
between, say, an only child and his parents. The importance of education, then, lies not in its intrinsic capacity for acting as an index of social
class, but rather in its function as a means of gaining occupational
prestige.

Voting behaviour is still correlated strongly with social class, though
definite conclusions are dependent on the interpretation of social class
employed—whether class membership is based on occupation or some

other "objective" criterion, or alternatively if it is dependant on subjective assessment. Subjective views of class are of great help in predicting the vote of border-line cases whose income and occupation are on
the dividing line between the middle and working classes. Alford's
work[71] certainly shows the extent to which class voting occurs in
Britain compared with Australia, the United States and Canada. For
each country, Alford computed an index of class voting derived by
subtracting the percentage of middle-class persons voting for Left-wing
parties from the percentage of working-class persons voting Left. Not
only does Britain have a higher index of class voting than the other
countries concerned, but this class voting also overrides regional
loyalties—except in Scotland and Wales where class voting is intensified
by such loyalties. Over the 25 years covered by Alford's investigations,
the incidence of class voting has been remarkably stable in Britain;
indeed, it was on the increase between 1945 and 1959. This was because
the Labour Party had a sizeable minority of middle-class support in
1945 and it was this support which was gradually eroded in the subsequent 15 years. More recent experience suggests that the Labour Party
has regained a measure of middle-class support just as the Conservative
Party has always acquired a substantial proportion of votes from manual
workers.[72]

Conclusion: The Changing Class Structure

Weber conceived of class as the common market situation of groups
of people possessing specific goods or capabilities. Building on this
approach, Giddens[73] has recently argued, in his discussion of "class
structuration", that a three-class system is endemic in capitalist society:
an "upper", "middle" and "working" class related to three kinds of
market capacity—ownership of property in the means of production,
possession of educational or technical qualifications, and possession of
manual labour-power. However, the shape of class systems in particular
capitalist societies is seen as a specific configuration dependent on both
"mediate" and "proximate" factors. The former has to do with the

[71] Alford, R., *Party and Society*, John Murray, 1964.
[72] See Nordlinger, E. A., "The working-class Tory", *New Society*, 13 October 1966,
pp. 572–4.
[73] Giddens, A., *The Class Structure of the Advanced Societies*, Hutchinson, 1974.

extent of inter- and intra-generational mobility. "In general", claims Giddens, "the greater the degree of 'closure' of mobility chances, the more this facilitates the formation of identifiable classes." In addition, three "proximate" factors are postulated: the division of labour and authority relationships in the production enterprise, together with the influence of distributive groupings sharing common patterns in the consumption of economic goods. Each of these factors, "mediate" and "proximate", may harden or soften the way in which the three-fold class system is structured. The Weberian character of this standpoint is reflected in the following statement:

> The mode in which these (mediate and proximate) elements are merged to form a specific class system, in any given society, differs significantly according to variations in economic and political development. The problem of the existence of distinct class "boundaries" is not one which can be settled *in abstracto*: one of the specific aims of class analysis in relation to empirical societies must necessarily be that of determining how strongly, in any given case, the "class principle" has become established as a mode of structuration. Moreover, the operation of the "class principle" may also involve the creation of forms of structuration within the major class divisions. One case in point is that which Marx called the "petty bourgeoisie".

What this means, in essence, is that the class system is in a constant state of flux—which makes it scarcely surprising that it is difficult to draw a clear and coherent picture at any given point in time. Moreover, the fluctuating nature of the scene makes it even more difficult to make sensible predictions. Drawing on the past, however, Giddens argues that the rise of an organized working class and its incorporation into the system has helped to stabilize—rather than destroy—capitalist society: "Social democracy is the normal form taken by the systematic political inclusion of the working class within capitalist society." On the other hand, the stability of such a society, in what Giddens calls its "neo-capitalist" phase, merits the adjective "fragile". He properly notes that whilst union leaders may seek with Government and employers to regulate the economy, the resultant coalition is not easily sustained. It would be more straightforward during periods of economic growth, but in so far as the coalition implies attempts to regulate wages and negotiate long-term labour contracts, resistance from the rank and file may be expected. The intensification of that form of conflict, perhaps associated with movements for workers' control, may be translated into a new socio-economic order if capitalism is not able to generate real wage increases. It is this which leads Giddens to predict that "the renewal of class conflict, relating directly to the nature of industrial control, and thus spilling over into the political sphere", is a strong possibility.

In this chapter we have seen that the class pattern in Britain is undergoing some critical changes which exemplify the Giddens approach to "class structuration" and the influence of "mediate" and "proximate" factors. Members of what could be described as the "new" working class—high income manual workers—are closer today, in economic terms at least, to many lower middle-class groups than they are to the seriously deprived section of the population which occupies the base of the social pyramid. Similarly it appears that the socio-economic situation of many white-collar employees is altogether closer to the "new" workers than to higher-level managers and professionals. This is especially true of the growing body of clerical and technical staff who have only uncertain or limited career chances and who form, in effect, a kind of white-collar labour force. In other words, the distinction between manual and non-manual employment, as indicating a major line of class cleavage, is becoming a good deal less important than it once was.

This view is confirmed by trends in social mobility in modern Britain. It has become evident that the manual/non-manual dividing line is no longer a major barrier to occupational advancement or decline. Intergenerationally, if not in the work histories of individuals, it is frequently crossed, in both directions, though it must be stressed that much of this mobility is of a short-range kind. The pattern of a relatively high rate of limited mobility persists right through to the top of the class hierarchy, since even at the elite level—among higher civil servants and business circles—the circulation which occurs goes on within a restricted range, in which kinship is one of the major factors.[74]

Mobility is restricted in other ways, too. Education is of crucial importance[75] in determining level of occupational achievement; the possibilities of "working one's way up" from the kinds of job allocated

---

[74] See Lupton, T. and Wilson, C. S., "The social background and connections of 'top decision makers' ", *Manchester School of Economic and Social Studies*, Vol. 27, 1959, pp. 30–52.

[75] With the exception of the occasional entrepreneur, show business performer or sportsman.

to secondary modern school-leavers and their equivalents from comprehensive schools are few and diminishing. Moreover, occupational mobility is not necessarily the same thing as status or cultural mobility. Even when occupational barriers have been overcome, status and cultural barriers have yet to be surmounted—a recurrent theme in the modern English novel. Status exclusiveness, and cultural differences as an expression of this, are in fact those features of the stratification of British society which are most impervious to the egalitarian effects of an expanding economy. Nonetheless, these very economic pressures have forced the upper class—that 2 per cent of the population comprising the aristocracy, "Society" and a few important families whose common feature is the ownership of land—to assimilate a few *nouveau riche* captains of industry into their ranks.

The general increase in the earnings of industrial workers has produced a fall in their level of class consciousness and hence less class conflict, at least along the lines predicted by Marx. Today only a minority of workers see society as divided into two warring camps of bosses and labour, and allow this concept to shape their entire social outlook; those who do are invariably concentrated in the least prosperous and most alienated sectors of the working population.[76] In part, this declining hostility stems from the decay of the tightly knit, homogeneous communities where feelings of in-group solidarity and conservatism were readily formed. At the same time, as Goldthorpe and his associates have shown, the affluent worker retains his working-class values and attitudes; while pursuing the goals of a consumption society, he rejects the status-striving values of the middle class. The affluent worker automatically resents the status superiority which middle-class people still seek to preserve even when their economic superiority has vanished—and, in the eyes of the worker, this status superiority is itself illusory. As one Dagenham wife said, "In Ilford they're all fur coats and no drawers", and another remarked "They're all show and no breakfast."

[76] Similar observations have been made in the United States. A sample survey of manual workers in Detroit in 1960, for example, showed that extremely militant class consciousness was highest among unemployed Negroes belonging to trade unions; employed whites were least class conscious of all. See Leggett, J. C., *American Sociological Review*, Vol. 29, No. 2, 1964.

On the middle-class side, the most important changes are occurring among the lower white-collar groups, since it is these who are threatened by the affluent manual workers. Because the white-collar workers feel insecure, they retain their middle-class ethos (and claim to separate identity) with grim determination, yet simultaneously there are signs that they are abandoning the traditional individualism of the middle class in favour of collective action. These deep-seated changes have been described by Zweig[77] as "de-bourgeoisement". They are manifested in various ways, including bureaucratization, namely, a transformation of the middle classes from independent, self-reliant merchants, industrialists and professionals into salaried office-holders; the erosion of middle-class values; the declining economic, social and political status of the middle classes; the progressive appropriation by the middle classes of the armoury of working-class struggle in collective action via trade unions, quasi-unions and other militantly active pressure groups. Zweig further perceives a growing alienation among the middle class, itself a dialectical counterpart of the growing dis-alienation of the working classes, and leading to such phenomena as withdrawal, partial withdrawal of participation (apathy), some withdrawal of investment, and even the withdrawal of persons themselves (emigration). While this account must remain somewhat speculative, it is notable that surveys show some difference of opinion within the middle classes themselves. On matters concerning the social services, for example, the lower middle classes express more positively favourable judgements, perhaps because these services are now an essential part of their well-being and security.

At the extremes of the British class structure, attitudes and styles of life remain relatively fixed, reflecting the rigidity in the structure at these points. In the middle ranges, socio-economic changes are forcing individuals into new conceptions of their social worlds and new appraisals of their values and interests. Even if this were not true, we could never hope to get an absolute picture of social class in its totality, for there is no such uniformity in people's thinking or behaviour. Different people do not necessarily mean the same things by terms like "working class" or "middle class", and indeed the same person may at different

[77] Zweig, F., *The New Acquisitive Society*, Barry Rose for the Centre for Policy Studies, 1976.

times or in different contexts use them in different senses and locate himself (and others) differently. It is scarcely surprising that this should be so, since it is an inevitable concomitant of the class-structured society which we are trying to describe.

CHAPTER 4

The Socialization Process: Education

We rightly ask of our educational system that it should give equal opportunities to climb a ladder irrespective of income or social class.
(Sir Edward Boyle, then Minister of Education, *Guardian*, 6 September 1962)

Social and educational policy have not successfully seized on the enlarged occupational opportunities since 1945, in such a way as to realize either an egalitarian or a meritocratic society.
(A. H. Halsey, *Towards Meritocracy? The Case of Britain,*
Oxford University Press, 1977)

Save our Grammer Schools.
(Protest banner)

Introduction

The importance of education lies not only in its power as a factor in social stratification but also in the rather obvious fact that the prosperity of the country depends ultimately on the quality and quantity of education received by its citizens. A democracy can never work efficiently unless all its members possess at least a reasonable degree of literacy. It was the realization of this fact which led to the enforcement of elementary education for all in 1880, *after* the vote had been extended to almost all the male population. Similarly, an industrialized country can never maintain its level of wealth, in the face of technological and economic competition, without continued attention to scientific training and the effective deployment of manpower. Thus, for example, talent is wasted if a potentially gifted individual is forced to remain an agricultural labourer all his life, as doubtless occurred often before education became free and compulsory, and before competitive examinations replaced nepotism as the chief source of recruitment to most occupations. The complexity of industrialization, the development of more occupations requiring detailed technical knowledge and skills, creates a massive demand for the maximum utilization of potential abilities and aptitudes at every level. This means an educational system specifically designed to weed out and exploit such abilities and aptitudes.

This is not to say, however, that the argument for education is merely a question of economic utility. In Britain the aims of educators have been directly affected by the ideas of philosophers and social reformers such as Matthew Arnold and John Stuart Mill, who visualized education as contributing to the social rather than the economic development of society.[1] In its modern form this doctrine is exemplified in the belief that training in, say, engineering should be accompanied by education in the traditional humanities or social sciences. Such ideas are a legacy of the whole-hearted commitment to a liberal education which characterized the universities and lesser educational institutions at the beginning of the nineteenth century. This liberal education, while not in itself fitting the recipient for any particular occupation, was intended to develop his moral and intellectual faculties irrespective of any ends to which he might put them, and it was thought that such an education was calculated to induce habits of rational thought and analysis. As Sanderson[2] has remarked, however, "such an education fitting for no special livelihood was particularly apt for those who had no need to earn a living or whose position was assured". And a paradox began to emerge in that the content of large parts of a liberal education was also directly applicable to the most common career followed by graduates, namely, the Church. In the later eighteenth century and the first half of the nineteenth, half of all Cambridge graduates and two-thirds of those from Oxford went into Holy Orders. Then, by the middle of the nineteenth century, it began to be argued that although a liberal education prepared for no special vocation, it did enable the student to approach and solve problems in almost any field—thus justifying its use as a basis for entry into the Home and Indian Civil Services.

> This attempt to link liberal education with almost any form of career was some-what of a retreat from the more mandarin defence that it was the attribute of the gentleman or an intellectual end in itself. . . . Much of this ambivalence of attitude was tied up with attitudes to social class and to technology. A liberal education was successful at the older universities and could be seen to lead to success in its pupils because they already came from an elite whose wealth and contacts opened

[1] Williams, R., *Culture and Society 1780–1950*, Penguin Books, 1958.
[2] Sanderson, M., ed., *The Universities in the Nineteenth Century*, Routledge & Kegan Paul, 1975.

opportunities and future prospects for their sons. When attempts were made to transplant an Oxbridge liberal education to the north . . . the results were deeply disappointing. A lower social class of pupil found such curricula totally unsuitable for their needs"[3]

Naturally, occupational success is often uppermost in the minds of those who seek to achieve educational qualifications, but most educational theorists, when asked the question "what is education for?" would go beyond the narrow economic justification. It is no part of this book to answer these philosophical inquiries, but it is relevant to make the point that if the British educational system does appear to be disorganized and to lack clearly unified objectives, this is precisely because it is the result of pressures busily competing for attention and domination: economic, idealistic, religious, and political.

In conjunction with the family, education is plausibly the most influential medium for socialization in our society. It supplies, both formally and informally, the behavioural norms, roles, values and social skills which the individual requires (to a greater or lesser degree) in order to become an accepted and acceptable member of adult society. The significance of this process will be discussed in more detail later, with special emphasis on the problems created if the socializing influences exerted in the school conflict with those supplied by the home. And, of course, we must consider the relationship of education to social class and the extent to which the educational system, as a socializing agent, acquaints the individual with and reinforces his "place" in society.

The Development of Education in Britain

The first major expansion of education in this country occurred as a direct consequence of industrialization. Education in the eighteenth century was either inadequate or non-existent for the majority. For the rest, access to satisfactory schooling (supplied generally by private tutors and governesses) was limited virtually to those who economic position made this possible—in other words, the aristocracy. Thus there has been, from the beginning, a close correlation between the type of education received and one's socio-economic status. Even when the

[3] Sanderson, M., ed., *op. cit.*

1868 Schools Inquiry Commission recommended the establishment of three types of secondary school, these were to be distinguished by social gradings rather than by the mental abilities of the pupils. Children of well-to-do parents would be taught the classics and similar non-vocational subjects up to the age of 18; children from the middle strata of society would receive an education suited to their eventual position as artisans, up to the age of 16; and the rest would receive, up to 14 years of age, an education to fit them to be labourers. This scheme was based on the widely accepted assumption that an individual's occupation should depend primarily, if not completely, on his social origins and that the lower classes should not be educated above their station in life. Carried to its extreme the result would have been a caste system of the most rigid kind. Fortunately, in 1870 the Civil Service Commission had replaced nepotism by competitive examination as its chief method of recruitment. This decision was to have far-reaching repercussions for education as a whole.

But the pressures for change had been active well before 1870. The desire of the mercantile and landed middle classes to organize effective education for their children, coupled with their inability to meet the costs of private tutors, led to the foundation and expansion of what are now known as the public schools. These establishments were only public in that they catered for the middle classes rather than the aristocracy, though they did supply a channel of upward social mobility in the sense that many comparatively impecunious individuals achieved positions of eminence through them. Indeed, some of the ancient foundations had been set up with this purpose implicitly in mind, to provide recruits for the Church and the Law; Winchester, for instance, was formed to supply students to New College, Oxford. Until the end of the eighteenth century, such schools catered largely for children in their respective localities, but as the Industrial Revolution gained momentum and expupils achieved positions conveying occupational prestige, this was reflected on to the *alma mater* and the schools began to lose their local character. During the nineteenth century about seven public schools gained a national reputation and their pupils were primarily fee-payers. It was at this time, too, that the aristocracy began to patronize the public schools (which, of course, increased their prestige still further) instead of employing private tutors.

Some headmasters remained conscious of their obligations towards the poor, despite opposition from parents of fee-paying pupils. Various devices were adopted, such as segregation in the playgrounds, but the system finally succumbed and the public schools assumed the character which they have maintained, virtually unchanged, to this day. There are currently about 80 in the group of better-known private boarding schools. A more precise indication of the total numbers may be derived from the Headmasters' Conference, whose membership is restricted to a maximum of 200, including girls' schools. The most vital qualification for admission to this select body is "the measure of independence enjoyed by the governing body and the headmaster". In all, pupils in schools represented at the Headmasters' Conference amounted to 113,028 in 1974 (a modest gain of 3.3 per cent over the previous year), or about 5 per cent of all children in the 13-year-old age group. [4]

The nineteenth century also saw a formidable expansion in the grammar-school system as a training ground for the increasing range of black-coated occupations required to administer Britain's empire and commercial concerns. These grammar schools modelled themselves closely on the public schools in terms of both organization structure and curriculum design. Their non-vocational and "literary" emphasis could be attributed to the fact that this type of tuition was thought to be more suitable for budding teachers and clerks; organizationally they relied upon a "house" system, prefects, obligatory games and the development of corporate loyalty. Many grammar schools had a long and honourable history, while others were established by local education authorities under the 1902 Balfour Act.

In 1900 admission to such schools depended either on parental wealth or on exceptional promise shown in the elementary stage. Today, admission to education of the grammar-school type (though hardly ever conducted in grammar schools as such) is rather more dependent on the child's abilities and his chronological position within a specified age-range. Moreover, secondary education is now an accepted phase in the

[4] On the face of it, a continuing increase in the numbers at public school is surprising given the economic climate and the continuously rising fees. In 1975, Eton was charging £1287 a year and current fees are approaching £2000. The cause of the rise in numbers lies in the very success of comprehensive re-organization, which has meant that there are fewer grammar schools to which parents unreconciled to the comprehensive system can send their children.

whole educative process whereas in 1900, for most children, teaching stopped at the age of 14 after 9 years continuously in the elementary or primary school. Credit for these changes must be attributed partly to the Hadow Commission[5] which recommended that at the age of 11 *all* children should proceed to some form of secondary education. Three types of school were advocated to meet the estimated demand: secondary, grammar, junior technical and "modern" schools. Broadly speaking, these schools could be differentiated in terms of the educational attainment of their pupils, although the Hadow Commission preferred to confine themselves to the remark that the "modern" schools would have a more practical and vocational bias. Theoretically, too, the new "modern" schools (in some cases no more than senior departments to existing elementary schools) were to enjoy "parity of esteem". In practice the staffing ratio and equipment were almost invariably less generous than in the grammar schools. Of the technical schools, some of which had existed since 1900, the Spens Report[6] had more to say. It was firmly expected that such schools would enjoy equality of status with the grammar schools but that after the age of 13 the pupils would specialize in more practical subjects.

The concept of the tripartite system, which as we have seen was first mooted in 1868, was further reinforced by the Norwood Report.[7] Norwood reiterated the assumptions made by Hadow and Spens, that at the age of 11 all children should pass into secondary schools, of which there should be three types. All three should enjoy parity of conditions and amenities, with a broadly uniform curriculum for the first 2 years at all schools to facilitate transfer for late developers. Pressure from the Norwood Committee and the cumulative effects of earlier Commissions led directly to the 1944 Education Act, which revolutionized secondary education, firmly established the tripartite system, and incorporated the then novel concept of equality of opportunity. Henceforth no child, however poor his parents, would be denied access to the type of secondary education most suited to his intelligence and aptitudes. The realization

[5] The Hadow Report: *Education of the Adolescent*, H.M.S.O., 1926.
[6] The Spens Report: *Secondary Education with Special Reference to Grammar and Technical High Schools*, H.M.S.O., 1938.
[7] The Norwood Report: *Curriculum and Examinations in Secondary Schools*, H.M.S.O., 1943.

of this principle and its obvious implications for the universities and the public schools was to preoccupy politicians and sociologists for years to come.

Nowhere does the 1944 Act mention the tripartite arrangement of grammar, technical and "modern" schools, since this would have been regarded as unjustifiably restrictive so far as the future progress of education was concerned. In practice there now exists an enormous variety of arrangements for post-primary education, a consequence of the considerable autonomy which each local education authority enjoys. Although the Act does specify that the duty of the Minister (now Secretary of State) is "to secure the effective execution by local authorities under his control and direction of the national policy for providing a varied and comprehensive educational service in every area", local education authorities are subject to few restrictions so long as their provision is "adequate".[8] These authorities are themselves made up of Greater London, 36 large metropolitan districts inside six English metropolitan counties (such as Manchester, South Yorkshire, and the West Midlands), 39 non-metropolitan counties in England, eight counties in Wales, and a number of similar counties in Scotland.[9] In theory, section 101 of the Local Government Act, 1972, does permit counties to arrange for the districts in their areas to carry out functions for them, and vice versa, but in practice most of the non-metropolitan counties have retained direct control over the performance of their education responsibilities.

The school-leaving age was raised to 15 in 1947 and became 16 in 1972.[10] Clearly the enforcement of increased school attendance,

---

[8] However, the interpretation of "adequate" is left to the Secretary of State and his advisers. In recent years it has been equated with the comprehensive system rather than the previously prevailing arrangement of grammar, technical and "modern" schools.

[9] This pattern is a direct consequence of the Local Government Act, 1972, whose changes were introduced on 1 April 1974 (in Scotland from 1 April 1975). In essence, the Act has created 422 local authorities in England and Wales (outside London) from a former pattern of 1391 councils of varying kinds.

[10] Proposals to alter the leaving age to 16 were incorporated in the Crowther and Newsom reports. See *15 to 18*, Vol. 1 of the Report of the Central Advisory Council for Education (England) (The Crowther Report), H.M.S.O., 1959; *Half Our Future*, a Report of the Central Advisory Council for Education (England) (The Newsom Report), H.M.S.O., 1963.

coupled with the 1944 Act's demand that secondary schools should be housed in different buildings from primary schools, created great pressure on education authorities, in terms of both financial resources and teacher recruitment. This pressure, at its height during the onset of post-World War II austerity, prevented the improvement in educational facilities from keeping up with the rise in the school population to over 9.8 millions in 1972. By 1974 the numbers had risen to over 11 millions, with nearly 450,000 at independent schools. One of the major reasons for this rise, apart from the later school-leaving age, has been the increased willingness of pupils to remain at school beyond the age of 16, though that general assertion conceals significant regional differences in the United Kingdom. For England, the proportion of pupils wishing to remain at school dropped from nearly three-fifths to less than a quarter in 1974, whereas for the previous 10 years a greater number of pupils from England had decided to stay on at school after their 15th birthdays than in any part of the United Kingdom. The 1974 figures, in detail, showed that the pupils electing to remain at school in England constituted 23.1 per cent of the total, compared with 36.3 per cent in Northern Ireland, 35.1 per cent in Scotland, and 27.5 per cent in Wales.[11] Within England itself, the north no longer held the dubious distinction of having the greatest share of the country's reluctant pupils. East Anglia, where 55 per cent of the pupils had stayed on when the school-leaving age was 15, had dropped to 17.7 per cent in 1974; the North-west had 18.1 per cent staying on, the North 18.5 per cent, the East Midlands 18.7 per cent, and Yorkshire and Humberside 20.2 per cent. As always, the South-east had the greatest share of pupils remaining at school, with 30 per cent, but even that figure was a considerable fall from the earlier peak of more than 60 per cent. Of the 681,500 school-leavers aged 16 or more in 1974, 83,000 had achieved at least two passes at G.C.E. Advanced Level and 60,400 had obtained five or more Ordinary Level passes, plus a further 166,400 with between one

---

[11] See *Education Statistics for the United Kingdom, 1974*, H.M.S.O., 1976. The reasons for remaining at school beyond the minimum school-leaving age are not all connected, of course, with a single-minded pursuit of knowledge and qualifications. In certain areas, notably Northern Ireland, the lack of employment opportunities for school-leavers must be a potent factor.

and four Ordinary Level passes.[12] The figures for Advanced Level had been fairly static since 1972, but there had been a conspicuous rise in the proportion of Ordinary Level passes, perhaps connected with the greater acceptance of the Certificate of Secondary Education (C.S.E.), whose Grade 1 pass is included in these statistics as equivalent to a pass at G.C.E. Ordinary Level.

The 1944 Education Act reflected the egalitarian ethos of Britain at the end of World War II. Until that time it had been recognized that social class raised barriers to equal opportunity, and the task of reform was to ensure equality of access—for the children of comparable ability, regardless of their social origins—to the available institutions of secondary, further and higher education. In so far as social class had an effect on educational performance (as distinct from opportunity), the problem was seen as a material one: how to mitigate the handicaps of poverty, malnutrition and overcrowding by using schools as social agencies—by distributing free meals and milk to necessitous children and developing school medical services. Selection for entry into the grammar school was to depend on objective criteria, such as intelligence tests, attainment tests (particularly in arithmetic and English), proficiency tests in certain subjects, teachers' reports and primary school records. Local education authorities were free to develop their own procedures and consequently attached varying importance to each of these factors—indeed, some were omitted entirely.

Unfortunately it soon became apparent that no amount of tinkering with the selection system could remove the social class bias inherent in the concept of the tripartite pattern. Although about 25 per cent of all children at the secondary stage were successful in achieving grammar-school places, the middle class was heavily over-represented in this group. A major contributory factor here was undoubtedly the high value placed on education by middle-class parents which in turn transmitted itself to the children, but also important was the fact that the grammar school as a social system heavily embodied the middle-class style of life and was thus unacceptably alien to many working-class

---

[12] These figures do not include those who subsequently obtain G.C.E. qualifications by full-time or part-time attendance at establishments of further education. In 1974, for example, the total numbers with at least two Advanced Level passes, from schools and further education together, amounted to 155,600.

entrants. Parents with children attending grammar schools were almost invariably required to sign an undertaking to keep them at school until 16, since the grammar school's curriculum was based on G.C.E. (or its forebears) and 16 was the age at which the G.C.E. Ordinary Level examinations were normally taken. Although such agreements were not legally binding, they exerted significant moral pressure and the parents' willingness to sign was a vital factor in the marginal child's chances of gaining entry to grammar school. Moreover, the marginal child of middle-class parents benefitted in other ways. At the point of interview the child's appearance, manners, demeanour and speech patterns were all likely to be regarded favourably by selectors who were themselves middle-class, and it is not therefore unreasonable to suppose that the "halo effect" had some impact on the final decisions. Even if working-class children were admitted to grammar school, their performance was almost invariably worse than that of their middle-class equivalents, their behaviour was more likely to be deviant (when evaluated against grammar-school norms) and they were more prone to leave school at the first opportunity.

Although we have said that 25 per cent of all children received a grammar-school education, too, the proportion varied significantly between different local education authorities, from as much as 40 per cent to as little as 10 per cent (it is arguable that in a fully developed tripartite system, about 33 per cent of all pupils should have the opportunity of going to grammar school). In other words, while the average Intelligence Quotient (I.Q.) "cut-off" level for grammar-school pupils might be 115, in some areas it could rise to 125 or even higher while in others it could be as low as 105. Wallasey allowed 32 children out of every 100 to go to grammar school, while in Burton-on-Trent only 13 could do so. Since the children in these areas are likely to have the same range of abilities, then about 19 children out of every 100 in Burton-on-Trent were being denied the grammar-school education which they would have had if they had lived in Wallasey.

Because of these manifest absurdities and contradictions, various attempts have been made to dispense with the tripartite system, and these attempts are now focused on the comprehensive school, which absorbs all children of secondary-school age regardless of their intellectual ability. It is alleged that this procedure overcomes the social stigma of failure attached to the secondary modern school and its occupants,[13] promotes social integration because it compels children of different academic interests and capacities to mix throughout the school, and achieves all the advantages accruing from the economies of scale in that specialist staff and equipment can be justified when deployed in larger establishments. Once inside the comprehensive school, however, the children may be streamed as much as if they had gone to separate schools, though as far as the external essentials are concerned (such as uniform and facilities) they appear equal. Alternatively, pupils may be placed in classes not according to their overall ability but rather according to their aptitude in individual subjects. Thus a child may be in the A stream for Art, the D stream for Mathematics and the C stream for English. This arrangement generally satisfies the advocates of the comprehensive theory in that each pupil usually excells in some sphere of his scholastic endeavours and subject streaming enables him to feel a strong sense of achievement in at least one course of study. In yet other cases the headmaster may elect to discard streaming altogether so that each class incorporates a random spread of ability—on the assumption that the less able children will be motivated towards improving their performance by the presence of academically more gifted children.[14] A recent survey of 15,000 16-year-old children, however, found that most schools still use traditional forms of streaming from 12 or 13 upwards. A third of the sample were in schools that used streaming, more

---

[13] This reputation for failure is to some extent a natural reaction to the image of the grammar school as a passport to occupational success. In the immediate post-1945 period, the declared philosophy of the modern schools comprised the somewhat negative doctrine that they would be free from the narrow, hide-bound teaching imposed by examination syllabuses. Instead, teachers would be free to pursue any topic in which their pupils showed interest, without fear of wasting time more properly devoted to examination-directed studies. The application of this belief meant that many children of average intelligence left the schools with no marketable qualifications at all, and hence much reduced chances of obtaining any form of employment among increasingly certificate-conscious organizations.

[14] There is little or no evidence to support this view: like so much published thought in the field of education, it is stimulated by ideological commitment rather than empirical observation. It could be argued, equally convincingly, that less able children will be demotivated and disheartened by being given a frequent opportunity to make ample invidious comparisons between themselves and other children with superior intellects.

than a third in schools that put children into sets, and about a sixth were in mixed-ability classes.[15]

Whatever the type of organization employed, the comprehensive school offers (at least in theory) far more flexibility than the tripartite system. Late developers have a genuine chance of making up for lost time as against the rather spurious and potentially traumatic experience of transfer from one school to another. Yet the debate continues on the educational standards found in comprehensive schools: do they really open doors, as their advocates claim, or are they so bound up with doctrinaire egalitarianism that they have a levelling-down effect? Pedley's figures[16] suggested that comprehensive education is more successful in encouraging children to proceed to further and higher education, and that the percentage of children successfully obtaining G.C.E. passes is higher for comprehensive schools than for the tripartite system they have replaced.

True, from 1965 to 1972, a period of marked comprehensive growth, there was a 28 per cent increase in G.C.E. A-level passes in the secondary system. But it is impossible to show that this rate of increase was greater than it would have been without comprehensivization, or was greater in the comprehensive sector than elsewhere. During the same period, it is significant to note that, although there was rapid growth in sixth forms of all kinds, the expected increase of 44 per cent in the number of school-leavers with two or more A-level passes turned out in practice to be one of only 23 per cent. At the same time, a small sample of 12 mature comprehensive schools was being examined in detail.[17] The result was that only in 5 out of 11 schools (for which the question was appropriate) were the proportions of pupils attaining five or more G.C.E. Ordinary level passes at or above the national average. As regards two or more A-level passes, only 1 of the 11 schools was at or

[15] Fogelman, K., ed., *Britain's 16-Year-Olds*, National Children's Bureau, 1976. The survey further reveals that most of the children were in schools with fewer than 1000 pupils. More than half the sample were in classes of between 20 and 29 for mathematics and English—but 28 per cent were in classes of more than 30 for these subjects. Only 4 per cent were in schools which had no uniform.

[16] Pedley, R., *The Comprehensive School*, Penguin Books, 1963. His findings partially reflected improved standards over time, but none the less they were still significant.

[17] *A Critical Appraisal of Comprehensive Education*, National Foundation for Educational Research, 1972.

above the national average. Another study, concentrating on a direct comparison between tripartite schools and comprehensive schools on achievement in mathematics, has found that the standard of attainment of O-level candidates was actually higher in secondary modern schools than in comprehensive schools. The advocates of the comprehensive system dismiss such evidence as misleading, perhaps because the continued presence of grammar schools in many areas during the 1960s automatically meant that the comprehensive schools were denied their fair share of able pupils, or alternatively because parents, given some freedom of choice, have preferred to send their children to established types of school rather than establishments symbolizing a new departure in educational thinking. Nonetheless, the point remains that there is little evidence to indicate conclusively that comprehensive schools—even when staffed by committed enthusiasts—can surpass the best achieved in well-developed tripartite systems, let alone match up to the national average.

Scrutiny of the relationship between comprehensive schools and the universities shows that students from this particular background differ in some respects from the university population in general. In the first place they are more likely to have been late developers. One student in eight, from Neave's sample,[18] was an 11-plus failure. Second, the comprehensive school entrant was likely to have passed a mixture of science-cum-arts/social science subjects at Advanced level; and third, he was more likely to be following a science-based degree course at university. As far as social class is concerned, a far higher proportion of students from such schools came from working-class homes than is the case with university students generally. More students from comprehensive schools, too, selected as first choice a university which was near to home, and fewer students applied to Oxbridge from this type of school.

If anything, the amount of variety and diversity in educational provision for the post-16 age group is even greater than that found within primary and secondary education.[19] Apart from the traditional sixth form, sixth form colleges, sixth form centres, and so forth, pupils—who

[18] Neave, G., *How They Fared: the Impact of the Comprehensive School upon the University*, Routledge & Kegan Paul, 1975.
[19] For a detailed analysis of this topic, see King, R., *School and College; Studies of Post-Sixteen Education*, Routledge & Kegan Paul, 1976.

at this stage begin to be called students—can enter the world of further education, where technical colleges, the descendants of Mechanics' Institutes, no longer confine themselves specifically to the training of craftsmen, technicians and technologists. Most of the institutions of further education—whether designated as polytechnics, colleges of higher education, or by some other fancy name—interpret their roles very widely and provide courses in a wide range of categories: technical, commercial, vocational, non-vocational, recreational. In 1973 there were 30 polytechnics with 156,700 students, plus nearly 600 other colleges and 7000 evening institutes, with between them a total of over 3 million students—though it must be remembered that this figure included all part-time as well as full-time students. Just over 200,000 students were studying for advanced qualifications at (roughly) degree or post-graduate level, many of these being degrees awarded by the colleges themselves under the supervision of the Council for National Academic Awards (C.N.A.A.).[20] Long courses—of one academic year or more—may be undertaken on a full-time or part-time basis or as a "sandwich" programme with alternate periods in college and in industry. If the student is college-based, then the college arranges with companies to supply him with relevant practical experience. More commonly, students are recruited by an organization, paid a trainee's salary, and handed over to the college for theoretical tuition. The advantage of the former arrangement is that the college can organize the course on wider lines, with more emphasis on liberal studies. On the other hand, the company-based trainee is paid a salary and the college does not have to worry about his future occupational placement.

Membership of most professional organizations is normally obtained through a combination of examination success and practical experience. Though these organizations are very numerous and differ widely in the extent to which they enjoy social acceptance, they resemble each other in that they stipulate certificates and diplomas as more appropriate than a university degree taken by itself. This is not to say that a degree is valueless, but it must invariably be supplemented by more specific training, experience and examination successes if it is to be

---

[20] C.N.A.A. criteria include the presence of staff who can devote themselves exclusively to high-level work; a liberal study element in all courses; an adequate and efficient library; and acceptable residential facilities.

acceptable to the professions. After all, the English universities largely held aloof from specific occupational training until after the middle of the nineteenth century, when they variously began to provide efficient and examined education in such fields as law, medicine and engineering. Hitherto John Stuart Mill's famous assertion that there was "a tolerably general agreement" that a university was "not a place of professional education" had held sway in the older seats of learning. As the polytechnics and other colleges have never been inhibited by such considerations, it is in this sector that most training for the professions[21] is undertaken, in fields such as accountancy, company secretaryship, and personnel management.

In the period immediately after 1945, the Government was naturally preoccupied with building primary and secondary schools. Between 1946 and 1952, over 27 times as much money was spent on primary education as on further education. More recently, however, the Government, conscious of the vital connection between technology and economic survival, has been treating further and higher education with increasing urgency. Advanced courses of technology and management within polytechnics and the colleges, new technological awards of degree status, increased Exchequer aid—all these moves, and more, have helped to bring education more into step with industrial and economic demands. Not that such a relationship is entirely a novel affair: the universities, for example, have never been immune to such pressures. During the nineteenth century, the older universities began to disengage from the Church and, emulating the newer ones, they became more closely involved in the secular areas of national life. One of the most important of these areas was industry and commerce. Many of the new civic colleges, subsequently to become fully-fledged universities, had been founded by businessmen to develop science and training for local industry—most notably was this true for Leeds, Birmingham and Sheffield. Even in those cases where industrial motivation was not explicit other universities relied heavily on industrial finance for their very existence. Even Cambridge—which, like Oxford, had relied

[21] For an analysis of the components of a "profession", see Greenwood, E., "Attributes of a Profession", in Mosow, S. and Form, W. H., eds., *Man, Work and Society*, Basic Books, 1962.

largely on the wealth of its landed property—began to feel that it should get into closer touch with industry whose lucrative sources of finance were being poured into the newly chartered civic universities. Thus the universities emerged as major suppliers of new industrial technology with specialized centres developing fortes of expertise in relation to local industry: Leeds pre-eminent in textile design, metallurgy at Sheffield, brewing at Birmingham, electrical physics at London.

In view of these facts, it is slightly ironic that each university is extremely jealous of its independence and of the maintenance of its academic standards. In general they strenuously resist any attempt to make them too narrowly vocational and degrees are seldom related to the requirements of any particular profession (apart from law, medicine and education, plus other more dubious categories such as management including its derivatives). The Robbins Report[22] prophesied a need for 560,000 places in full-time higher education in 1980–81 compared with the 216,000 places available in 1962–63. The statistical work behind this recommendation fills Appendix I of the Report and demolishes the "more means worse" or "pool of ability" arguments. Of the 560,000 places, Robbins proposed that 350,000 should be in the universities, i.e., the existing foundations plus six entirely new establishments (which have been created at York, Colchester, Coventry, Canterbury, Lancaster and Norwich), translations of status among the former colleges of advanced technology (such as Bristol and Bradford), promotions among the technical colleges, Scottish central institutions (the Scottish equivalent of technical colleges) and the teacher training colleges, which were renamed colleges of education. Most of these changes have by now been implemented, with the addition of colleges of higher education created from former technical colleges and the like.

These changes and developments have been accompanied by some alarming fluctuations in the demand for higher education. Whereas during the 1960s the number of people seeking places in higher education was consistently higher than forecast, since 1970 the situation has been reversed and each year fewer young people than anticipated have been opting for higher education. For example, Education Planning Paper No. 2 published in 1970 followed the trends of the 1960s and

[22] *Report* of the Committee on Higher Education, H.M.S.O., 1963.

projected 835,000 full-time students in higher education in England and Wales by 1981. But by 1975 the Secretary of State announced that 640,000 full-time students then appeared a reasonable target for 1981 and current indications are that an even lower figure would not be inconsistent with recent trends in the numbers of qualified school-leavers wishing to enter higher education. An inquiry into the reasons for this fall (which is still likely to produce 1981 numbers in excess of those predicted by Robbins) has found that two factors are principally responsible: the falling growth rate in the proportion of young people staying at school beyond the minimum school-leaving age, and the falling proportion of leavers with G.C.E. A-level passes seeking entry to higher education institutions.[23]

Among 16-year-olds, Williams and Gordon found a group of "hard core" leavers consisting of over a third of the boys and nearly a quarter of the girls who claimed never to have considered staying on beyond the minimum school-leaving age.[24] At the other extreme, a third of the boys and well over 40 per cent of the girls were proposing definitely to continue full-time education either at school or in a further education college. Most members of this group showed few signs of having ever seriously contemplated any other alternative. This left about a third of the boys and a sixth of the girls who could be viewed as susceptible to influences and pressures at or near the time of leaving. Among 18-year-olds, not surprisingly, the proportions were somewhat different because they had already, to a degree, committed themselves by remaining at school for 2 years. About 70 per cent (both boys and girls) proposed to proceed directly to higher education; only 6 per cent proposed to move straight into a job. Also, around 13 per cent of the sample proposed to take a break between school and higher education; of these, 54 per cent claimed they would definitely re-enter education within 5 years. At this age, it seemed that the most potent single factor affecting

[23] Williams, G. and Gordon, A., *Attitudes of Young People to School, Work and Higher Education* (preliminary report), University of Lancaster, 1976.

[24] The fact that over half these boys and a quarter of these girls proposed to do part-time study while working could probably be attributed more to the requirements and the regulations about day release, in their chosen employments, rather than to any strong desire by most of them to undertake further study.

attitudes towards higher education was being fed up with study, but a further significant group saw no economic value in a degree.

There is a very close relationship between staying on beyond the minimum school-leaving age and social background. This occurs within comprehensive schools as well as within the system as a whole, so it cannot be attributed simply to biases in selection at the age of 11. However, it is less marked within any type of school than within the sample as a whole, and it is likely that the differences are the end result of differences that accumulate throughout the period of compulsory education and even earlier. At the age of 18, social class differences are less noticeable among those continuing into higher education, but there are some variations in the types of institution selected by individuals. Middle-class children show a greater propensity to go to Oxbridge, while those with working-class backgrounds are slightly more likely (as we have seen already) to choose the former colleges of advanced technology, polytechnics, and the like. Among all social groups, the evidence indicates that perceptions of earnings and career opportunities (however misguided) do influence the educational decisions of many students. Unfortunately, it is not yet possible to justify any claim that changes in the growth of demand for further and higher education are *caused* by changes in the perceived economic advantages of educational qualifications. On the other hand, there is some tentative support for such a view, namely, that occupational choice is rationally based on relative earnings. Thus the authors of *Social Scientists at Work*[25] conclude: "We have shown that possession of a social science degree entailed average earnings higher than those for graduates as a whole during the 1960s and we have suggested that this may have accounted at least in part for the rapid growth in the number of social science students during that decade." Armed with such assumptions, the study predicts that the proportion of sociologists will fall during the next few years, followed to a certain extent by the number of psychologists; business studies courses will remain popular; the expansion of economics will continue; and the decline in geography is perennial.

[25] Williams, G., Westoby, A. and Webster, D., *Social Scientists at Work*, Society for Research into Higher Education, 1976.

Education and Society

Socialization is a process of cultural transmission whereby people learn the rules, practices and norms of the social groups to which they belong. Formal education is only one of the many agencies[26] through which the socialization process is enacted, but it is particularly crucial in advanced industrial societies because of the amount of time it occupies during the individual's formative years. As education proceeds, and prolongs itself by the development of extensions to the system beyond the minimum leaving age, it produces recruits for the specialized roles required by industrialization. Equally, education communicates informal values which are eventually internalized by the recipient, on aspects of behaviour concerned with occupational advancement, honesty, individual competitiveness and others. These ideals may not always be imparted deliberately—they may be, in Merton's terminology,[27] a *latent* rather than a *manifest* function of the education system —but they are nonetheless real. For example, if the majority of teachers are middle class, their judgement of children's behaviour will tend to be based on middle-class standards, with the result that the majority of children, in order to avoid criticism or worse, will learn to conform with middle-class norms. This process creates no particular difficulties if the socializing agencies to which the child is exposed—school, family, friends—are all transmitting a similar pattern of values and social skills. However, this is not always the case. It is against the background of education as a means of socialization that we must now consider the contribution of the British educational system in facilitating individual achievement, occupational advancement and social mobility.

In entering this discussion, certain assumptions have to be made about the nature of human abilities (principally intelligence, or whatever is measured by I.Q. tests) and the contribution of education in developing these abilities for purposes of personal success (however

[26] Others include the family, religious organizations, work, and so on. It is important to bear in mind that socialization is something that continues throughout life, as we pass through a succession of roles—child, adolescent, husband, father—and have to acquire new patterns of behaviour. Socialization even continues at the point of death. Hospital staff try to socialize their dying patients into dying in a "good" and "proper" manner, as defined by the staff's own expectations. See Sudnow, D., *Passing-On*, Prentice Hall, 1967.

[27] Merton, R. K., *Social Theory and Social Structure*, Free Press, 1957.

defined). Herrnstein's[28] theories about class differences in I.Q. are based on the following propositions: if differences in mental abilities are inherited, and if success requires these abilities, and if earnings and prestige depend on success, then social status will be based to some extent on inherited differences between people. Herrnstein clearly believes that, as society becomes more complex, then I.Q. is becoming more crucial for success but (as we have briefly outlined in Chapter 1) there is violent disagreement on the proportion of I.Q. which is attributable to heredity—and therefore on the extent to which Herrnstein's prediction of social castes, self-recruiting intergenerationally, will be fulfilled. Eysenck, for instance, points out that intelligent parents tend to have children with lower I.Q.s, thus regressing towards the mean.[29] Jencks and his colleagues[30] argue that many researchers into the subject have made the crucial mistake of underestimating the influence of the environment. A person who is genetically well endowed with intelligence will tend to be born to parents who have created an above-average family environment, so that these people have a double benefit (as opposed to those at the other end of the I.Q. scale, who experience a double disadvantage). Having admitted that the data base for making generalizations about heritability is still too weak to justify precise estimates, Jencks nonetheless suggests that genotype explains about 45 per cent of the variance in I.Q. scores, that environment explains about 35 per cent, and that interaction between the two explains the remaining 20 per cent.[31] Although this still leaves heritability as the major factor influencing I.Q., generalizations about heritability in populations are of little use in predicting the degree of heritability of sub-populations and even less in predicting it of individuals in sub-populations. And the figures produced by Jencks leave open the question of whether it is possible significantly to alter I.Q. by manipulation of the environment (e.g., by increasing educational opportunities).

[28] Herrnstein, R., *I.Q. in the Meritocracy*, Allen Lane, 1973.

[29] Eysenck, H. J., *The Inequality of Man*, Temple Smith, 1973.

[30] Jencks, C., *et al.*, *Inequality*, Basic Books/Allen Lane, 1973.

[31] In a footnote, Jencks draws attention to the fact that the relatively homogeneous environment of Britain tends to produce a larger genetic effect than has been observed in the U.S.A.

Not only is there conflict over the respective influences of heredity and environment on I.Q., there is also disagreement on the importance of I.Q. (and educational attainment) for success in life. Eysenck has compared the status of various occupations with the average I.Q. of those in the jobs. He has found an almost perfect agreement between the social prestige of an occupation and the average I.Q. of those in that occupation. The link between I.Q. and earnings is weaker, he admits, but there is no doubt that success in life "defined either in terms of income or social prestige (and thus defined essentially in terms of what the man in the street thinks) correlates quite well with I.Q." Jencks, however, concludes (with evidence drawn principally from the United States) that there is only a slim connection between a person's inherited I.Q. and his success in terms of status or earning capacity. He calculates, for instance, that the fifth of Americans with the highest I.Q.s have incomes at most 40 per cent higher than the fifth with the lowest I.Q. This difference is rather small in the United States where the top-income fifth of the population earns six times as much as the bottom fifth.

At the same time, Jencks finds that the most important influence on a person's ultimate social status is education, even though its precise impact is modified by the operation of luck during each individual's lifetime. After all, the distribution of earnings in an economy is the result of a complicated interaction of variables, many of which can only be measured approximately and some of which no one has yet succeeded in measuring at all. Yet it does appear that this complex of variables does have one desirable feature rarely encountered in the study of social phenomena, namely, that of forming a sequential causal chain: many of the variables are clearly antecedent to others, being causes but not themselves effects. Thus the impact of home background makes itself felt early in an individual's life, causing (but not being caused by) the amount and quality of schooling he or she receives. A variable like neighbourhood environment influences educational achievement both before and during school attendance, but once again the causal effect largely runs in one direction. How much, then, do genes and home environment alone contribute to personal earnings? The evidence suggests that the impact is very limited. Inequality in earnings between identical twins, whether reared together or apart, as well as between brothers reared together, is almost as great as it is between random males in the population.[32] Jencks's final conclusion is that "there is nearly as much income variation among men who come from similar families, have similar credentials, and have similar test scores, as among men in general. This suggests either that competence does not depend primarily on family background, schooling, and test scores, or else that income does not depend on competence". If we know certain characteristics about an individual, according to Jencks, this permits us to predict his income with only a 60 per cent chance of being right. The large remaining element of chance makes it doubtful whether education, by itself, can achieve equality of opportunity. Both Eysenck and Jencks agree that even if examinations and I.Q. tests were abolished, this would not necessarily make it any easier for coloured people or individuals with working-class backgrounds to climb the social ladder.

The presence of a widespread belief—amounting almost to blind faith—in the efficacy of educational opportunity led to increasing pressure for the large-scale provision of secondary education throughout the early years of this century. Of boys born between 1910 and 1929, only 14 per cent of those from state elementary schools were able to proceed to secondary school. Initially, it was assumed that the 1944 Education Act would remove all these inequalities once secondary education—based, admittedly, on a tripartite pattern—became universally available. Nothing could be further from the truth. In practice the tripartite system became a means of solidifying and reinforcing the existing arrangement of social classes in Britain, both because of the occupational implications of the type of education received and also

---

[32] It is, of course, questionable whether I.Q. is measured successfully by any set of allegedly culture-free tests, and it is even more questionable whether nature can genuinely be separated from nurture. It is quite likely that able children are treated differently by their own parents, thus in effect creating a different environment for themselves. Likewise, home background characteristics are typically measured by family income, father's occupation, and so forth; if what matters is the degree of achievement-motivation which parents succeed in instilling in their children and if this element is not itself highly correlated with visible signs of parental social status, it may then be that the influence of home background is being seriously underestimated. At every point in the analysis, therefore, questions arise as to whether the researchers have measured what they really ought to be measuring. Nowhere is this more apparent than in the implicit interpretation of "success", particularly in American research, in financial terms as opposed to other possible criteria.

because of the criteria of selection imposed, both explicitly and implicitly, for admission to each type of school. The subjectivity of the procedures is ironically illustrated by the fact that local education authorities which have used teacher ratings for allocating children to grammar schools at the age of 11 actually admitted *fewer* working-class children than those which used I.Q. based examinations. Even currently and despite the proliferation of comprehensive schools, only five in 1000 children from homes within Class V (the unskilled) stay on at school beyond the age of 16, whereas almost one in four young people from classes I and II remain in full-time higher education beyond 20. The proportion of working-class university students remains at roughly 25 per cent—the same as in the 1930s—and only 15 in every 1000 from semi-skilled or unskilled homes ever attain passes at G.C.E. Advanced level.[33]

The grammar school was the earliest focal point for criticisms about the inegalitarianism of educational opportunity. Dent[34] argued that the grammar school had always concentrated on the acquisition of superior social status. Banks[35] saw the grammar school unequivocally as an agent of social selection, with its status borrowed from the occupations for which its pupils were being prepared. Ever since competitive examinations had become the chief source of entry into the major professions, education had been recognized as a potential passport to the relative security and prestige associated with white-collar occupations. The significance of this becomes even more overwhelming when one recalls the vast expansion of professional and quasi-professional careers, all requiring educational qualifications of some kind, and all reflecting a large range of desirable positions in the middle areas of the job hierarchy. As automation proceeds and mental skills replace manual skills, so the professions become even more highly prized. The grammar schools performed a crucial role as an essential prelude to entry into the coveted careers; this being so, parity of esteem among all types of secondary education was nothing but an idle dream.

[33] Reid, I., *Social Class Differences in Britain*, Open Books, 1977.
[34] Dent, H. C., *The Educational System of England and Wales*, London University Press, 1961; also Dent, H. C., *Secondary Education for All: Origins and Developments in England*, Routledge & Kegan Paul, 1949.
[35] Banks, J. A., *Parity and Prestige*, Routledge & Kegan Paul, 1955.

These comments apply with even greater force if the public schools are considered, for there is little doubt that a public-school education confers a unique advantage on those fortunate enough to have experienced it—though here, following Jencks, it could be argued that the real benefit is not the public-school education as such, but the proximity to parental wealth and status which enables the public-school education to be received. In some respects the best public schools are superior to the majority of those in the State system—as regards staffing ratios, academic qualifications of the teachers, and imaginative extra-curricular activities—but social considerations are clearly uppermost in the minds of parents willing to meet the costs of such education. Recruitment to the old elite occupations, like the Civil Service and the Church, has been very dependent on public-school products and graduates from Oxbridge (who are themselves more likely to be former public-school pupils). Some 90 per cent of the higher Civil Service attended either Oxford or Cambridge. In 1961, out of 78 ambassadors and senior officials in the Foreign Office, 63 were ex-public-school. In 1971, more than one-quarter of the personnel in the Diplomatic Service, the army and navy, and the judiciary had fathers listed in *Who's Who* (itself dominated by public-school products), thus putting them in an elite of 24,000 out of the 55 millions in the United Kingdom. While it has to be conceded that many of this elite reached their position through the possession of intelligence and subsequent educational attainment, it is likely that there are many others, of equal or greater intelligence and attainment, who are not among the elite.

On the other hand, even if it were once true, as Lewis and Stewart[36] claimed in 1968, that the public-school boy had about 10 times as many opportunities to get into management as the general population, and the old Etonian had the most opportunities of all, there is no guarantee that this remains a permanent feature of the business world. The larger managerial bureaucracies and corporations have partially adjusted their recruitment policies to cater for the nation-wide catchment area available since 1944. This fact, combined with the unavoidable hurdles of competitive examinations as modes of entry to many careers, has compelled the public schools to concentrate on intellectual

[36] Lewis, R. and Stewart, E., *The Boss: The Life and Times of the British Businessman*, Phoenix Press, 1958.

training rather than merely rely on their reputations as breeding grounds for a social elite.

A separate problem concerns class representation in the secondary school system itself. Having admitted that grammar schools provided a superior education in every sense of the word, did all social classes have an equal chance of obtaining such an education? The manifest intention of the 1944 Education Act was to throw open entry to the grammar schools to anyone with the requisite ability, regardless of social origin, yet a multitude of studies (to some of which brief reference has already been made) have revealed that the middle class was heavily over-represented and the lower working class—with about 15 per cent of grammar-school places—proportionately under-represented. To express this another way, children from professional and managerial families accounted for 15 per cent of the total population, 25 per cent of the grammar-school population and 44 per cent of the sixth-form population. There appeared to be a steady decline in academic performance from children progressively lower in the social scale (as measured by the occupations of their parents). Even if a working-class child was admitted to grammar school, his performance there was likely to be below average, he would probably leave early and would rarely reach university. Not only are such observations made in the United Kingdom: Husen's work[37] involving such other countries as Denmark, Sweden, Holland, West Germany, the United States and Canada shows that selective systems of education, in which pupils have to pass successive hurdles before going on to the next grade or the more academic school, discriminate against working-class children in the sense that fewer and fewer "stay the course". A slightly moderating factor, however, is that social class does not appear to produce such marked differences between children from different social classes once they have achieved the same grade.

A mass of statistical evidence, collected by the National Survey of Health and Development of Children since 1946, supports the conclusion that the working-class child is relatively disadvantaged in terms of educational opportunity and achievement. Covering a national sample of more than 5000 British schoolchildren born in March 1946,

[37] Husen, T., *Social Background and Educational Career*, O.E.C.D., 1973.

the survey suggests that a third of the primary school pupils who should have gone to grammar school, judged by their ability at the age of 8, did not in fact get there. At successive stages in their development—the ages of 8, 11 and 15—the children were given tests of both mental ability and academic achievement. They were also grouped into four social classes according to their fathers' occupations and the educational and social origins of both their parents. Even at the age of 8 there were wide differences in the average test scores of children from these different classes; but during the next 3 years, at each level of measured ability, the middle-class children improved their performance relative to the rest of the children, and the working-class children fell behind.

Taking their ability at the time of the 11-plus selection examination, a quarter of the children who should have got places were excluded—and virtually all these children came from poorer-than-average family backgrounds. When the 11-plus results of the children who showed slightly above-average ability (I.Q. 105) at the age of 8 were compared, it was revealed that only 12 per cent of the children of lower manual working-class parents subsequently went to grammar schools, compared with 46 per cent of upper middle-class children. The lower manual working-class children, whose intelligence (as measured by I.Q. tests) seemed to fall by an average of several points between 8 and 11 years old, were further penalized by the working of the selection examination itself. For those at the I.Q. margin, especially in areas where there were relatively few places in grammar schools, there was further corroboration of the belief that examiners may be unconsciously prejudiced in favour of a neat and clean appearance as distinct from a good academic record.

The importance of the kind of longitudinal study undertaken in the National Survey[38] lies principally in its revelation that social class is not a simple barrier to opportunity but rather a complex cluster of influences on the development of ability. In general, middle-class parents take a greater interest in their children's education; middle-class children go to better primary schools; their families are smaller and their housing conditions are better. These factors overlap, but the

[38] See Douglas, J. W. B., *The Home and the School*, MacGibbon & Kee, 1964.

National Survey shows that each has an independent influence on the measured ability, even within the same social class.

Parental attitudes and encouragement (or lack of it) are particularly crucial in affecting the educational attainment of children. The National Survey indicated that most children in the lower manual working class already had lower than average ability at the age of 8, and this was observed to decline quite sharply if their parents took little interest. Specifically, Douglas notes that 73 per cent of upper middle-class parents wanted their children to go to grammar school, and 78 per cent wished them to leave school late, compared with corresponding figures of 49 per cent and 13 per cent among lower manual workers. Elizabeth Fraser's 1959 study, *Home Environment and the School*, found a 0.60 correlation between parental encouragement and I.Q., and a 0.66 correlation between parental encouragement and school marks, among a sample of Aberdeen pupils.

Another study, of 88 clever working-class children in a northern town who made their way into the middle class by means of the grammar school, shows the way in which the children and their parents coped with the resulting clash of value-systems,[39] a clash which is equally relevant to the environment of the comprehensive school. The children soon found it desirable to adapt their broad Yorkshire accents into standard English at school, yet if they spoke standard English at home they were regarded with contempt. Some attempted to meet their parents half-way. One got a holiday job on the railways, and remarked: "I enjoyed working with my hands. I felt quite proud and when I came home at night, since I was not half as tired as I thought I would be, I used to say to my parents: 'There you are, you see!' because it's funny: my parents have a queer idea of work. Reading a book is not work; only doing things with your hands." Other children made no attempt to accommodate themselves to the situation at all; one of the respondents said "I thought my parents were terrible, and very badly educated. They were always doing the wrong things." Parents found the relationship equally distressing from their point of view, as this conversation by a working-class father indicates:

[39] Jackson, B. and Marsden, D., *Education and the Working Class*, Routledge & Kegan Paul, 1962.

"Many a time you'd be out and the neighbours would say, 'Eeh, is your lad still
at school? What's he going to be then?'
And I'd have to say, 'I don't know what he's going to be yet.'
And they'd say, 'Doesn't he know yet?' And then I'd come home and I'd sit
opposite our lad in the chair, and I'd say 'What do you think you'll be when you
leave school?' 'I don't know, and I don't know at all, don't bother me,' he'd say
and that was it. When the neighbours bothered me, I hadn't got an answer and I
felt soft. They'd look at you as much as to say, 'Staying on at school all that time
and don't know what he's going to be, well!' "

This precisely illustrates the potential conflict between socializing
agencies to which we referred earlier. In most cases of this kind, the
individual withdraws from the conflict, accepts the socialization process imposed by one set of norms and ignores, or consciously fights, any
alternative norms. In his study of a northern grammar school, for instance, Lacey[40] describes the formation of an "anti-school culture"
composed partially of boys from working-class backgrounds and partially of others who found academic and social achievement difficult
and thus drifted into an alliance with the working-class "deviates".
This process had all the characteristics of a self-fulfilling prophecy.
Teachers reacted against the anti-school culture because it represented
a threat to their social values; the boys came to believe in their role and
to live up to it, thereby confirming the teachers' hostility. Lacey shows
how academic and social criteria of behaviour become confused as the
vicious circle escalates: children who are behaving badly are also
assumed to be stupid and this affects their assessment in written work
and examinations. Willmott[41] found that about a tenth of the boys in
his Dagenham sample had gone much further than a mere anti-school
culture: they had rejected both the working-class standards of the local
community and the middle-class norms of the school; they hated school
itself and did not get on with their parents. These comments, however,
should be taken in context. Rebelliousness is a phase common to most
adolescents, and in Willmott's Dagenham group it may well have been
a perfectly natural escape route from intolerable clashes of authority
with parents and others.

There is some evidence that working-class attitudes to education are
becoming more favourable. As long ago as 1956, Floud, Halsey and

[40] Lacey, C., *Hightown Grammar*, Manchester University Press, 1970.
[41] Willmott, P., *Adolescent Boys of East London*, Routledge & Kegan Paul, 1966.

Martin[42] reported that in both Middlesbrough and south-west Hertfordshire "numerous" working-class parents expressed a willingness to keep their children at grammar school until 16 years of age. One-quarter of the Middlesbrough group even contemplated a leaving age of 18. In a comprehensive survey of two adjoining "commuter villages" north of London, Pahl[43] asked parents the age at which they would like their offspring to leave full-time education. In conformity with the now-familiar pattern, only 15 per cent of the working class mentioned a leaving age of 18 or over compared with 82 per cent of the middle class. On the other hand, only a quarter of the working class mentioned 15 years (that being the minimum school-leaving age at the time the survey was conducted) as the most appropriate age; 27 per cent would have preferred a leaving age of 16 years and 16 per cent of 17 years. Attention has already been drawn in this book, too, to regional variations in the propensity of children to remain at school beyond 16: the most popular areas for this practice are concentrated in the South-east (e.g. Harrow, Richmond, Barnet, Brent, Bromley, Sutton and Kingston) while the localities with the lowest numbers of post-16 schoolchildren are the smaller industrial towns in the North and the north Midlands (e.g. St. Helens, Oldham, Barnsley, Salford, Warrington, and Stoke) together with places like Ipswich and Barking. Perhaps a major influence on these regional variations and differences in working-class attitudes to education is the social mix of the community in general, together with such economic factors as, say, the proximity of rapidly growing industries like electronics or a high level of unemployment. In general, very few parents ever refuse the opportunity of a longer and more academic type of education for their children. Although this may be mainly due to the increasing value placed on education itself (even if it is seen only as a means to an end, namely, a way of enhancing secure employment opportunities), it must also be attributed, in part, to the reduced impact of material factors. Poverty caused ill-health and low attendance at school; study facilities were absent in the slums; families would desperately need the extra income provided by adolescent earnings. Few of these considerations are relevant today.

[42] Floud, J., Halsey, A. H. and Martin, F. M., *Social Class and Educational Opportunity*, Heinemann, 1956.
[43] Pahl, R. E., *The Sociological Review*, Vol. 11, No. 2, 1963.

Another important aspect of class in pre-determining educational success is the extent to which the middle class are aware of the technicalities in the educational system and are prepared to manipulate them to advantage. We have already seen how middle-class mothers prepare their children more constructively for school and how the middle-class home is likely to be a more favourable framework for the transition to an educational environment. For example, middle-class mothers are more inclined, when choosing toys for their children, to stress the value of toys in stimulating the child's curiosity and emotional and cognitive development. This concept conforms closely to the concept of toys and play which the child finds at the infant school. In the survey on the connection between toys, parental attitudes and child development, conducted by Jones and her associates[44] among 360 mothers of 5-year-old children, it was found that the mother's conception of play has a strong correlation with her child's performance score, 1 year later, on the Wechsler intelligence scale for children. But Jones goes further. "Because of their superior status and knowledge, middle-class mothers are better equipped to monitor and participate in school activities." Working-class mothers, on the other hand, were more prone to want a firm boundary between themselves and the school ("the teacher's got his job, and I've got mine"), possibly because they are intimidated by the school system.

Middle-class parents have been more adept, too, at realizing that the critical point in the education of their children is the choice of primary school, for this very often has a powerful influence on the particular school entered at the secondary stage. When most local authorities relied upon the tripartite system, the success of primary schools was often calculated on the proportion of its pupils passing the 11-plus, but even if there is no explicit selection procedure parents still show great concern that their children should go to certain "good" schools rather than others. By middle-class parents in particular, a "good"school—in the comprehensive sector as in any other—is defined as one which sends a high proportion of its pupils to university. Jackson and Marsden[45]

[44] Jones, J., "Social class and the under-fives", *New Society*, 22 December 1966, pp. 935–36.
[45] Jackson, B. and Marsden, D., *op. cit.*

illustrate the inequalities which can arise from this situation. So far as middle-class parents were concerned,

> When they chose a primary school they chose with care. They chose one which not only promised well for a grammar school place, but pointed firmly in the direction of college or university. This turned out to be quite a feasible forecast. . . . Of these ten sons and daughter (of middle-class parents), nine were placed in what our calculations show to be Marburton's leading primary schools for long-term results.

Working-class parents paid very little attention to long-term goals, by contrast:

> Mrs. Black chose in this way for her little girl: "Yes, there *were* two schools in Broadbank but we didn't know much about them. Well, there were some children passing on the road and I said, 'Which school do you go to?' and they told me the Church School. So I told our Doreen, 'Those children go to the Church School. Would you like to go to that school?'"

It would be scarcely surprising that, since these individual experiences are repeated many times among parents within each social class, a kind of ecological effect is created among primary schools—and similarly among comprehensive schools at the secondary stage (bearing in mind that primary schools are 'comprehensive' for children in their particular age-range). The schools which attract middle-class children, with speech and behaviour patterns similar to those of many of the teachers, can easily create a climate conducive to effective learning. Teachers find the environment pleasant and are less likely to leave. In working-class surroundings, on the other hand, difficulties of pupil assimilation and parental support rapidly accumulate; teachers do not find the schools rewarding and leave quickly, thus producing a constant turnover of teaching staff, which is disruptive to continuity and learning effectiveness. As in many other areas of social life, the schools become caught up in a self-fulfilling prophecy, where success breeds success or failure breeds failure. These ecological influences are virtually unavoidable, moreover, since primary schools (rather more than comprehensive schools) serve very localized neighbourhoods which themselves tend to be socially homogeneous—predominantly middle-class, working-class, and so on.

Further support for ecology can be derived from the National Survey of Health and Development of Children.[46] Primary schools with a very good academic record (as measured by 11-plus successes) showed a continued high success rate even among children receiving little parental encouragement. In schools with poor academic records, even children receiving much encouragement from their parents did badly. Since a much larger proportion of middle-class than of working-class children entered primary schools with good academic records, *and* a larger proportion of their parents gave them strong encouragement, school and family reinforced each other positively. The contrary was true for working-class children. This process continued into the secondary stage of education when, if anything, its effects became more pronounced. Working-class children were more likely to find themselves in secondary modern schools, tarred with the brush of failure. According to Elder,[47] such schools were "typically staffed by less qualified personnel" who got less money than their grammar-school counterparts and had less equipment to help them. In contemporary terms, this still applies where secondary modern schools exist, where allegedly comprehensive schools operate alongside selective schools for the higher ability ranges, or even where different comprehensive schools (with their own characters and reputations) serve a similar locality. Whatever type of school is involved if children feel themselves to be failures, then they think little of their abilities and conscientiously perform in accordance with that self-estimate: Douglas showed that secondary modern I.Q. scores actually registered a fall over the years as children progressively dodged any demands made on their mental powers. Naturally the combined effect of poor primary school and inferior secondary school produces, at the very least, significant alienation from society in adult life. Elder quotes a Gallup survey of social and political attitudes, which showed that former grammar-school boys, even those with manual occupations, tended to approve of British society and institutions. Modern-school products, even those with non-manual jobs, were far less confident, far less satisfied with society as it is, and more inclined to claim that they would not bother to vote.

Floud, Halsey and Martin[48] have shown that family size is an im-

[46] Douglas, J. W. B., *op. cit.*
[47] Elder, G. H., *Sociology of Education*, Vol. 38, No. 3, 1965.
[48] Floud, J., Halsey, A. H. and Martin, F. M., *op. cit.*

portant environmental influence on educational chances. There can be no doubt that children from small families, whatever their social origin, tend to do better in intelligence tests and therefore in selection procedures. Working-class families are likely to have more children than those at higher levels in society, and therefore suffer from this further handicap. Several reasons have been suggested for the apparent (relative) backwardness among children in large families. It may be that the child with a large number of siblings learns verbal skills less effectively from his contemporaries, whereas the only child has many more opportunities for conversing with adults. The evidence from Middlesbrough indicated that the disadvantages of a large family were less marked for Catholics, perhaps because intelligent Catholics were less prone to practise family limitation. Thus the general level of intelligence among large Catholic families was higher than that among large non-Catholic families (where birth control was largely a function of intelligence).

We also need to take account of the theoretical and experimental work on language and the learning process which has been led by Professor Bernstein.[49] Bernstein is concerned with language as an implicit mode of socialization. In choosing a form of talk to regulate a child's activity and to tell him about the world, a mother is implicitly conveying an attitude to him, towards school and towards knowledge. Having analysed the speech of both parents and children, Bernstein concludes that there are considerable differences in the vocabulary and syntax of the language typically spoken by members of the middle classes and by members of the lower working classes. In general, the latter type of family is particularistic in its attitude to knowledge, positional in its view of its members and context-bound and restricted in its speech code; and, the argument runs, these characteristics are associated causally with educational failure.

Bernstein argues that the lower working class typically speaks a "public" or "restricted" language: with simple grammar, sentences often unfinished, poor syntactical form and little use of impersonal

---

[49] See Bernstein, B. and Henderson, D., "Social class differences in the relevance of language to socialization", *Sociology*, Vol. 3, No. 1, 1969; Bernstein, B., "A sociolinguistic approach to socialization: with some reference to educability", in Gumperz, J., and Hymes, D., eds., *Directions in Sociolinguistics*, Holt, Rinehart & Winston, 1970; Bernstein, B., ed., *Class, Codes and Control: Volume II*, Routledge & Kegan Paul, 1973.

categories such as "one". The middle classes, on the other hand, use a "formal" or "elaborated" code, characterized by a more complex grammatical and syntactical form, a more extensive vocabulary, and so on. While there are enormous problems in isolating and classifying these differences, they have special significance in the case of the working-class child's encounters with the educational system. As Bernstein comments:[50]

> Many mothers in the middle class (and it is important to add not all), relative to the working (and again it is important to add not all by any means), place greater emphasis on the use of language in socializing the child into the moral order, in disciplining the child, in the communication and recognition of feeling. Here again we can say that the child is oriented towards universalistic meanings which transcend a given context, whereas the second child is oriented towards particularistic meanings which are closely tied to a given context and so do not transcend it. This does not mean that working-class mothers are non-verbal, only that they differ from the middle-class mothers in the *contexts* which evoke universalistic meanings.

The school concentrates, says Bernstein, on

> the transmission and development of universalistic orders of meaning. The school is concerned with making explicit—and elaborating through language—principles and operations as these apply to objects (the science subjects) and persons (the arts subjects). One child, through his socialization, is already sensitive to the symbolic orders of the school, whereas the second child is much less sensitive to the universalistic orders of the school. The second child is oriented towards particularistic orders of meaning which are context-bound, in which principles and operations are implicit.

The working-class child is less able to express his own particular response to situations, because he relies heavily on standardized sayings within his community, such as proverbs; also he is less capable of expressing his feelings in detail because he has a more restricted vocabulary than the middle-class child. Since most schools are dominated by (middle-class) teachers using the "formal" or "elaborated" speech code, the working-class child suffers from the handicap of having to learn these speech patterns in order to qualify for social and academic approval; speech patterns which are taken for granted by both teachers and the middle-class pupils, though neither group is likely to have consciously conceptualized the issue. The dilemma of the working-class child is perhaps rather similar to the problems experienced by, say, a

[50] Bernstein, B., "Education cannot compensate for society", *New Society*, 26 February 1970, pp. 344–7.

Nigerian commencing a course on industrial relations in a United Kingdom context, and finding it necessary to assimilate unspoken cultural frameworks before he can understand or participate in what is going on.

Having concentrated so far on the social class implications of primary and secondary education, and some of the factors impinging on attainment and performance at these stages, perhaps it is now appropriate to discuss how far educational and social policies have succeeded in equalizing "life chances" in Britain so far as university entrance is concerned. In this context, the Nuffield College Social Mobility Project[51] has recently published a major study which examines the chances of going to university both before and after the 1944 Education Act. The analysis concerns the educational achievements and social origins of these men born between 1913 and 1931, and those born between 1932 and 1947. Only 2.6 per cent of the total age group in the earlier years obtained university degrees while in the later years this rose to 6 per cent. Every social class group increased its output of graduates in the intervening years—but the proportions of graduates remained closely linked with social background, and the differences have *increased* rather than diminished. Thus, while in the pre-1944 years 15 per cent of those boys in Class I obtained university degrees, 27 per cent of the post-1944 generation obtained degrees. Similar increases were observed in Class II. The semi-skilled and unskilled categories also increased their graduate prospects, from 0.9 per cent to 2.4 per cent. But while the chances of graduation have risen more proportionately for the sons of unskilled and semi-skilled workers, the absolute percentage increases offer a more realistic picture. An extra 1.5 per cent of working-class children found their way to the universities after the 1944 Act compared with an extra 13 per cent of upper middle-class children.

There is thus no clear trend towards the elimination of class inequality in educational attainment. Class I has fallen from having 5.76 times the average chance of getting a degree to 4.50, but Class V has worsened its previously disadvantaged position, from having just over to just under one-third of the average chance. On the other hand, whereas before the 1944 Act above-average chances were shared by

[51] Halsey, A. H., *Towards Meritocracy? The Case of Britain*, Oxford University Press, 1977.

sons from the top social groups down to and including all white-collar workers (amounting to nearly 30 per cent of the population), superior chances in more recent periods have accrued only to the sons from Classes I and II (rather less than 15 per cent of the population).

Any commentary on the recent incidence of social mobility through educational attainment relies implicitly on comparisons with earlier periods. During the nineteenth century, factors like capital accumulation, market acumen and on-the-job promotion were more important than education in facilitating upward mobility. In the first half of that century, for example, nearly a third of Cambridge students came from families whose fathers were in the Church (32 per cent) and about the same proportion from landowners (31 per cent). Law and medicine each accounted for 8 per cent and other backgrounds were of negligible significance. At Oxford from 1752 to 1886, 90 per cent of students came from a gentry, clergy or military background; high fees and a costly life-style had squeezed out all students from humble social backgrounds. The future occupations of the Oxbridge students were equally narrow, so that, in effect, the universities were largely receiving the sons of clergy and gentry and returning them to the same careers. Their impact on change in the social structure was minimal. But during the latter half of the century, the universities became more attractive to the professional, commercial and industrial middle class; by 1910, the landed and clergy groups had fallen to a mere 23 per cent of the total intake. Final career choices also became more diversified, with a radical fall in entry to the Church being offset by increases in recruitment to administration, business and the professions.

Such changes signified the fact that educational attainment had become a major mediating factor in occupational success. A shift in occupational structure over more recent generations has produced more opportunities at the top and more net upward mobility in British society as a whole. Like all other advanced industrial societies, Britain has been gradually reducing its proportion of unskilled, low-paid jobs while increasing the number of professional, technical and managerial occupations. While it is true that people today tend to be chosen for jobs less in terms of what their fathers did and more on what qualifications they themselves have managed to achieve, nonetheless the family into which a child is born is actually having an increasing effect on the sort of education he receives. Halsey remarks that "Class weights the dice of social opportunity and 'the game' is increasingly played through strategies of child rearing which are umpired by the schools. . . . The direct effect of the class hierarchy of families on educational opportunity has *risen* since the war." Perhaps a major reason for the growing discrepancies between the classes, in Halsey's view, is that schools are less immersing than they used to be. Thus the degree to which individuals are educationally successful is less under the control of schools and school-teachers than once was the case; hence what happens within the family is commensurately more important.

The Halsey evidence is history: the analysis is about people who have already gone through the educational process and does not take account of the impact of comprehensive education which was intended, at least partially, to overcome all the social factors so far discussed. In the early 1950s, Crosland[52] envisaged the future as follows: "All schools will more and more be socially mixed; all will provide routes to the universities and to every type of occupation, from the highest to the lowest. . . . Then, very slowly, Britain may cease to be the most class-ridden country in the world." The kind of facts about inequality of educational and occupational opportunity which actuated the desire for social change among reformers like Crosland have already been discussed in detail within this chapter, but nonetheless it would be helpful to supply further amplification of the arguments. The middle classes have been over-represented in higher education, not only in Great Britain, but also in almost every country in the world, even in the communist nations with their commitment to the advancement of the proletariat. It is generally recognized that the expansion of higher education typically benefits the middle classes, at least in the short term.[53] Of course, it is possible to argue that greater opportunities for young

[52] Crosland, C. A. R., *The Future of Socialism*, Cape, 1956.

[53] In the United States, for example, middle and upper income groups are substantially over-represented in higher education. An 18-year-old from a family earning more than $15,000 a year is almost four times as likely to attend college as an 18-year-old from a family earning less than $3000 a year. It may be argued that fewer young people from low-income homes attend college because they place less value on a college education as a result of their cultural environment. However, even those who do plan to attend college are less successful in achieving this ambition than high-school graduates from more prosperous homes. See Scott, P., *Strategies for Post-Secondary Education*, Croom Helm, 1975.

people from middle-class families to attend universities and colleges. that were once the almost exclusive preserve of a tiny elite does represent social advance of a kind. And reformers often believe—on somewhat intangible grounds—that in the long term the expansion of higher education will extend educational opportunities to all classes in the community.

Yet the elite shows itself remarkably resistant to change. The *Who's Who* study of the social and educational backgrounds of key posts in eight occupational groups (to which brief reference has already been made) suggests that the rate of upward mobility among elite personnel[54] did not increase significantly between 1939 and 1971.[55] Where there was upward mobility, it was more associated with Oxbridge than with other universities, and more with Oxbridge than with the well-known public schools. The public schools account for nearly 40 per cent of the intake at Oxbridge and, of the closed and restricted scholarships and exhibitions 82 per cent at Oxford and 76 per cent at Cambridge are tied to a public school. Among ambassadors, army officers and clearing bank officials, the proportion from Oxford and Cambridge is actually increasing, while in the judiciary Oxbridge graduates have consistently accounted for at least 75 per cent of the group. Only in one of the eight occupational categories, the Church of England hierarchy, was there a slow decrease in Oxbridge graduates, though even here they still make up about 78 per cent of bishops. Boyd suggests that continuity in the elite is exemplified by selection systems for the Civil Service. As many of the selectors are themselves people with an Oxbridge background, they tend (consciously or unconsciously) to select individuals in their own image; if this in turn discourages students from red-brick universities from applying, then the bias in favour of Oxbridge (and hence in favour of elite succession) becomes a self-fulfilling prophecy. A predilection for arts graduates may also have helped Oxbridge; graduates in scientific and technical fields, often from the newer universities, have

[54] To discover the extent of social mobility the subjects' parents were looked up in *Who's Who* or *Who Was Who*. Where fathers were listed, this was taken to indicate elite succession, and where they were not was interpreted as elite mobility. The eight occupational groups were the Civil Service, the judiciary, the Diplomatic Service, the Royal Navy, the Army, the Royal Air Force, the Church of England and the clearing banks.

[55] Boyd, D., *Elites and Their Education*, National Foundation for Educational Research, 1973.

not been selected for administrative posts to any significant extent. One more reason, claims Boyd, is that "Very possibly these graduates (from Oxbridge) were of high quality. Since the war, Oxford and Cambridge have chosen from the finest students in all British schools. Pupils who are sufficiently competent to pass the competitive examination of the Civil Service are thus likely to have attended Oxford or Cambridge." The plausibility of this point, however, is somewhat diminished by revelations about the large numbers of public-school products accepted by Oxbridge, and even the geographical bias in Oxbridge's catchment area, given that one would normally expect the United Kingdom to contain a random distribution of intellectually able pupils. For example, 10 per cent of all sixth formers lived in Yorkshire and Humberside in 1974–75, whereas only 4 per cent of Cambridge's new students came from that region. Nearly 22 per cent of sixth formers lived in the South-east outside London, yet they made up 32 per cent of those accepted by Cambridge.

The study of 1960 graduates by Kelsall and his colleagues[56] began by confirming what was already known. Only a quarter of the men and a fifth of the women came from families with manual working fathers— and even this minority was in important respects not typical of the working-class age group of which it nominally formed part (this will be discussed below). But the study showed that unequal chances persisted well beyond the point of graduation, so that both the job aspirations and eventual careers of the 1960 graduates (whatever their subject, degree class or university) were found to vary according to social origin. This finding casts some doubt on the validity of such descriptions of the role of education as that given, for example, by Floud and Halsey when they described it as "a process of cultural assimilation through the reconstruction of personalities previously conditioned by class or race.".[57]

The Sheffield data indicated that social class operated in at least two

[56] See Kelsall, R. K., Poole, A. and Kuhn, A., *Six Years After*, Department of Sociological Studies, Sheffield University, 1972; also, same authors, *Graduates: The Sociology of an Elite*, Methuen, 1972. The survey was a 6-year follow-up examination comprising every woman and every other man who completed first degrees in most British universities in 1960, in subjects other than medicine, dentistry and veterinary science.

[57] Halsey, A. H., *et al.*, eds., *Economy and Society*, Free Press, 1961.

important ways. On the one hand, family background, peer groups, school and university all helped to shape the level and type of aspirations of particular graduates, effectively "limiting" the horizons of those with less privileged circumstances. On the other hand, potential employers also had a role to play in reinforcing these tendencies, for graduates from manual working-class backgrounds were actually found to be less successful competitors in the higher status employment sectors than their colleagues from non-manual homes. In particular, those few who had thought of a career in the older professions had something of the order of a 10 per cent poorer chance of realizing their ambitions than men from middle-class homes with similar aspirations; and in the administrative and managerial sector their chances were even more slender. The result was the under-representation in education (as a career) of the graduate sons of professional and intermediate non-manual workers; and the very pronounced under-representation in the legal profession, general management or the administrative class of the home Civil Service, for graduates with manual working-class fathers. In essence, therefore, the chances of going to a university, for working-class children, appeared to be little better than they would have been before World War II; and, having graduated, their attitudes and aspirations were likely still to be heavily influenced by social background, imposing severe limitations on career choice. As against this, we should remember that set against the general population these graduates were all in high-status jobs 6 years after graduation; and also that graduates themselves, despite the expansion in higher education since Robbins, are only a tiny minority of the population as a whole. Of the men born in England and Wales between 1930 and 1949, 6.88 per cent reached a university compared with 2.6 per cent of those born before 1930 (those who went to school before the 1944 Education Act).

When the Sheffield researchers examined those relatively few children with fathers in manual occupations who did manage to get degrees, they were found to be by no means typical of the rest of their working-class peers. The usual sociological procedure—of defining social class of origin in terms of the father's occupation—had to be modified by references to other influences on the family's social standing, such as the parents' education, their social backgrounds, and the mother's occupation. In the ordinary way most of these various factors are positively inter-related, so that the average manual worker will have left school at the minimum leaving age or soon after, and will usually marry someone of similar education and occupational level to himself. Occupation is therefore, normally, a reasonably reliable indicator of social standing. But the exceptions become crucial when examining the causes of individual social mobility. First of all, upwardly mobile people tend to come from families with smaller numbers of children than is usual on average in their social class. We have already drawn attention to this factor; Jackson and Marsden[58] comment on it in relation to their 88 upwardly mobile subjects; and Kelsall found that the average family-of-origin sizes of graduates from manual and white-collar backgrounds were exactly the same at 2.24 while in the general population of the same generation there was a marked difference between the two groups. Secondly, most of the manual-worker families from which the graduates came held high status within the working class as a whole: something like four out of five had fathers of skilled manual status.

Other factors were connected with evidence for status dissonance within the kinds of working-class families which produced graduates. The father may have received education incommensurate with his occupational level, or his wife may differ from him in her educational or occupational level. Or a parent may have undergone some downward mobility and still retained contact with the class of origin. About 3 in every 10 parents in the working-class sample, for instance, had received more than an elementary education themselves, having been to grammar schools, technical schools or their equivalents. In about a quarter of the families concerned, one or both parents had had some form of further education after leaving school. Several of the fathers had experienced some downward mobility during their lifetimes: some 26 per cent of the graduates' paternal grandfathers had been in white-collar jobs. These sorts of characteristics were fairly evenly distributed throughout the working-class families in the sample, so that most of them possessed at least one distinguishing "middle-class" characteristic, which may have been crucial in triggering the parental encouragement which (as we have already shown) is often vital to educational attainment.

[58] Jackson, B. and Marsden, D., *op. cit.*

As the Sheffield authors succinctly conclude, "the more an individual already has in common with members of his class of destination the more likely he is actually to succeed in reaching it".[59]

Against influences as disparate (yet often mutually reinforcing) and pervasive as these, it is doubtful whether a comprehensive schooling system can achieve anything more than a slight modification of class divisions. A 1966 study[60] does indicate that, certainly in Sweden, comprehensivization encourages working-class children to opt for academic courses and to stay on longer at school. The survey, of a 10 per cent stratified random sample of all students born in 1948, was undertaken at a time when about half the school districts in Sweden had introduced the 9-year comprehensive school on an experimental basis, so that it was possible to compare results and pupils' aspirations in both the comprehensive and the parallel selective systems. It was found that although choice of an academic course was higher in the upper classes, even when social class was held constant, choice of an academic course was consistently higher in the comprehensive system. Also children from rural backgrounds in particular benefitted from the new arrangements. This research, therefore, provides ammunition for those who believe that comprehensive education can broaden educational opportunity and raise educational aspirations.

A recently-published study of a large comprehensive school at Banbury[61] echoes the same position. This research found little evidence

---

[59] The advent of the Open University does not appear to have done a great deal to change the state of affairs so far as educational opportunities for working-class individuals are concerned. Once housewives are excluded, there is a strong white-collar bias. In every year from 1971 to 1975 inclusive, new students entering the Open University have been such that about 90 per cent consist of (in rough rank order) : educational personnel (mainly teachers); houseworkers; technical personnel; professional and arts; clerical and office staff; administrators and managers; scientists and engineers. However, examination of the social origins of the *parents* of Open University recruits does show that the children of blue-collar workers constitute a much greater proportion of the intake than do the children of blue-collar workers at conventional universities and polytechnics. It is possible (though not yet established), of course, that the families of these individuals display much the same sort of quasi middle-class characteristics as the working-class group in the Sheffield analysis. See McIntosh, N. and Woodley, A., *Paedagogica Europaea*, Vol. 9, No. 2, 1974.

[60] Quoted in Husen, T., *op. cit.*

[61] Newbold, D., *Ability Grouping; The |Banbury Inquiry*, National Foundation for Educational Research, 1977.

to suggest that bright children were held back by being in the same class as the less able; and conversely, low-ability pupils gained positive advantages from learning alongside the clever ones. The report does concede that a child's academic performance at the end of the first 2 years of secondary school is determined chiefly by factors outside school control, but it argues that the main benefit of all-ability classes is the better social integration of the bright and not-so-bright, together with the development, among less able children, of more positive and favourable attitudes towards school in general. It is asserted that there is no reliable criterion for streaming pupils who come straight from primary school—assessments by primary school teachers are inconsistent, and tests of the 11-plus type do no more than deal out rough justice—and at least the consequences of a wrong assumption about a pupil's potential will be less serious if he enters an all-ability class or an all-ability school.

On the other hand, the relationship between comprehensive education and social stratification in Britain has been the subject of a far less hopeful (from the point of view of the advocates of comprehensivization) analysis by Julienne Ford.[62] She based her research on a sample of fourth formers in a medium-sized mixed comprehensive school plus two control groups from a secondary modern school and grammar school respectively, all in the London area. The comprehensive school used a system of academic streaming, somewhat modified by the fact that the children were allocated into mixed-ability houses. Miss Ford found that "social class (measured by the father's occupation) correlates with stream placement in the comprehensive school as in any other sort of school." In other words, the streams were, like those studied by other researchers, startlingly homogeneous in terms of social class background—and perhaps it is hardly surprising therefore that their aspirations were equally homogeneous. In response to questions about job preferences, over half the working-class A stream in the comprehensive school indicated that they were aspiring to middle-class jobs, compared with one in ten in the C and D streams. The house system did little to effect this homogeneity. The comprehensive children were as prone as those from the other schools to choose their friends from their own academic streams, regardless of

---

[62] Ford, J., *Social Class and the Comprehensive School*, Routledge & Kegan Paul, 1968.

house "loyalty". As one middle-class girl in a C stream said, having indicated that her only friend was the other middle-class girl in the same form, "I think friends should be people who think like you. You can trust them then."

Miss Ford even suggests that in some respects the comprehensive school may increase rather than reduce class consciousness. If a working-class child is successful in the 11-plus, he may well be able to avoid any obstacles created by his lack of acceptance among middle-class children, so long as he goes to grammar school. But if he merely enters the "grammar" stream of the comprehensive school, then he is not so emancipated from the influence of class background in determining his social relations. These working-class "successes" neither accept their middle-class form mates as equally suitable as friends, nor are they accepted by them. It is at least plausible that the tripartite system, seen in this light, promotes more genuine social mobility (from the working class to the middle class) than the comprehensive system is able to achieve. Miss Ford's work must certainly call into question the belief that sending children of different abilities and backgrounds to the same school will *in itself* break down barriers of class in interpersonal relationships—and that belief must be undermined almost totally if one considers the powerful impact of pre-school and extra-school factors such as those outlined in this chapter.

CHAPTER 5

Leisure and Pleasure

Leisure and pleasure must not be confused.
> (Appleton, I., ed., *Leisure Research and Policy*, Scottish Academic Press, 1975)

> *He is to be observed leaving the Saturday afternoon football match, clutching a transistor to his ear, stopping on his way home in a pub where he will drink, play bar billiards and talk about the Australian cricket tour while watching out of the corner of his eye, "The Generation Game" on the pub TV. He hurries home for "Desert Island Discs" which he listens to while exercising with his chest expander. Off to a movie and home in time for "Match of the Day", during the dull parts of which he does a crossword puzzle, sorts out his Sunday morning fishing tackle or looks through brochures for his next holiday. The lesiure freak is the twentieth-century equivalent of the Renaissance man.*

> (Stan Cohen)

Introduction: What Leisure is About

The modern dictionary definition of leisure as "freedom from business, occupation or hurry; unoccupied time or time at one's own disposal" seems in some ways less apt than the Middle English meaning of "opportunity afforded by unoccupied time". More and more people (though not all) see time off as a chance to do something resourceful, active and creative, perhaps reflecting a modern version of the eighteenth-century notion that leisure consisted of scholarly and artistic accomplishments, good manners, and the cultivation of an appropriate style of life. In contemporary sociological terms, Dumazedier[1] has defined leisure as "a number of occupations in which an individual may indulge of his own free will either to rest, amuse himself, add to his knowledge and improve his skills disinterestedly and to increase his voluntary participation in the life of the community after discharging

---

[1] Dumazedier, J., *Sociology of Leisure*, Elsevier, 1975.

193

his professional, family and social duties". The defining characteristics of leisure, then, include its freedom from obligations, its disinterested character (serving no immediate lucrative, utilitarian or ideological end), its hedonistic nature and its personal rather than societal function by allowing an escape from routine and recovery from work.

It may seem strange to regard leisure as a "problem", but undoubtedly it does raise questions of an empirical, moral and ideological kind. Has there, in fact, been a reduction in working time and if so how will non-working time be divided between the idle time of traditional societies and modern free time? Should there be a lengthening of compulsory schooling and/or an earlier age for retirement? Is leisure a necessary part of happiness, despite the survival of earlier moral imperatives concerning work, the family, politics and religion? In Western societies, such dilemmas have come to the fore as a by-product of post-1945 affluence combined with a general move towards shorter working hours. In Britain it is estimated that by the year 2000 there will be 72 million people working 30- to 35-hour weeks, driving 31 million cars and taking 60 million holidays a year. Between 1970 and 1975 the average number of hours worked each week fell, with male manual employees working a full 2 hours less even after overtime—thus leaving a proportionately greater number of hours available for leisure. More than three-quarters of the population are now entitled to at least 3 weeks' paid holiday a year. In 1975 the total of holidays taken amounted to roughly 50 million, though a survey in 1974 found that of those with weekly household incomes of less than £15 per week, only half had a holiday in the previous year, and nearly one in five had not had a holiday for more than 10 years. But already there is concern about too many people in too little space with too much time, coupled with a fear that this increasing amount of time should be spent "improperly", no doubt recalling the old adage that "Satan finds work for idle hands to do." There is, of course, a danger that for moralists the "proper" use of leisure merely reflects their own views on the matter. On the other hand, there is more than a grain of truth in the idea that in the rush to reduce working hours (though this has been partially offset by increased overtime), those most directly involved have tended to assume that leisure will look after itself. It does seem ironic that trade unions should have struggled for generations to gain shorter hours and more adequate pay packets, yet made little or no effort to encourage their members to utilize their leisure periods to best advantage.

The case for leisure cannot be argued without reference to work. Leisure presupposes work, and these areas affect each other in complex ways. With the erosion of some traditional work values, for example, people may seek the properties of leisure in work itself: as C. Wright Mills wrote, "today work tends to be assessed by the criteria of leisure". But in general the dichotomy between work and leisure, still widely accepted today, is a product of the Industrial Revolution and, more specifically, the emergence of the factory system. Prior to 1750 it was very difficult, if not impossible, for an employer to secure a regular, disciplined labour force. The Protestant ethic made industrialization possible by advocating hard work and abstinence; yet the natural corollary of this belief was an attitude of hostility towards the leisure pursuits of the working classes. The playgrounds of the poor were reduced by the inexorable growth of the towns, and the constant superiority of hard economic pressures produced urban congestion of the most demoralizing kind.[2] Sunday leisure for the manual worker was limited to the pubs, which only opened for a few hours.

In view of the exorbitant hours worked during the initial boom of industrialization, it is surprising that the working classes had any time for leisure at all. As Plumb[3] notes:

> The poorest working men today would have found the lives of their ancestors almost unbearable. The hours of work were 14, 15, or even 16 a day, 6 days a week throughout the year except for Christmas Day and Good Friday. This was the ideal time-table of the industrialists. It was rarely achieved, for the human animal broke down under the burden; and he squandered his time in palliatives—drink, lechery, blood-sports.

For many people, the long hours of labour, in wretched conditions that have been fully documented elsewhere,[4] produced such desperate

---

[2] "After 1815 there was an actual worsening of conditions in the rapidly developing factory towns, where houses were being run up wholesale by contractors intent chiefly on cheapness, and the older residential areas were being rapidly converted into slums as the well-to-do citizens moved further out." From Cole, G. D. H., and Postgate, R., *The Common People 1746–1946*, Methuen, 1946.

[3] Plumb, J. H., *England in the Eighteenth Century*, Penguin Books, 1950.

[4] For the situation among rural labourers, see George, D., *England in Transition*, Penguin Books, 1953; for the conditions of industrialization, see Pinchbeck, I., *Women Workers and the Industrial Revolution, 1750–1850*, Routledge & Kegan Paul, 1930; also Thompson, D., *England in the Nineteenth Century*, Penguin Books, 1950.

fatigue that time spent at home was chiefly time spent in recuperation. Many girls and women, for example, claimed that Sunday (their one day of rest) had to be spent in bed.

The entrepreneurs of the Industrial Revolution could be praised for their application and perseverance, their energy, thrift and courage—virtues which are generally regarded as the very epitome of Victorianism. But the other side of the picture is far less attractive, both morally and aesthetically. It is interesting, for example, to consider the energy and perseverance shown by these same entrepreneurs in whittling away the number of holiday days on which the Bank of England was closed. These were reduced from 47 in 1761 to about 6, thereby cutting off a further source of leisure time for all sections of the community—leisure time which, to the industrialists, was so much unproductive waste. It was characteristic of the period that even when Jedediah Strutt entertained "the female hands" to "a sumptuous *dejeuner*" to celebrate the passing of the 1832 Reform Act, they had to work off the extra holiday at the rate of an extra hour a day for 2 weeks.[5] Despite the fact that Britain pioneered the introduction of official Bank Holidays—they were hailed as "oases of rest and quiet for the ordinary man" when Sir John Lubbock's Act of 1871 was passed—almost every country in the world now has a larger number than Britain.[6]

The secular holiday is traceable partly to earlier religious festivals and pilgrimages, but derives mainly from men's interest in their physical health. The sixteenth century saw a revived trust in the virtues of mineral springs, formerly appreciated by the Romans. Certain inland waters like Bath and Buxton began to attract health seekers in Tudor days and by the end of the seventeenth century over 100 such springs had been "discovered". However, the heyday of the watering place or spa—principally centres like Bath, Cheltenham, Tunbridge Wells and Scarborough—was the eighteenth century and the early nineteenth century, though the inland resorts soon found themselves challenged by

[5] Quoted in Fitton, R. S. and Wadsworth, A. P., *The Strutts and the Arkwrights, 1785–1830*, Manchester University Press, 1959.

[6] England and Wales now has 7 Bank Holidays; every other nation in the Commonwealth and every country in Europe surpasses this figure. France and Germany have 10 full national holidays; Belgium and Sweden have 11; Italy and Spain have 13. Apart from Kenya (with 8), no country in the Commonwealth has fewer than 9 Bank Holidays (or their equivalents).

the craze for sea water as a "cure". Various contributory factors accelerated the spread of the holiday as a social institution. For example, just as the Industrial Revolution brought with it an increasing degree of geographical and occupational movement, so this was in turn possible by the development of mechanized modes of transport and communication during the nineteenth century. The railways, which made cheap (and tolerable) travel a reality for the poorer classes after 1830, were especially important in this connection. As early as 1851 the Census showed that 15 selected "watering places" (4 inland and 11 seaside) had grown at a faster rate in the previous half-century than any other class of town.

Higher standards of living among all sections of the community have facilitated the growth of industries catering for private transport in this century: the bicycle, the motor-cycle, the car. The increasing availability of these modes of conveyance not only created new forms of leisure in themselves (cycle touring, car outings, even car cleaning and maintenance), but also largely promoted the growth of the suburbs, since people could now live at greater distances from their work. The suburbs offer far wider scope for the more satisfactory use of leisure time than did the crowded collection of narrow slums built in the shadow of the factories. If nothing else, the density of houses per acre in the suburbs is generally sufficient to allow a garden area for each property.

Starting with the wealthy and fashionable classes, the habit of taking an extended holiday away from home spread to the middle classes. It took longer to spread further. But the railways did bring short excursions and day trips within the reach of manual workers and their families. Periodic factory legislation achieved a steady reduction in working hours; the Bank Holiday Acts specified three free Mondays after traditional religious festivals and an entirely new Monday holiday in August. Walvin, for example, shows that football, subsequent to the founding of the Football Association in 1863, was reabsorbed by the new working class which, for the first time, had the opportunity, money and inclination for organized leisure—though Walvin rightly stresses how this differed from earlier leisure: it was as timetabled, disciplined and regulated as the industrial society which had created it.[7]

[7] Walvin, J., *The People's Game: The Social History of British Football*, Allen Lane, 1975.

During the nineteenth century, too, there was a growing movement in favour of holidays with pay, justified on the grounds that if people were expected to work regular hours, they should have regular times set aside for holidays. It was also argued that holidays act as a restorative force and even indirectly result in increased productivity. Nonetheless in 1925 it was estimated that only 1½ million workers had paid holidays, and it was not until the 1938 Holidays With Pay Act that a framework was created for a big expansion in collective and voluntary agreements for paid holidays. By 1939 over 11 million workers received holidays with pay, and after 1945 paid holidays applied to virtually the whole employed population. Currently a significant number takes more than one holiday per year, a phenomenon almost unknown in the years before World War II, though holidaymakers are noticeably more likely to cater for themselves and go camping and caravanning. Moreover, as one might reasonably expect, the incidence of holiday-making is not constant through all social classes. In his impressionistic account of the 1950s, Hoggart[8] said of the working-class man:

> Nor does he travel a great deal, in spite of the great changes in transport during the last 50 years. There are "chara" trips, football excursions and perhaps an annual holiday, and occasional train trips to the funeral or wedding of some member of a branch of the family. . . . Before he married, he may possibly have gone to the Continent, or seen some distant parts of England by push-bike; he probably travelled a great deal during war-service or National Service. But after marriage, and if we leave aside the occasions just mentioned, the speed and extent of his travel are not much different from what they would have been 30 years ago.

To some extent this picture is endorsed in a comprehensive survey of Derby by Cauter and Downham.[9] Among those interviewed, one in four of the middle classes had made a journey out of Derby in 1952, compared with only 10 per cent of the working class (1-day or 2-day trips were excluded). Today such studies are principally of historical value in highlighting the dramatic contrasts of a changing society. Previously sharp class differentials, in holiday experiences, have been eroded by the affluence of the manual worker, the relative fall in the price of holidays abroad, the development of "package" arrangements, and the changing

[8] Hoggart, R., *The Uses of Literacy*, Chatto & Windus, 1957.
[9] Cauter, T. and Downham, J. S., *The Communication of Ideas, a Study of Contemporary Influences on Urban Life*, Chatto & Windus, 1954.

occupational framework, which in turn has meant that the vast majority of employees enjoy a working week of limited dimensions (including a 5-day pattern without the need for Saturday working) and paid holidays amounting to at least 3 weeks a year.

Sociologists have long been aware that leisure interests are inseparably interwoven with other significant aspects of life, such as social prestige, age and occupation. It is important to remember, too, that to meet the need for leisure pursuits in a prosperous market economy, leisure has been commercialized. There are now powerful specialists in fulfilling the mass demand for spare-time activities, and these large-scale enterprises—inspired not so much by philanthropy as by the profit motive—are often important media of communication for certain ideas and beliefs. For example, there is a decided tendency to place a higher value on "active" as opposed to "passive" pursuits, yet this distinction is more subtle than it at first appears. It may well be nothing more than a by-product of middle-class social commentators, who look down on working-class leisure habits primarily for status reasons. If middle-class leisure is more active, it may be a natural consequence of the fact that middle-class people are frequently engaged in sedentary occupations and therefore need the exercise. The fact that the middle class indulges in sporting activities (as distinct from spectatorship) more often than the working class need not reflect any fundamental difference in outlook but merely normal physical limitations. Perhaps it is worth noting, though, that the British in general spend more than any of their European neighbours, except perhaps the Danes, on recreation and entertainment. Much of this is of the "passive" sort, including meals out and drinking, total expenditure on which has climbed continuously within the last decade.

The Five Ages of Leisure

Patterns of leisure on contemporary Britain are heavily influenced by the teenager, enjoying the first of what Dr. Mark Abrams calls the five ages of leisure.[10] During this period, a high proportion of non-working time is spent outside the home and in the company of the teenagers'

[10] Abrams, M., "The five ages of leisure", *Observer*, 19 November 1960.

own age groups—at cinemas, dance-halls, evening classes, clubs, cafes, attending mass spectator sports, taking part in team games, walking and cycling. In recent years, the period between the minimum school-leaving age and the attainment of adulthood has attracted the attention not only of those authorities concerned with the welfare of the adolescent, but also of the economic interests in society. This financial emancipation of the inarticulate—the C and D streams suddenly faced with the problem of spending relatively large sums of money each week has naturally been fed by commercial enterprises which know that a sizeable proportion of the national income goes into the pockets of young earners. As a result, teenagers have been transformed into a highly self-conscious stratum in society, with a socially marginal and distinctively non-adult "youth culture" whose artificial insulation from adult roles was previously confined to schools and universities. Dr. Abrams comments:

> By and large one can generalize by saying that the quite large amount of money at the disposal of Britain's average teenager is spent mainly on dress and on goods which form the nexus of teenage gregariousness outside the home. In other words, this is distinctive teenage spending for distinctive teenage ends in a distinctive teenage world.[11]

How do teenagers occupy their non-working hours? One major contribution to knowledge in this sphere is a birth cohort study of 14,000 boys and girls who were 16 years old in 1974.[12] The notion of teenagers slumped in front of the television in their leisure hours is given some support from the figure of 65 per cent who gave T.V.-watching as one of their main spare-time activities. Added to this, 24 per cent said they never, or hardly ever, read books other than those connected with their school or homework. However, 38 per cent played outdoor games or took part in sports on a regular basis; 19 per cent went often to parties in friends' homes and 39 per cent regularly went to dance halls or discos. Thirty per cent were involved at some time in voluntary work to help others; a further 16 per cent said they would like to spend some time in this way but lacked the opportunity. Most of the sample went out only about once or twice a week, but 15 per cent went out five times or more.

[11] Abrams, M., *Teenage Consumer Spending in 1959* (Part II), London Press Exchange Ltd., 1961.
[12] Fogelman, K., ed., *Britain's Sixteen-Year-Olds*, National Children's Bureau, 1976.

Half of the sample did spare-time work in term time, thereby making the point that affluent youth is not confined to those in full-time employment after leaving school altogether. One in 10 worked more than 15 hours a week (earning £6 or more), but most worked for between 3 and 9 hours to earn something between £1 and £3. Half did baby-sitting at home, while almost two-thirds did baby-sitting for other families. Average pocket money, not surprisingly, involved rather smaller amounts. A quarter of the teenagers received between £1 and £1.50 a week from their parents, the most common figure among the sample, but 21 per cent, the next biggest proportion, were given between 50 and 75 pence. Only 6 per cent received £3 or more, but just under half the teenagers were expected to pay for clothing, travel or meals from their pocket money.

Examination of teenage expenditure patterns shows that about a third of the average youth's expenditure goes on drinks, cigarettes and entertainment admissions, while nearly 40 per cent of the average girl's spending concerns clothes, shoes and cosmetics. These consumption preferences, however, are primarily located in the mostly working-class majority of young people who are not receiving full-time education at school or college, or who are not in the armed forces. Not only have the real wages of young people risen enormously since 1945, but also, because parents too are more prosperous, children typically retain a much higher proportion of their earnings to spend on themselves. It is not surprising that whole industries cater exclusively for this clientele: records and record-playing equipment, soft drinks, magazines, distinctive clothes, motor-cycles, and cosmetics.

The emphasis on the working class is not misplaced, for "The aesthetic of the teenage market is essentially a working-class aesthetic", in the phrase used by Dr. Abrams. Just as middle-class and working-class adolescents could once be differentiated by the comparative poverty of the latter, so today it is the middle-class youth who is poor and his working-class counterpart who is characterized by (relative) affluence and his own peculiar spending habits. Yet curiously teenagers are less powerful as an economic force than one might expect. Their tastes change very rapidly; each year a proportion of their number defects through marriage or increasing age. As a result, the commercial interests geared to the demands of the teenage market must find new ways to attract the support of the new teenagers constantly emerging from the chrysalis, and this means a constant search for new fashions, new gimmicks, new sensations, most of which derive from the United States where the teenage market is so much bigger. Nevertheless, some factors remain constant. The pop-music market, for example, has become an established ritual of so-called "stars" coming and going at regular intervals, accompanied by a similar sequence of musical styles. The fact that most of these pop singers and group instrumentalists are male reflects nothing more than the overwhelming dominance of the young male in the 15 to 20 age group. He is numerically stronger than girls, he earns more, and disposes of about two-thirds of the total teenage spending money.

One of the implications of the so-called "youth culture" is that it contributes to the alleged disunity of the modern family. This point of view is hotly contested by Fletcher[13] who remarks that, when thinking of the period before industrialization, "The picture of the large, contented family practising its manifold recreations in the cosy firelit homestead is itself something of a caricature." Nowadays, the range of activities for leisure hours has not only increased, but so has the actual opportunity for participating in leisure, particularly for young people. Assuming that the teenage consumer market is calculated to appeal to teenagers and to nobody else, then it follows quite naturally that their parents will be, if not actively hostile, then passively bewildered. Brew[14] may have been right when he wrote that "Young people have never been under more heavy fire; their manners, their spending habits, their love of modern dancing and modern music, have all been the subject of abuse." On the other hand, there is little support in *Britain's Sixteen-Year-Olds* for the idea that there has been a serious breakdown in family life. "The concept of the 'generation gap'" says the report, "is part of popular mythology. However there is little evidence in our findings for its widespread existence. The great majority of both parents and children reported harmonious family relationships." Eighty-six per cent claimed they got on well with their mothers, and 80 per cent with their fathers. Even though the teenagers admitted that they quarrelled fairly frequently with brothers and sisters, many said this "did not mean there

---

[13] Fletcher, R., *The Family and Marriage*, Penguin Books, 1962.
[14] Brew, J. M., *Youth and Youth Groups*, Faber & Faber, 1957.

was anything wrong with the underlying relationship". Dress and hairstyle were the main causes of friction between parents and children but they led to frequent disputes for only 11 per cent; disagreements over these issues occurred "sometimes" for 35 per cent. Trouble over times of getting home at night or going to bed created disagreements "often" for 8 per cent and "sometimes" for 26 per cent. Doing homework and choice of friends of the same sex led to rather fewer disputes.

Where disputes between parents and teenage offspring do occur, it is likely that the conflict is a reaction to the fact that, for teenagers, approval by a peer group is emphatically more valuable than approval by adults. Even if this were not true, expressions of hostility from adults could scarcely be considered, given current values about the acceptance of parental authority, an effective way of restoring behaviour to a more conforming pattern. Indeed, there is some evidence that adult society has built up an adolescent stereotype whose internal coherence has to be maintained at all costs. According to Tanner,

> A picture is painted . . . of the suddenly accelerated youth, staggering under the impact of his newly acquired hormones, urged forward by glimpses of personal independence but hesitant and uncertain in the ways of social life; embarrassed, erratic and unhappy, and turning now and again for relief to the solidarity of a gang and the anodyne of aggressive behaviour. Undoubtedly this picture has some degree of truth, but only in certain circumstances and with certain qualifications. It is the picture of the adolescent seen largely through the eyes of stabilized middle age.[15]

That 16 is in some ways still a "difficult" age, even for the modern teenager, is borne out by parents' observation of the youngsters' behaviour in the home, as reported in *Britain's Sixteen-Year-Olds*. Parents were presented with a list of characteristics—restlessness, fidgeting, fighting with others, bullying, disobedience, and so on, and were asked to say to what extent these types of behaviour were visible in their children. Most frequently noted was a tendency to be solitary. Next came irritability—being "quick to fly off the handle"—and then being "fussy or over-particular". On the other hand very few found their youngsters destructive, aggressive to others or frequently disobedient. The category "Often destroys or damages own or other property" was considered inapplicable in 97 per cent of all cases—though such responses may have

[15] Tanner, J. M., *Growth at Adolescence*, Blackwell, 1962.

to be qualified by reference to an understandable level of parental loyalty. If this was the case, incidentally, then it points still more decisively to the continuance of family relationships.

If there is a leisure problem among adolescents, it is associated principally with the "identification period of working-class non-academic youth", according to Miller.[16] This period, normally lasting from 14 to 17 years of age, is when "the healthy individual should develop a firm feeling of self" and establish relevant reference groups towards which his behaviour will be adjusted. The child who remains at school until 17 or 18 will have few difficulties in completing the "identification period" satisfactorily, at least when compared with the non-academic child who leaves school at 16. The academic child has little genuine leisure time and experiences no problems in allocating it satisfactorily; the fact that he remains at school beyond 16 generally means that he has adjusted well to the school environment. The non-academic child has an absurd excess of leisure time, so much so that it may be interpreted as "a devaluation of their productivity and an assessment that society considers them worthless". Very likely it was this group which figured prominently in the 30 per cent, from the 16-year-old sample, which claimed that they did not like attending school, to say nothing of the 11 per cent who considered that school was largely a waste of time. Teachers (who were consulted in the survey) estimated that 8 per cent were regular truants, but 52 per cent of the teenagers said they had stayed away at some time or other; of these, 20 per cent said they had stayed away simply because they were "fed up with school". Miller argues that society has been insensitive to the real needs of the children at the lower end of the intellectual continuum, and has merely handed them a combination of dangerous toys: "drugs, scooters and motorcycles, with empty acres of time in which to play with them". Faced with a steady devaluation of their egos (which, in the recent economic climate, may be compounded by the experience of prolonged unemployment immediately on leaving school), it would hardly be surprising if such young people felt discontent and boredom. Such emotions may be translated into riotously aggressive or subtly self-destructive behaviour, which in turn provokes a vicious circle of adult

[16] Miller, D., "Leisure and the adolescent", *New Society*, 9 June 1966, pp. 8–10.

TABLE 5.1. Leisure Activities of 16-year-olds Expressed as a Percentage

	Often	Sometimes	Never or hardly ever	Like to but no chance
Reading books (apart from school work or homework	27	46	24	3
Playing outdoor games and sports	38	35	24	3
Swimming	21	44	27	8
Playing indoor games and sports	25	32	32	10
Watching television	65	29	5	1
Going to parties in friends' homes	19	48	26	7
Dancing at dance halls, discos etc.	39	31	24	5
Voluntary work to help others	7	30	46	16

resentment expressed in a confused tangle of punitive sanctions and rehabilitation.

From the moment they marry, set up a home and have children, most young working-class couples have to become accustomed to entirely new spending habits, a transition for which they have usually not been well prepared. Indeed, they have to make the change twice over: once when they get married, even though the wife (as is typical for the middle classes, too) still continues at work; and again when the wife has to give up her employment in order to have a child. This latter change is generally the more drastic of the two, since the couple may have acclimatized themselves to a standard of living based on their joint income. Not only does the income of one of the partners disappear, but also there is another mouth to feed. For all social classes this is the second main stage of life, extending from the wedding to the period when the children are entering their teens. Today nearly 70 per cent of young women and 55 per cent of young men are married before the age of 25. Family building is, in turn, concentrated into a comparatively short period. Only 10 per cent of all babies are born to women aged 35 or more. In these circumstances young married people must perforce spend their leisure time largely at home. Their recreational activities tend to consist of watching T.V., reading, gardening, do-it-yourself, listening to the radio, knitting and sewing.

Over 90 per cent of these young households have a T.V. set which, for an increasing minority, provides pictures in colour rather than black-and-white. Overall weekly hours of viewing increased from 18.6 in 1971 to 19.9 in 1975, and the attraction of the medium seems to be evenly spread throughout the social structure, though Reid[17] argues that professional and managerial families (in all age categories) watch television for less than 12 hours a week compared with an average of $14\frac{1}{2}$ hours for the majority of the population. Certainly class differences in the ownership of T.V. sets have been largely ironed out, although this was not true in, say, 1954, when there was a strong correlation between set ownership and weekly income. This was presumably due to the higher price of T.V. sets at that time, relatively speaking, coupled with the status-conferring prestige to be gained from the presence of a set in the home.[18] There was once a close relationship, still vaguely discernable, between T.V. set ownership and educational attainment, which is also worth noting. In this case the relationship was curvilinear: that is, those with elementary education and those with further or higher education had a low proportion of sets, compared with a high proportion for those with secondary education. Today the T.V. set is regarded typically as a normal item of furniture in the vast majority of households, and the availability of rental arrangements has largely removed any economic restrictions on the habit.

What changes has television brought, if any, to the lives of the British people? Certainly it has altered the domestic habits of countless families. On the one hand it now matches the weather as a staple topic of conversation, both inside the family circle and outside, while on the other it does encourage the family to remain at home during their leisure time. This view again contradicts the pessimism of those who postulate the continuing dissolution of the family under present-day circumstances (though the pessimists then shift their ground to attack the debilitating effects of television itself). Almost any publican will

[17] Reid, I., *Social Class Differences in Britain*, Open Books, 1977.

[18] 1954 was a year after Queen Elizabeth's coronation. The typical pattern for watching this event was not in individual households, but rather in larger gatherings around the TV sets owned by privileged relatives or friends.

testify to the increasing tendency of his customers to take their bottles home rather than spend their evenings in the pub.[19] As Abrams[20] notes, "Once, the working-class husband sought to escape from the crowded shabbiness of his home to the warmth and conviviality of 'pubs' or the club rooms of voluntary associations. . . . But now, as far as shabbiness and smartness are concerned, the boot is on the other foot; so the new man stays at home."

Yet the very universality of television renders it susceptible to critical onslaught, from those who categorize it as "moving wallpaper" to those who see some causal relationship between violence on television and increasing levels of physical aggression in society. In fact the evidence is nothing if not ambiguous on this point, though it must be conceded that the defenders of television espouse a strange paradox when they argue that violence in T.V. programmes does not induce violent behaviour in certain sections of the audience, while advertisements on T.V. do induce behavioural changes of an appropriate kind. Himmelweit and her colleagues[21] showed that television does negligible harm to children, while Noble[22] argues that television, through its power to expose the young child to the wider society, is a positive agent of socialization. When children were born into small, stable village communities, where roles and relationships were clearly defined, each child was exposed to the entire range of roles which he or she would be called upon to fulfil in later life. Noble believes that it is mainly through interaction with stable figures in his environment that the child acquires the skills essential to effective social functioning; this was made easy in small, localized communities by the child's contact with his extended kin. With the Industrial Revolution, the village community became less stable, more mobile and more complex, and as a result socialization itself became a more complicated process. Whereas in the village all

[19] Perhaps this is connected with the increasing consumption of alcohol in Britain. Between 1966 and 1976, the amount spent on alcohol (at constant prices) rose from 6.6 to 9.0 per cent of total incomes, although some of this increase may be a result of the fall in the *relative* price of alcohol compared with the upward movement in prices for other goods.

[20] Abrams, M., "The home-centred society", *The Listener*, 26 November, 1959.

[21] Himmelweit, H., Oppenheim, A. and Vince, P., *Television and the Child*, Oxford University Press, 1958.

[22] Noble, G., *Children in Front of the Small Screen*, Constable, 1975.

members of the community contributed to this process and the whole of society was visible to the developing child, now the burden of socialization rests upon the nuclear family and only a few of the social roles which the child will later be required to fill are clearly visible within such a restricted context. According to Noble, watching television can compensate for lack of direct social experience because the child is not simply a passive viewer but rather "interacts" with familiar T.V. personalities. This "para-social" experience derived from television can transfer to a real-life context and help the child to deal with otherwise unfamiliar situations. While this hypothesis is interesting it must remain so far unproved, and in any event it could still be used as a basis for the contention that individuals "learn" violence (or other socially destructive behaviour) from television, as opposed to the suggestion that watching violence on T.V. serves a cathartic function.

With more and more families assuming the responsibilities of house ownership, the home is likely to take up a major proportion of the husband's (and the wife's) leisure time. True, unskilled manual workers rely heavily on rented accommodation: fewer than one in four have mortgages and more than half live in council homes. But the extent of home ownership increases rapidly further up the social scale. Willmott and Young noted that in Woodford, two-thirds of the inhabitants lived in privately-owned houses.

> For the men, their houses provide almost endless opportunities for work. Cleaning windows, washing down walls, interior painting, repairing house and furniture form an annual routine to set against a 5-year plan of improvement and conversion. Why this pre-occupation with the house ? The most obvious reason is the sheer pride of ownership. . . . He can identify himself and his house and feel that as he improves it he is also in a sense adding to his own stature, in the eyes of his wife and his children, his neighbours and himself. A second reason is that the house is an opportunity for using and developing his capacity as a craftsman. The work of the day, in office or factory, may be becoming more and more boring. To compensate for this, the work of the night or week-end may be becoming psychologically more and more rewarding. The third reason is that the house is regarded as a sort of business.[23]

The connection between work and leisure, here mentioned by Willmott and Young as a hypothetical explanation for do-it-yourself activities,

[23] Young, M. and Willmott, P., *Family and Class in a London Suburb*, Routledge & Kegan Paul, 1960.

has been a subject for sociological investigation for many years. In an early study, Lundberg defined leisure as

> the time we are free from the more obvious and formal duties which a paid job or other obligatory occupation imposes upon us. In accepting this definition we are not overlooking the independence of work and leisure. Such terms are merely pragmatic ways of designating aspects, rather than separate parts, of life. It remains a fact, however, that nearly all people can and do classify nearly all their activities according to these two categories in a way that is deeply meaningful to themselves.[24]

Choosing to participate in craftsman-type do-it-yourself hobbies, therefore, can be seen partly as an adjustment to technological changes which have virtually eliminated any interest, creativity or initiative from many jobs, manual and non-manual alike. Such arguments would be more acceptable if there were the slightest evidence that do-it-yourself activities were concentrated among those who, for technological or other reasons, felt least involvement with their work. Not only is there no such evidence; if anything, the facts point in the opposite direction, namely, that individuals who perceive their work to be psychologically rewarding and stimulating are more likely to engage in creative leisure pursuits. In essence, then, we cannot ignore the more down-to-earth explanation that do-it-yourself is a once working-class activity which, in response to the post-1945 shortage of plumbers and decorators, increasing labour costs, and the relative decline of middle-class prosperity, has become classless and more ambitious, a question of necessity rather than of voluntary preference. There are now do-it-yourself sports cars, electronic organs, complete central-heating kits, and it is estimated that 4 million people in the United Kingdom seriously pursue practical interests of this kind, spending upwards of £450 millions in the process.

House maintenance and improvement, together with ancillary tasks like gardening, is not typically an end in itself nor is it a leisure activity in the usual sense. It is what has been called a non-work obligation—or more accurately an obligation to undertake work out of working hours as the more or less inescapable consequence of owning or renting a house. Studies of leisure patterns among American and British families show that doing odd jobs around the home and working in the garden are among the few spare-time activities which are not significantly

[24] Lundberg, G. A., Komarovsky, M. and McInery, M. A., *Leisure: A Suburban Study*, Columbia University Press, 1934.

related to social status or occupational prestige. Yet this does not necessarily prove that people *enjoy* these tasks. Indeed, it seems more likely from the evidence that the middle-class white-collar professional will regard, say, gardening as "work" and his paid employment as "leisure" in the sense that he would quite possibly continue to do his job even if it were not economically required of him. Manual workers typically express an equally strong desire to continue working if they did not have to, but with the powerful proviso that they would not be willing to continue doing manual work. Because their jobs are narrowly defined and subdivided, they must look elsewhere for their real satisfactions in life. It ought perhaps to be stressed here that these are very broad generalizations which within them encompass many exceptions. Large numbers of manual workers, not only those who have had their jobs enlarged or enriched in a deliberate attempt to generate more involvement in their work, regularly experience the kind of autonomy and satisfaction which is often associated with high-level occupations: drivers and dustmen, for example. Conversely, many administrative and managerial employees, ostensibly in responsible positions, experience minimum levels of commitment—either because the work itself has been diluted or because the employee has to function in an endemically restrictive environment (as in the large public-sector bureaucracies). But there is no reason to suppose that, for example, the latter group comes to regard do-it-yourself in the home with noticeably greater feelings of enjoyment; and even if this were the case, it would not be an acceptable basis for arguing that perceived enjoyment in do-it-yourself was *caused* as a reaction to lack of job satisfaction in the individual's paid employment.

As they pass their middle thirties, so the compulsive home ties on parents begin to slacken. They cease to have children, and their existing children either start to go out to work or, if still at school are regarded as being capable of looking after themselves in the evenings and at weekends. For the married woman, this loosening of the domestic ties does not mean increased leisure: she characteristically uses the additional time in order to work. Some of the extra money acquired from these two sources—wives and children at work—is spent on extending the home-centred leisure activities acquired during the early years of marriage. Gardening and do-it-yourself projects become more elaborate and require more expensive equipment; there is a little more home entertaining; T.V. viewing takes place in front of a bigger and a coloured screen. But the most important change is towards leisure activities outside the home. Although church-going continues to decline—the Church of England and the Roman Catholic Church lost active worshippers between 1971 and 1976 in almost equal proportion —altruism, or enlightened self-interest, has not been affected by secularization. The volunteers of the Samaritans' organization, for example, increased by several thousand from 1971 onwards, the income of the Save the Children Fund increased by more than £1 million, and the Consumers' Association registered an increase in membership of 110,000. Cultural activities are better patronized, though participation follows closely the distribution of income among the social classes. There was an increase of a third in public support for all museums between 1971 and 1975; visitors to National Trust properties, who numbered a million in 1960, were estimated at 4½ million in 1975. Well over 400,000 caravans are now in use, about half being located at static holiday sites; if hired, these caravans are mainly used by families with one or more children for a fortnight at a time, the majority having above-average incomes. Equally, camping now enjoys the patronage of over 3 million people. The average camper is 40, married, with one to three children, camping as a family unit, and 90 per cent of all tents used today are frame types. The significance of this last point is that frame tents require a car for transport: indeed, most of the pursuits mentioned in this paragraph are symptomatic of the geographical emancipation presented by large-scale ownership of the motor-car.

The fourth main stage in the development of leisure activities concerns the age group 45 to 64. In such households there are few young children—in all families where the housewife is aged between 45 and 64, only 18 per cent contain a child under school-leaving age—and on average the family contains two earners. Of these latter, the subsidiary earner is usually an adolescent, but more than 20 per cent of all married women in this age group go out to work. Whatever the source of the income, however, this period is the most prosperous in the whole family life. Mortgage repayments form a decreasing proportion of total expenditure; the majority of the main consumer durables have been acquired by this stage; and if the principal earner is in an occupation where advancement has been possible, his actual salary (even in real terms) represents a substantial increase on the amount he received earlier in his career.[25] Generally, too, geographical mobility has virtually ceased for the principal earner and his family, with the result that he can build up a stable circle of friends and acquaintances. On the other hand, this period of comparatively greater affluence and stability coincides with slackening physical energy. Thus the individual is typically characterized by a marked increase in home-based leisure activities, such as eating and drinking, or watching television. If outdoor pursuits are still practised, they tend to be of the quieter, less energetic kind—like golf[26]—or the individual continues to sustain his interest for more intensive pastimes but changes his role from that of active participant to that of passive observer.

Although consumption of alcohol is by no means confined to this age-group—*Britain's Sixteen Year-Olds* indicated that about half of the sample had drunk some alcohol in the week before they were interviewed and some 20 per cent claimed to have had a drink in a public house, albeit illegally—it would perhaps be appropriate at this stage to comment on changes in drinking habits. Beer was only a shilling a pint in 1945, but that was expensive at a time when the average manual worker's income was 121s 4d a week (one shilling equals 5p in decimal currency). However, Britain has remained a nation of beer drinkers, for although the *per capita* annual consumption was 186.8 pints in 1945, it had risen marginally to 201.2 pints by 1975. The more dramatic changes have been in the field of wines and spirits. In 1975 the nation drank 11.3 pints of wine per head compared with 0.7 pints in 1945, and 6.6 pints of spirits compared with 1.9 pints in 1945. This increase has been mainly attributable to the efforts of people in the South-east after World War II, when the region was more affluent than others and sent more people abroad for their holidays.

---

[25] For the manual worker, by contrast, the experience may be one of gradually declining income, as he withdraws from shiftwork, finds overtime more onerous, or moves away from the more physically arduous types of manual task like assembly-line work.

[26] Golf courses have risen to slightly over 2000 in number since World War II, but the number of golfers has more than doubled to well over a million. Other activities in the same general category include angling, with a total support of over three millions, and river cruising.

The final phase of life, so far as leisure is concerned, begins at 65. This is the age when most people retire (despite an increasing tendency for the age of retirement to be brought forward to 60 or even 55), their incomes drop sharply, their time available for leisure increases markedly but their physical and mental skills and energy are waning. Against this background, it is scarcely surprising that the leisure occupations of the old chiefly take the form of inexpensive or even free pursuits. In an average week, only 5 per cent go to a cinema (despite the fact that many cinemas have special prices for old age pensioners) and only 15 per cent visit a pub. In Bethnal Green, one of the most often-quoted reasons given by old people for relinquishing their long association with the pub was that although they could afford to buy the odd pint for themselves, they could not afford to stand a round for their friends and acquaintances. Rather than face the humiliation of having to refuse, they stayed away. A small sample survey of 101 retired men in north-west London[27] found the same link between money and status. "Men sat at home and watched the television night after night. 'It's better to stay at home if you can't pay your way,' a man commented."

Beveridge thus found that the most commonly undertaken activity around the house was watching television: 93 of the 101 men possessed sets and looked in fairly regularly. During the fortnight before the survey interviews, 86 said they had helped with the housework; 49 said they had gone for a long walk; 45 had read a book of some sort; 33 had taken part in an indoor hobby (rug-making, oil painting, carpentry); 71 said they worked regularly in the garden. As regards external pursuits, 24 had watched sport outdoors during the fortnight in question; 17 had gone to a social event of some sort (bingo, whist, old folks' club); 15 had taken part in an outdoor sporting activity (golf, angling, cycling); 14 had attended a church service and 13 had been to the cinema. In general, it has been found that since no more than 15 per cent of old people live in households with a car, occasional drives to the seaside or the country are rare, and only 40 per cent of people over 65 ever manage to take a holiday away from home. Radio is nearly as common as

[27] Beveridge, W. E., "How worthwhile is retirement?" *New Society*, 3 June 1965, pp. 14–16.

television, and on a typical afternoon the most frequent pastime is having a sleep. The older generation reads fewer magazines and newspapers than the rest of the adult population, which is partly a reflection of economic pressures and partly the result of declining powers of concentration. Their contacts with the outside world, such as they are, take on a a more parochial, direct and personal form. Most of them are visited quite frequently by nearby relatives, friends and social workers (either voluntary or professional). Indeed, the satisfaction and pleasure to be gained from retirement depend heavily on these personal relationships.

Part of the difficulty lies in the attitude to retirement which regards it as a period of decrepitude leading merely to the graveyard. "You're not wanted; you're on the scrap-heap" was the way one man described his feelings in the Beveridge survey. Yet as Ronald Fletcher writes: "If old people could be materially secure, there is no reason why the period of retirement should not be regarded in a positive constructive way, as a time when many interests and activities, for which there has been neither time nor opportunity earlier, can now be undertaken."[28] In many ways it seems ironic that many men have so few leisure resources on which to call that they will search desperately for another job in order to pass the time tolerably. In large measure such problems are a consequence of inadequate preparation for retirement: Beveridge found that less than half the men he interviewed had made any plans for retirement even during the final 6 months of their working life. But as Beveridge realistically concludes, "Society has offered them few satisfactions apart from work and, when society proposes suddenly to take away their work and its satisfactions, they can think of little else to live for."

Leisure, Status and Social Class

It would perhaps be appropriate to begin this section by outlining the arguments in Thorstein Veblen's influential book, *Theory of the Leisure Class*, published in 1924. Veblen suggests that people are basically motivated, in everything they do, by the desire for status. Since

[28] Fletcher, R., *The Family and Marriage*, Penguin Books, 1962.

status is not acquired easily, they generally pursue the acquisition of wealth as a compensatory mechanism. By emulating the expenditure patterns of the upper strata of society, in other words, they hope in turn to achieve the social position they so much admire. Eventually material wealth becomes intrinsically honourable because it is a passport to social prestige, and to membership of the leisured class whose distinguishing feature is freedom from the necessity to undertake paid employment. The corollary of this view is that work is degrading because it is associated with social inferiority. Veblen makes the interesting point, however, that the manufacture of goods by manual labour is more expensive and wasteful than using machines, and so the handmade product, despite its crudeness and imperfections, exudes an air of costliness which is a highly potent status symbol for the wealthy. For this reason, hand-carved and hand-painted pottery and hand-blown glassware are cherished possessions in the upper-class home.

Veblen's theory is still relevant in contemporary Western society, although the view that conspicuous and ostentatious expenditure is alone sufficient for the acquisition of social prestige has been discarded. Other more subtle criteria have been established as membership qualifications for the social elite. According to MacCannell,[29] for example, the new post-industrial leisure class is principally devoted to the quest for "reality" and "authenticity", a compensation for the discontents of modernity, and a reaction (in an attempt to sustain status differentials) against the democratization of leisure which has produced millions of "tourists" evidently content with such inauthentic experiences as the fake flamenco dance on the Costa Brava.[30] Hunting, shooting and fishing may have originally been the sole prerogative of the upper classes, and discovery of the medicinal qualities present in sea-water initially benefitted only the wealthier sections of the community. However, development of the mass media of communication has familiarized many sections of the community with upper-class methods of enjoying leisure. At the same time the affluent society has encouraged the growth of such expensive pursuits as yachting, ski-ing, underwater exploration,

[29] MacCannell, D., *The Tourist: A New Theory of the Leisure Class*, Macmillan, 1976.
[30] MacCannell introduces the notion of "negative sightseeing", exemplified by a special 3-week package deal to stay in West Virginia "with some of the poorest people of the United States".

motor-car racing and rallying, and holidays abroad. If status differentials are to be sustained in these areas, therefore, they must inevitably take more subtle forms.

Clearly there are ways in which the classes can be distinguished by reference to leisure interests. Cauter and Downham's survey of Derby revealed that the group going most frequently to the cinema is that composed of working-class people aged between 16 and 24, 87 per cent of whom were said to attend the pictures regularly (compared with only 25 per cent of the 65–69 age group). Newspaper and periodical readership can easily be analysed, in market research terms, according to social class criteria. The audience for *The Times* and the *Guardian* is scarcely comparable with that which reads the *Daily Mirror* and the *Sun*, whether one considers mere numbers, or wealth, occupation, and educational attainment. It appears, too, as if the middle classes are more likely to read books and to join public libraries; according to Reid,[31] some 67 per cent of social classes I and II say they read books more than a dozen times a year, compared with 28 per cent in classes IV and V. In Derby those borrowing at least one book a week from the public library constituted about one in six from the working classes and people with elementary education, and one in four from the middle classes and people with secondary and/or further education. Forty per cent of the middle class and 26 per cent of the working class were reading a book at the time of the interview; those who had never read a book comprised 12 per cent and 23 per cent respectively. More recently, too, sample surveys of audiences at London's theatres and concert halls have shown that 61 per cent came from the professional classes, 19 per cent from managerial occupations, with only 5 per cent being made up of manual workers; the only proviso to be made here is that these proportions may not be replicated in theatre attendances for the provinces, where the social composition of the locality (and the prices) may be different.

In some cases, the combined effects of democratization, increasing affluence and respectability have enabled certain leisure activities to throw off their more conspicuous class connotations. This is certainly true of gambling. At one time there seemed to be an unconsciously orchestrated attempt to categorize betting as an almost exclusively

[31] Reid, I., *op. cit.*

working-class phenomenon, the argument presumably depending on the assumption that the manual worker, confined to a dull job and constantly frustrated by his inability to make ends meet, reacts with dreams of sudden wealth and something for nothing. This theory is supported by the supposedly working-class ethos which discounts saving and encourages short-run hedonism. Orwell noted, during the 1930s, how the incidence of betting, far from declining in that period of high unemployment, actually increased:

> Even people on the verge of starvation can buy a few days' hope ("something to live for" as they call it) by having a penny on a sweepstake. Organized gambling has now risen almost to the status of a major industry. Consider, for instance, a phenomenon like the football pools, with a turnover of about six million pounds a year, almost all of it from the pockets of working-class people.[32]

Football pools still provide the greatest draw, attracting over 60 per cent of the population, and they remain principally an activity for working-class families. However, recent research by Downes and his colleagues[33] has provided a great deal of useful information about the major forms of gambling in Britain, about the differential involvement of various social groups, and about the variables which influence this involvement. It gives the lie to the notion that Britain is becoming "a society of gamblers" and it undermines the myths about the overcentration of such practices in the working class. While in terms of absolute numbers the working class may appear predominant, an important qualification which must be noted is the fact that the average amount of money wagered by each working-class individual is relatively small. At the other extreme, an insignificant number of wealthy people can bet with very large stakes in a gaming club and thereby counteract the economic contribution to gambling statistics made by the working class *en masse*. On the other hand, Downes does show the strong positive link between lack of job interest and betting (though, as we have seen already, lack of job interest is by no means the exclusive preserve of the manual worker). Parental gambling is firmly established as the most important predictor of gambling behaviour (whether this be football pools, betting shops,

[32] Orwell, G., *The Road to Wigan Pier*, Gollancz, 1937.
[33] See Downes, D. M., Davies, B. P., David, M. E. and Stone, P., *Gambling, Work and Leisure: A Study Across Three Areas*, Routledge & Kegan Paul, 1976.

fruit machines or even club bingo). The old hypothesis about working-class fatalism and belief in luck being a natural determinant of gambling is laid to rest, as is the idea that bingo is essentially a pastime for middle-aged women.

As regards interest in various forms of sport, a 1975 survey[34] confirmed that football led the way in almost every aspect of public interest. Football had even strengthened its position, compared with surveys in previous years, while nearly every other sport had lost ground. Golf commanded a total interest level of 36 per cent of the sample. Yet 11.3 per cent, as Table 5.2 demonstrates, actually practised the sport of golf, which places it second only to football, and not by all that much. The most unpopular sports were rowing, sailing and cycling, but it should be remembered that many sports—like ice hockey—were not even thought worthy of the statisticians' attention in this particular study. Perhaps more significant omissions were squash and ski-ing, the one showing a spectacular advance in recent years, the other enjoying a steadily rising popularity since package tours brought Alpine holidays within most people's purses.

Sociologists have also noted that in terms of functional analysis, leisure pursuits often serve both manifest and latent purposes. Thus membership of a golf club may be highly valued by those anxious to

TABLE 5.2. Interest Levels in Various Specified Sports, Measured as
Percentages of a Total Sample of 577 Males

	Foot-ball	Ath-letics	Box-ing	Cricket	Golf	Horse racing	Rugby union	Tennis
Takes any form of interest in	76.8	40.7	47.8	42.1	36.0	23.4	22.5	39.7
Takes part in	15.1	4.2	0.3	8.1	11.3	0.3	2.9	7.5
Follows on TV and/or radio	72.8	39.0	46.4	38.3	33.8	22.9	21.3	35.4
Follows in press	57.2	19.4	26.9	21.5	16.1	13.9	9.4	15.3
Goes to meetings/ matches	38.1	5.5	4.7	13.7	5.7	5.9	6.4	5.7
Follows in other ways	0.9	0.5	—	0.5	1.6	0.5	0.7	1.2

[34] "Who watches what, and where", *The Times*, 12 April 1975.

play golf, but also satisfies a number of other objectives. A study of spare-time activities in America by Clarke[35] discovered that membership of golf clubs increased steadily as one moved up the social scale, but that actual participation in playing golf was at a maximum in the middle-status groups, especially among those who classified themselves as "salesmen". "This would appear to be consistent with the widespread conception that golf offers an excellent opportunity for pursuing business relations under informal and pleasant surroundings," comments Clarke.

> It should also be noted that among the participant sports, golf represents perhaps the most pertinent example of how an activity is being transformed from the exclusive pastime of a few wealthy individuals to a popular pastime for many, representing diversified backgrounds in income and social status. The possible instrumental nature of this activity suggests, however, that membership in the "right" golf club could still be accepted as an important index of social status.

When the idea of leisure is extended to include clubs and societies of all kinds, then the implications of status are unavoidable. Clubs organized around the performance of certain prestige-conferring leisure activities, for instance, may deliberately engineer their membership regulations in order to preserve their exclusiveness. In Woodford, Willmott and Young[36] noted that although most clubs were not explicitly selective in their membership, there were exceptions: some controlled entry through the enforcement of high fees or more indirect means (such as the need for approval by a majority within the club's committee, or the operation of the black-ball, which means that if one member of the committee vetoes the applicant then he is automatically rejected). "Supposing a plasterer or someone like that applied to join", one club member said. "We want something a little bit higher social standard than that." Compared with Bethnal Green, there were fewer meetings for a chat in the street, but more clubs and organizations. Women were members of the Women's Institute, the Townswomen's Guild or the tennis club. The survey concluded that 35 per cent of the

[35] Clarke, A. C., "The use of leisure and its relation to levels of occupational prestige", *American Sociological Review*, Vol. 21, 1956, pp. 301–7.

[36] Young, M. and Willmott, P., *Family and Class in a London Suburb*, Routledge & Kegan Paul, 1960.

middle-class population had attended at least one club in the month previous to the interview, compared with only 18 per cent of the working class. Reid[37] indicates that more than 70 per cent of men in classes I and II belong to a club (which, of course, is not necessarily the same as attendance), compared with less than 50 per cent for class V.

Bottomore's "Squirebridge"[38] apparently reflected the same pattern Nearly all the town's voluntary organizations were characterized by a strong influence towards segregation along lines of occupational (and hence social) status. In some cases, the tendency was obvious and even pardonable—in the trade and professional bodies, for example. Other factors were sometimes involved, however, such as the fixing of a high subscription or the establishment of a standard of behaviour unattainable (or seemingly so) for individuals of low occupational status. As Bottomore points out, the individual sees a club, society or association not only as a means of satisfying certain of his interests or needs, but also as a group of people with whom he may or may not feel that he can mix freely. Indeed, the latter factor is likely to be much more important for most people, as there is evidence that people choose friends principally from people whom they perceive as being like themselves (in attitudes, educational background, occupational status, and so forth).[39]

Bearing these last points in mind, we can say that leisure may be a mark of status or, alternatively, a means of achieving status. Of the latter possibility, Bottomore argues that it is exceptional to find an individual seeking to climb the social scale by deliberately joining an organization whose members possess high occupational status. Upward mobility depends more on educational or occupational advancement, and membership of a particular voluntary group is more a confirmation of newly acquired status than a step towards acquiring that status. In general, too, the avenues towards higher social standing through leisure activities are narrow and limited. Trade union or political activity may bear fruit in this respect, or well-known figures in the field of sport can become what C. Wright Mills calls "celebrities". On the

[37] Reid, I., *Social Class Differences in Britain*, Open Books, 1977.

[38] Bottomore, T., "Social stratification in voluntary organizations", in Glass, D. V., ed., *Social Mobility in Britain*, Routledge & Kegan Paul, 1954.

[39] For this tendency among children, see Ford, J., "Comprehensive Schools as social dividers", *New Society*, 10 October 1968,

other hand, a study of political party organization in Greenwich[40] revealed that the officials in both the main party organizations came from higher status categories than the party rank and file, supporters and voters. Homogeneity in the Labour Party was greater than among the Conservatives. To put it another way, the Conservative party organization represented a wider cross-section of the community than the Labour party, which was heavily over-weighted with manual workers. In Bottomore's "Squirebridge" it was found that the Conservatives had a higher proportion of women members, a higher average age level, and larger numbers of members from the top occupational categories. Of the 16 Conservative party local officials, 12 were from Group A, 4 from Group B and none from Group C (in a threefold classificatory system), although 40 per cent of the party's membership came from the latter group. Membership of Conservative organizations was apparently regarded as a means of achieving prestige, whereas Labour organizations did not carry prestige and often aroused active disapproval. Of the 18 members in the local Labour constituency leadership, 1 was from Group A, 1 from Group B, and 16 from Group C. In general, active party workers seemed to be no more than a small minority of the party's supporters, probably those with more leisure at their disposal than the majority.

Class may be significant in another way, inasmuch as an individual may be deterred from joining a leisure organization if, according to his own evaluation, the members of that organization belong largely to a different social stratum. In Squirebridge, for example, the cricket club had a high proportion of Group A members (according to the same three-fold classification) and the working class generally regarded it as rather "snobbish". This subjective appraisal undoubtedly intimidated many potential members in the lower occupational categories, even though, in some cases, the impression of status exclusiveness was erroneous. In fact the Squirebridge cricket club drew half its membership from the lower layers of the social structure.

In those organizations whose membership extended to all three occupational groups (A, B and C), official leadership was concentrated on the members with high social status. There is nothing necessarily

[40] Benney, M., Gray, A. P. and Pear, R. H., *How People Vote: A Study of Electoral Behaviour in Greenwich*, Routledge & Kegan Paul, 1956.

sinister in this situation—the leaders may have been chosen because of various qualities of character or personal effectiveness that were originally responsible for their high status. The large numbers of so-called vice-presidents in the local Conservative constituency association, for example, played only a negligible part in the party's affairs and must have been selected primarily for reasons of status—and also because their acceptance of honorific positions placed upon them a strong moral pressure to contribute generously to party funds. Distinctions of status used to be vitally important, too, in the charitable societies discussed by Chambers,[41] where a clear dichotomy between benefactors and beneficiaries could be observed. Until comparatively recently, the leading individual in each Red Cross branch, Women's Institute or Women's Voluntary Service centre was almost invariably the most prominent woman in the upper classes. Even where the rules required some of the organizing members to be appointed by election, the results were usually a foregone conclusion. As a consequence of World War II, the advent of the Welfare State, and the general process of economic and social change, this position has altered. But the transition has gone largely unnoticed by those working-class women who, according to Chambers, often criticize women's organizations on the grounds that their members are superior, patronizing and condescending.

Today, minor positions of authority are held in the Red Cross, W.I. and similar movements by women of all social levels, though some organizations (like the National Housewives' Register, predominantly directed towards graduate wives) are specifically designed to meet the needs of a group that is bound to be concentrated within a limited range of the class structure. Participation in community service— largely a wartime development—has been continued and extended, though the lowest status groups are still in a minority. In many of these voluntary organizations, the vital condition for success seems to be the presence of a key woman surrounded by a group of enthusiastic satellites. In some areas this key woman is still in the upper-class category, but more often she is middle-class (the wife of a business man, perhaps). At the lower levels, working-class are given their chance to

[41] Chambers, R. C., "A study of voluntary organizations", in Glass, D.V., ed., *op. cit.*

contribute, although some are necessarily ruled out by such intangible factors as, say, the lack of a telephone or access to a motor-car. Chambers contends that class consciousness is, on the whole, less evident among women: they join an organization to perform a specific function and are not worried by the different social origins of the other women in the group.

A number of factors influence status differences within leisure organizations; the first of these is *size*. A small group functions as a whole, and its members are more likely to develop a common system of values whereas, in the larger organizations, sub-groups emerge which almost always follow lines of occupational status. A clear instance of the latter concerned an informal social club in Squirebridge with 200 members, of whom 25 per cent were in Group A, 25 per cent in Group B and the remainder in Group C. There were no organized activities, and members attended merely to drink, talk, play billiards and darts. In practice there was practically no contact between members of Group C and the other two groups, and the club officials all belonged to Group A. Comparable examples may be quoted from the United States. Warner[42] found in Jonesville that "there is, in general, a sharp break between the upper middle and lower middle classes, with respect to the kind and amount of participation in associations. . . . There is little participation between the upper middle and lower middle classes". And Packard[43] notes: "Today, the two upper classes have substantially abandoned all associations, such as the lodges, that would bring them into contact with members of the three lower classes." The effect of such developments is that, in some respects, existing class divisions are enhanced by the provision of separate leisure organizations for varying status categories: Rotary Clubs on the one hand, Working Men's Clubs on the other. And the process goes further when minorities of various kinds organize themselves into clubs or societies with regular meetings, with the object partly of increasing their effectiveness as pressure groups, but also with group cohesion and continuity in mind. In the United States, for example, Muraskin[44] has written of the black Masonic movement,

---

[42] Warner, W. L., *Democracy in Jonesville*, Harper, 1959.
[43] Packard, V., *The Status Seekers*, Longmans, 1960.
[44] Muraskin, W. A., *Middle-Class Blacks in a White Society: Prince Hall Freemasonry in America*, University of California Press, 1976.

which has been second only to the churches in embodying the values of the Protestant Ethic for the segment of blacks who have risen into the ranks of the "respectable". It has emphasized sobriety, thrift, sexual chastity, self-help, the dignity of work, respect for property and education, responsibility and civic duty. The function of black Masonry for the negro petty bourgeoisie and skilled manual worker group has closely paralleled the role of Methodism in Britain—a role which has combined elements of socialization, escapist leisure activities, and status maintenance in the face of perceived external threats. For negroes in the United States, Prince Hall Masonry offers a model of a life-style which dominant white society denies to most negroes while nevertheless defining it as the only proper and worthy way to live. The Masonic movement therefore gives institutional support to ghetto blacks who hold on to this status-bearing life-style—precarious and precious— because it offers them a multitude of leadership roles and responsibilities not otherwise open to negroes. There are many similar groups, with similar manifest and latent functions, in Britain for minority categories of immigrants, women and the like.

Another side of the coin emerges when examining the smaller groups centred around specific activities. In Squirebridge one small hobbies club, with less than 20 members, emphasized the absence of occupational class distinctions within the organization, and suggested that interest and proficiency in the hobby were the only factors relevant to the achievement of high status. Their meetings were characterized by their informality, although the president was treated with some deference and not addressed by his first name—no doubt because he was a company director, a Justice of the Peace, and a founder of the club. Nonetheless it is true that when the leisure activity requires skill, prestige may be gained by the possession of that skill. This may produce a status system differing from that produced by occupation. On the other hand, the two status systems may coincide (and therefore be indistinguishable) if the skills required within the club are similar to those required in a business or profession, as in organizations like the Rotary Club or Round Table. For cultural and educational groups, too, membership is influenced by the individual's educational attainment, which is in turn closely correlated with occupational status. The Squirebridge branch of the Workers Educational Association, therefore, had only one weekly wage-earner among its 30 members. Cauter and Downham's Derby survey showed that 50 per cent of the middle class and 24 per cent of the working-class population had undertaken a part-time course of further education—usually an evening class—at some time or other. A partial explanation for this differential may be found in the reasons why people attend evening classes. The type of course chosen usually depends on the job, and people apparently enrol in the hope of promotion within their present occupation, not usually in order to change their form of employment. Hence evening classes are not particularly helpful to those in manual work where promotion chances are negligible.

A second factor influencing status distinctions within voluntary groups is the *nature of the organization's activities*. Among those clubs and societies having no specific function, there is no common interest to unite the members. This being so, there is a tendency for small groups to form, consisting of members who do have something in common— usually occupation—outside the club. By contrast, social differentiation in organizations exercising specific activities is more likely to be based, according to Bottomore, on the type of activity. This is especially obvious in the case of charitable organizations which include, as members, both the dispensers and recipients of charity, and for service and ex-service organizations where status distinctions are based on the "officer" and "other ranks" criterion. Since the ex-officers are usually those with higher occupational status in civilian life, however, membership in such societies usually follows the conventional pattern.

One aspect of Veblen's conspicuous consumption theory still remains valid in that money is of fundamental importance in gaining entry to certain socially desirable forms of leisure. Among clubs hoping to maintain their exclusive membership, high subscriptions help to eliminate the lower income groups. Even when an individual has gained access to the organization of his choice, finance again assumes great significance, especially where the organization indulges in a variety of optional activities. Prestige is acquired by those who participate most fully, and this depends largely on having sufficient time and money. Frequency of meeting is also important in accentuating or weakening status distinctions: the Rotary Club may hold a weekly lunch, while the horticultural society may only meet once a year at the annual show. Bottomore argues that members are more likely to enjoy a kind of "rough equality" if their organization meets frequently. Where meetings occur at rare intervals, there is no opportunity to break down social barriers.

Finally, it should be borne in mind that not all leisure pursuits are in any way correlated with occupational (or any other form of) status. With hobbies, for example, it appeared in Derby that 46 per cent of the working class had no hobbies, compared with 31 per cent of the middle class. On the other hand, those working-class members who did have hobbies typically undertook more (at least two) than their middle-class counterparts. Perhaps more important for the future are trends in population, specifically the changing age composition of British society. Those over 55 have increased by 40 per cent since 1951, those under 25 by 30 per cent. These two age-groups, which now make up well over half the total population in the United Kingdom, are both great consumers of leisure; more passive pursuits for the aged, active leisure for the young. Although some observers would argue differently, the existing level of provision for their specialized interests is such that there seems little justification for magnifying the "leisure revolution" into a major social "problem" for which direct goverment action is necessary. Moves of this kind, apart from their patronizing flavour, would inevitably contradict the idea of leisure as activity undertaken by choice rather than by compulsion.[45]

[45] For a more detailed discussion of this whole topic, see Parker, S., *The Sociology of Leisure*, Allen & Unwin, 1976.

CHAPTER 6

Social Controls and the Maintenance
of Order

The modern proletariat ends by believing that by flocking to the polls its direct participation in power will be ensured.

(Max Weber)

I enjoy shift work. Nights suit me best because I live locally, and at nights you can concentrate on really looking for trouble. You get a better class of criminal too.

(Police sergeant quoted in the *Evening Standard*)

I'm a very religious man myself. I pray every night before I go to bed: 'I love my chief superintendent and I hope he loves me.'

(Constable quoted in Cain, M. E., *Society and the Policeman's Role*, Routledge & Kegan Paul, 1973)

Introduction

All societies—large or small, formal or informal—establish mechanisms of social control in order to minimize and, if possible, prevent altogether any violations of the social rules which bind the society together. Many of these rules become so deeply internalized in the individual that he is hardly aware of their existence and could not articulate the rules even if he tried to do so. Indeed, the socialization process is directed largely to this end: rules are obeyed because the individual cannot visualize doing things any other way or because, although he can imagine other ways of behaving, he feels that his way has a superior moral justification. Such rules do not inevitably imply that everybody behaves in the same way, but merely that relationships between people are governed according to a particular pattern—just as the rules of cricket are designed to produce a complementary set of activities among

227

the players. Moreover, the rules themselves may be stated in very imprecise terms. Some rules are little more than values to which the society's members subscribe: "success", "tranquillity", "the good life" or similar abstractions. It is these values which hold society together and which legitimize many of the more specific rules that uphold and sustain the values themselves.

In an effort to achieve conformity, stability and social integration, societies establish a series of social-control mechanisms calculated to correct any tendencies towards deviation in behaviour. As usual, the effectiveness of these social controls depends on the operation of positive (reward-oriented) or negative (punishment-centred) sanctions, taken separately or together. The individual may be deprived of his life, liberty, physical comfort, and well-being or may be threatened with the imposition of economic sanctions; alternatively he can experience the benefits of conformity, in terms of social approval, respect and admiration. Consequently conformity with the rules and values of society, which are acquired through socialization, is further reinforced by the knowledge that society is prepared to substantiate its beliefs by enforcement procedures. Yet deviance may still occur. Indeed, if the deviant activities assume a greater strength than the social controls designed to prevent them, the controls may become self-defeating and actually contribute to further deviant behaviour. This process can be seen at work or in the school, where social controls are directed towards the achievement of academic success and where failure elicits the application of sanctions for "laziness".

> A boy who does badly academically is predisposed to criticize, reject or even sabotage the system where he can, since it places him in an inferior position. A boy showing the extreme development of this phenomenon may subscribe to values which are actually the inverted values of the school. For example, he obtains prestige from cheeking a teacher, playing truant, not doing homework, smoking, drinking, and even stealing. As it develops, the antigroup produces its own impetus. A boy who takes refuge in such a group because his work is poor finds that the group commits him to a behaviour pattern which means that his work will stay poor and in fact often gets progressively worse.[1]

Another explanation for deviance has been offered by Merton.[2]

[1] Lacey, C., "Some sociological concomitants of academic streaming in a grammar school", *British Journal of Sociology*, Vol. 17, No. 3, 1966, pp. 245–62.
[2] Merton, R. K., *Social Theory and Social Structure*, Free Press, 1957.

According to this view, the values of a society specify the ends which people shall pursue, and the rules specify the means by which these ends may be *legitimately* obtained. In the United States, financial success is highly valued but cannot be achieved by people who are very poor, unskilled and semi-literate. Thus many people in American society find themselves in a situation of "anomie"—they have internalized the value of pecuniary success but cannot attain it by legitimate means. Although many of them adapt to the situation by becoming "conformist"—pursuing success by the prescribed means even though the task is hopeless—a significant minority will either resort to illegitimate means for attaining wealth (by undertaking criminal activities) or will "retreat" from society and refuse to conform to its wealth-oriented values at all. "Sociologically, these constitute the true aliens. . . . In this category fall some of the adaptive activities of psychotics, autists, pariahs, outcasts, vagrants, vagabonds, tramps, chronic drunkards and drug addicts."[3]

The notion of adaptation figures prominently in the literature on job satisfaction, frequently in the context of an attempted explanation for the equanimity with which many industrial workers seem to regard their work. The idea is that whatever the latent potentialities and dormant needs which may lie within us, some people have been conditioned to expect less than others from their work. These people, necessarily spending their working lives performing tasks with little or no intrinsic satisfaction, can only preserve their psychic equilibrium or mental balance by altering their expectations so that they want nothing but money for their labours. Some writers seem unclear on whether in fact their expectations have been suitably structured before entry to work, or whether the major re-ordering occurs as a consequence of work itself. One general school of sociology, for example, in effect believes that society is external to man and constrains him through the operation of inpersonal social facts, so that the process of socialization gives him his social roles and determines how he will respond. An alternative conception is the so-called "Action frame of reference", which "argues that man is constrained by the way in which he socially constructs his reality. . . . Man makes society".[4] This being so, it is man's subjective

---

[3] Merton, R. K., *op. cit.*
[4] Silverman, D., *The Theory of Organization*, Heinemann, 1970.

perception of reality, or his "definition of the situation", which provides the basis for his adaptive behaviour, rather than any pre-existing and objectively-observable social phenomena. It seems most plausible in practice, to suggest that individual perceptions (and consequent behaviour patterns) are continually changing in response to both internal and external factors like, say, inflation, physiological growth and decay, and the general level of employment in the economy.

If the concept of adaptation is to be meaningful, it must imply a widespread—if not universal—desire for psychic equilibrium, with this equilibrium being most easily attainable through a conforming relationship with the immediate social environment. Yet adaptation may take many forms, and occasionally the notion is interpreted so generously that it loses all analytical precision. Goffman, for example, discussing the process whereby patients are assimilated into mental hospitals,[5] claims to identify four various forms of adaptation:

(1) *Situational Withdrawal*: "The inmate withdraws apparent attention from everything except events immediately surrounding his body."

(2) *The Intransigent Line*: "The inmate intentionally challenges the institution by flagrantly refusing to co-operate with staff."

(3) *Colonization*: "A stable, relatively contented existence is built up out of the maximum satisfactions procurable within the institution."

(4) *Conversion*: "The inmate appears to take over the official or staff view of himself and tries to act out the role of the perfect inmate."

This typology does have interesting parallels with the behaviour of people at work, especially when reactions to assembly line conditions are studied. As an illustration of "situational withdrawal", for example, Beynon[6] describes how the employees at Ford's Halewood plant say things like "When I'm here my mind's a blank. I *make* it go blank." Extreme illustrations of "colonization" and "conversion" appear in a recent study of American negro slavery, which shows that because only one-third of all overseers on plantations were white, slave labour was

[5] Goffman, E., *Asylums*, Penguin Books, 1968.
[6] Beynon, H., *Working at Ford*, Penguin Books, 1973.

virtually managing itself; somewhat naturally, slaves at all levels, from overseer to old hands, were trying to make the best of the situation in which they found themselves, and this generally meant a degree of real or apparent compliance with the system.[7] A milder instance of similar reactions is to be found in studies of industrial behaviour[8] which have demonstrated that shop-floor operatives produce a "ritualist" (or "colonized") response to questions on occupational advancement: they have rationalized their inability to obtain promotion by convincing themselves, for all sorts of "good" reasons (i.e. reasons "good" to the individuals themselves, thereby endorsing the Action frame of reference), that they would not want it anyway.

At the same time, the descriptive term "adaptation" does demonstrate an undesirable flexibility in conceptualization. It seems bizarre to categorize the "intransigent line" as a form of adaptation when Goffman explicitly admits that it is "typically a temporary and initial phase of reaction, with the inmate shifting to situational withdrawal or some other line of adaptation" (unless, of course, sufficient individuals pursue the intransigent line for it to become a type of adaptation in itself, as Lacey's anti-school culture indicates). What is implied here is that any psychic equilibrium offered by the intransigent line must be of an inherently unstable type, whereas individuals seem to prefer an equilibrium comprising large elements of stability. Indeed, there is some support for this in that Beynon's scrutiny of shop stewards at Ford—which is largely a study of individuals pursuing an intransigent line against the company's management—suggests that undiluted intransigence is a psychologically untenable position for any prolonged period, and that in practice the employees have, at least to some degree, to come to terms with their environment. One of the shop stewards is quoted as follows:

> I can see the time when the bomb goes up, you know. I can see myself leading the lads off my section and just destroying this place. I can see that happening. But you've got to cope with this plant as it is now, you've got to come in every day and represent the lads. That means you've got to set up some relationship with the supervision and with management.[9]

[7] Fogel, R. W. and Engerman, S. L., *Time on the Cross: The Economics of American Negro Slavery*, Wildwood House, 1974.
[8] See, for instance, Sykes, A. J. M., *Sociological Review*, Vol. 13, No. 3, 1965, p. 297.
[9] Beynon, H., *op. cit.*

Similar difficulties are inherent in Merton's approach, arising from his implicit assumption that value-systems and their accompanying social rules are consistent throughout society. In fact it is more realistic to visualize a "plurality" of norms and values, dependent on class, ethnic, sexual, religious and regional differences, and to recognize that these values may well be in conflict with each other. Thus, although occupational advancement may be highly valued by the middle class, it ranks as deviant if seen in working-class terms. What is at issue here, in essence, is the empirical accuracy of consensus and conflict tendencies of thought within sociology. The consensus-conflict debate spotlights different insights into society, different images about its unity and cohesion, and the extent to which there prevails within it any agreement over basic values. Broadly, in the study of crime, for instance, the consensus line emphasizes the way in which sanctions arise and vary with what is designated as criminal behaviour (which is itself classified as behaviour which departs from a model of society's agreed values); "problems", including economic problems, are correlated with the incidence of such sanctions. Conflict approaches prefer the view that both problems and sanctions arise from prevailing and inherited patterns of power, privilege and inequality. In those few cases where a determined attempt has been made to establish the general validity of either of these two approaches, the conflict model typically scores more points—but there are significant issues where a number of findings are clearly supportive of consensus ideas.[10] In fact, all societies are (whatever theories may imply) a mixture of consensual and conflictual elements, and it is as important to describe the mix as it is to weigh the separate components.

To some extent conflicts over values and social rules are reconciled through the operation of power and the political system, in that one group in society effectively makes rules for other groups and enforces these rules by means of penal and moral pressures. Although this is a reasonable pragmatic way of ensuring that there is some measure of apparent (if not real) uniformity in society's norms, and although a legitimate field for sociological inquiry is the nature and origin of the norms themselves, it should be clear that it is technically no part of the

---

[10] See, for instance, McDonald, L., *The Sociology of Law and Order*, Faber & Faber, 1976.

sociologist's function to advise on the specification of various norms or values.[11] With this in mind, we shall be considering three major mechanisms of social control in British society—religion, political institutions, and law enforcement. It must be borne in mind, too, that these social controls untidily reflect the heterogeneity of society itself: its class, ethnic, sexual, religious and regional differences. In practice, too, we shall concentrate on the impact of social class within these control mechanisms, since the evidence suggests that class is the major distinguishing element in the socialization process.

Religious Affiliations and Behaviour

Organized religion is merely one reflection of man's attempt to make sense of the world, to produce a systematic "belief system" which will account for the nature of the world, man's situation within it, the significance of human life and the distribution of resources among men. Although other philosophical constructs purport to achieve similar objectives, the distinguishing feature of religion is that it relates the world to supernatural forces and imposes moral standards sanctioned by supernatural beings. Individuals may adjust their behaviour in order to satisfy these moral standards, in the hope of some eventual reward, or alternatively they may espouse religious causes as a course of solace and compensation for an unpleasant existence.

[11] According to Lessnoff, the sociologist should confine himself to making statements about the expected consequences of various measures, and leave someone else to take decisions about which measures to enact (Lessnoff, D., *The Structure of Social Science: Philosophical Introduction*, Allen & Unwin, 1974). A similar standpoint is expressed in the view that "the social researcher can easily satisfy the demands made upon him by the various value systems if he does not confine himself to a static analysis of a given situation, but indicates also the *real* differences between different courses of action, which are implicit in the different decisions that the power-holding groups could adopt, and illustrates, therefore, to them the possible alternative policies with all their middle and long-range consequences. The social researcher as such does *not* take up a position. He simply clarifies to the decision-making group what is implicit in their decisions. He extrapolates for them the global and cumulative significance of their piecemeal approach. It is not up to him . . . to indicate ends or goals as 'good' or 'bad', as desirable or deplorable". See Ferrarotti, F., "Social Research and Industry in Europe", in *Social Research and Industry in Europe: Problems and Perspectives*, O.E.C.D., 1960. Ironically, these statements, while they commend the position of the sociologist as a "free professional", are themselves normative value-judgments.

There is little doubt that religion has a decreasing and (in some cases) an almost negligible influence over the lives of the majority of people in British society. In virtually all the studies of twentieth-century changes in religious activity—whether measured by figures for church membership, church attendance, rates of donation, etc.—there has emerged a definite decline in religious activity in Britain, compared with a steady state in America. In both countries, the implications of religious teachings have changed, receiving "a kind of passive acceptance that does not influence conduct".[12] For Britain, the trend has been towards a secularization of society, whereas in America it is the churches themselves which have become more secular.

Disillusionment with older systems of belief, cynicism generated by two world wars, the effects of scientific and rationalist thought, may all have contributed to this situation. On the other hand, even if organized religion is not an important part of our society, it may be argued that religious values are still crucial in controlling our behaviour. It is, in fact, a debatable question as to whether moral rules are ever generated, or are merely underwritten, by religion. If the latter is true, then the dominant values operative in society cannot be accurately described as religious at all. In any event, the attenuated role of religion can probably be described most satisfactorily by recalling that a religion is supposed to supply a general theory of the universe: it explains, provides a means of control, and enables predictions to be made. Today, scientific theories have eroded most of the religious explanations of life, and science certainly provides more efficient methods of control and prediction.

It would be a mistake to suppose, however, that religious beliefs are doomed to eventual eclipse. To argue in these terms is to ignore the fact that the very non-empirical character of religion enables it to perform psychological and social functions, particularly at the crises of life—birth, marriage, and death. As with the family, the State has assumed responsibility for many of the functions previously performed by the Church alone, including care of the poor and the sick, and this too has contributed to the decline of religious influence. In the United States, by contrast, the prevailing political philosophy has not permitted social

[12] Argyle, M. and Beit-Hallahmi, B., *The Social Psychology of Religion*, Routledge & Kegan Paul, 1975.

welfare to proceed to a comparable stage, and this suggests a possible, but only partial, explanation of the greater importance of organized religion in that country.

Several studies have thrown some light on the extent to which religious beliefs still exert control over people's thoughts and behaviour. Detailed examination of a rural village in Cumberland, for example, revealed a marked apathy towards the church which was by no means a recent phenomenon, although the blame was consistently placed on the shoulders of the new rector.[13] Religious rites accompanying birth, marriage and death were regarded as merely signifying some change in status, although Confirmation was viewed as a change in religious status alone. Indeed, Confirmation marked the climax of the most intensive period of church-going and religious instruction ever experienced in the individual's lifetime.[14] In Gosforth, the festivals with highest church attendances were also those which were secular holidays, but the general conclusion reached by the inquiry was that religion exercised a very weak influence over the behaviour and morals of the community as a whole.

In the Swansea area of south-west Wales, on the other hand, religion was still a very real social force despite the decline in its impact since World War I. Nearly half the population were church or chapel members (mainly the latter), and religious leadership was significantly linked with local government, political and trade union leadership. But because congregations were socially mixed, considerations of unity prevented individuals from discussing or determining social policy. The main factors in the decline of religious life were thought to be the growth of secular education and an increasingly materialistic interpretation of life, the democratic structure of chapel constitutions, and the influence of the Labour Party. The continuing strength of religion in this area, however, could be attributed chiefly to historical and cultural factors, and this is borne out eloquently by investigation into a semi-suburban London borough. Here only one-tenth of the population were at all closely associated with any of the churches, while at the other end of the scale, about two-thirds never or practically never went to church. True, the majority (80 per cent of the women and 65 per cent

[13] Williams, W. M., *Gosforth*, Routledge & Kegan Paul, 1956.
[14] Because of physiological and psychological changes, adolescence is the peak period for religious conversion, although the effects do not tend to be sufficiently long-lasting.

of the men) expressed a vague belief in God; the remainder felt doubts rather than active scepticism; and uncompromising disbelievers amounted to only 5 per cent of the total. Even of the Church of England churchgoers, under a third assented to the three basic tenets of the Creed, and 40 per cent doubted the possibility of an after-life. To most people, religion had come to mean little more than being kind and neighbourly, or doing good when the opportunity arose. Mogey's study of Oxford, too, revealed a very low frequency of church attendance. In Barton (the new housing estate) this could partly be accounted for by the absence of a proper church, but a significant number of people both in Barton and St. Ebbe's (the older residential area) explained that church-going was for children, youths and old people, not for them. Some men even regarded attendance at religious services as a feminine practice.[15]

Figures produced by a 1957 Gallup Poll—indicating that only 6 per cent of Britain's population was atheist and 16 per cent agnostic—suggested that there had been little decline in beliefs about God, but rather an increasing apathy towards institutionalized religion. Subsequent surveys have shown a distinct decline in doctrinal belief among the non-churchgoing majority, corresponding to an increase not in atheism but in vagueness. The majority now appears to believe in a metaphysical "something", but is less and less inclined to identify it with the personalized Christian deity. Paradoxically, too, a large segment of the population turns to prayer in times of great personal stress, and almost the entire population can relate at least one meaningful religious experience that they have undergone. Clearly the alleged secularization of Britain is a complex phenomenon, with many contradictions.

Nowhere is this illustrated more dramatically than in the figures for church membership and church attendances. In 1957, of the 78 per cent of the population believing in God, only 11 per cent of men and 16 per cent of women went to church. Only 9 per cent of those claiming affiliation to the Church of England actually attended religious services, compared with 20 per cent of the Free Church membership and 44 per cent of the Roman Catholics. As regards the proportion of the total population attending church, the Gallup Poll indicated that those who went to religious services once a month or more (including 13 per cent

---

[15] Mogey, J. M., *Family and Neighbourhood*, Oxford University Press, 1956.

who attended once weekly at least) totalled 26 per cent of the population. More recently, there were more people entitled to call themselves Anglicans in 1973 than in 1957, and the total, 27 millions, was nearly three-fifths of the population. If one adds to that those with at least a nominal claim to be called Jews, Roman Catholics, Nonconformists, Muslims, Sikhs and Hindus, the proportion rises towards four-fifths. The same is generally true of Scotland and Wales, although the relative strengths of the different denominations and creeds vary enormously. Yet less than 5 per cent of the population of England, about $1\frac{1}{2}$ million people, now receive the Easter Communion, which is usually accepted as a good rule-of-thumb test of committed church membership. On a typical Sunday, it is estimated that Mass attendance by Roman Catholics amounts to between $1\frac{1}{2}$ and 2 millions. The Methodist Church Church has about 550,000 members on its rolls, of whom a high proportion can be assumed to attend church fairly regularly, and nearly $1\frac{1}{2}$ million names appear on the so-called community roll of people wishing to be associated with the church. Age differences within the figures for church attendance suggest that older people predominate in congregations. This may be attributable to the fact that when people become older they begin to consider more seriously the implications of death, and also to the fact that older people may have fewer social or familial connections to keep them away from church (this is especially true if they have retired from active work). It is perhaps worth noting in this context, too, that the decade 1966–76 has been one of substantial change in liturgical procedures,[16] with the result that modern Christianity in Britain, with its own forms of interior life, is an alien sub-culture not only for those who have never belonged, but also for those who were once committed but who subsequently opted out. The decline in numbers and the sense that a visible distance now separates the churches from the mainstream of national life may have made the different denominations realize how much they have in common, in their beliefs and in their difficulties.[17]

---

[16] These changes include the new Anglican Series III services, the new English Mass, the new Free Church prayerbooks, all written in contemporary language like the many modern translations of the Bible now in general use.

[17] At least the churches can console themselves with the thought that far more people attend church on Sundays than football matches on Saturdays.

Turning to class differences in religious affiliations, the available evidence indicates that the working class is less active in this sphere, particularly as regards frequency of church attendance. The 1957 figures showed that while 30 per cent of non-manual workers attended religious services once a month or more, the comparable figure for manual workers was only 17 per cent. There are strong correlations between educational attainment and religious inclination, but as education is itself highly correlated with occupation and the other sources of class divisions, such figures can simply be interpreted as part of the class dichotomy. Booth and other observers at the turn of the century had similarly described the upper and middle classes as more active in religious terms, although Gorer, more recently, discovered a similar tendency among very poor people.

Between denominations, there is a slight likelihood that more members of the middle and upper classes belong to the Church of England rather than to Catholic or non-conformist churches. We have already seen, in the chapter on social class, that the upper reaches of the Church of England has been dominated by individuals with a public school and Oxbridge pedigree. Norman[18] has recently shown that this was a fundamental weakness for the radical thinkers among them, who could never understand why their progressive social ideas failed to bring the working classes flocking into the Church. In the United States, Jews belong generally to a social class above Protestants, with the latter in turn ranking higher than Catholics. The low position of Catholics may be partly due to the small incentive to achieve status which is characteristic of Catholicism and to the customarily low occupational status of many Catholic immigrants. Moreover, it is possible that the thrift, abstemiousnous and industriousness encouraged by Protestantism (when religion was more influential in impinging on human behaviour in non-religious contexts) results in the accumulation of wealth and upwards social mobility, as suggested by Weber.[19]

Argyle[20] argues that social class influences religion rather than vice

[18] Norman, E., *Church and Society in England 1770–1970*, Clarendon Press, 1976. Typical of this background was the comment by one Church of England cleric, made in all seriousness, that "Christ was the greatest public schoolboy who ever lived".

[19] Weber, M., *The Protestant Ethic and the Spirit of Capitalism*, Allen & Unwin, 1952.

[20] Argyle, M., *Religious Behaviour*, Routledge & Kegan Paul, 1958.

versa; Neibuhr, on similar lines, concludes that all churches reflect the interests of the social class of the majority of their members. Thus the American liberal Protestant churches personify the political conservatism, nationalism, optimism and acceptance of the *status quo* which are characteristic of the upper middle class. Bottomore's study of "Squirebridge"[21] identifies similar trends. Among those inhabitants who were at all religiously inclined, the church was regarded as an association with specific aims, to which a definite amount of leisure time was devoted and which interfered little with other activities. Church of England affiliation involved a relatively higher proportion of individuals from status groups A and B (in Bottomore's threefold classification). Indeed, the type of membership could, to some extent, be deduced from the style of life of the ministers. Those of the Church of England lived in fairly large houses (which they could no longer afford) while other ministers had fairly small homes. Nonetheless it was normal for leadership in church affairs to be assumed by those with higher occupational status, although social distinctions between the churches were declining in the face of a tendency for the squirearchy to be replaced by tradesmen and professional men in church organization.

The directionality of the causal relationship between social class and religion is also relevant to the reasons for founding new religious organizations and sects. Fallding[22] regards all religions as having their origin in sectarian protest, although he rejects the Niebuhr thesis that such protest necessarily arises from among the dispossessed. Rather Fallding sees new religions as matters of new aspirations, and as ways by which men "climb upward", an idea which can be illustrated by reference to movements as disparate as Buddhism and Islam on the one hand, and Quakerism and the Jehovah's Witnesses on the other. A specific example of the process is Moore's picture[23] of Methodism in the Deerness Valley (a coal-mining district close to Durham City) from the 1860s to to 1920s. In this context, Methodism was a supportive communal

---

[21] Bottomore, T., "Social stratification in voluntary organizations", in Glass, D. V., ed., *Social Mobility in Britain*, Routledge & Kegan Paul, 1954.

[22] Fallding, H., *The Sociology of Religion*, McGraw-Hill, 1974.

[23] Moore, R., *Pit-Men, Preachers and Politics: the Effects of Methodism in a Durham Mining Community*, Cambridge University Press, 1974.

institution which supplied a disproportionate number of miners' leaders in trade union and political life. These were pre-eminently the "respectable" working classes, hard-working, thrifty and responsible; more concerned with individual spiritual salvation than with radical social reconstruction. They co-operated with capital because they saw the interests of labour and capital as inseparable. The universalism of their religious beliefs and the communal nature of their religious institutions brought them closer to fellow-Methodists among the colliery owners and managers than to their non-believing fellow trade unionists. Only when the coal industry itself went into serious decline did the Methodist-led unions begin to use seriously aggressive industrial tactics. To a degree, therefore, Methodism in the Deerness Valley "fitted" the needs of capitalist society, and it could be argued that, by inhibiting class consciousness, it rendered the proletariat compliant and deferential.

Some writers have tried to show a distinction in the degree of religious attachment to be found in urban and rural areas. Gorer, for example, found considerably more activity round the church in rural areas, and similar observations have been made in the United States. If expressed on a graph, there would be a linear relation between religious activity and the size of the community—high for thinly populated rural localities and low for urban concentrations. One possible explanation for this greater activity in rural areas and small towns could be found in cultural lag—large towns, as in other things, taking a lead in the decline of religion. At the same time urban communities, because of their large populations, are able to support religious sects of various kinds, often originating as protest groups. In Britain the smaller sects—like the Elim Foursquare Gospel Movement and the Jehovah's Witnesses—have not increased their overall membership since 1900. They may even be declining in much the same way as small political groups which can never establish themselves firmly in the face of competition from a few very large political parties. A contributing factor to the decline may be that the sects are largely composed of poor people. As the incidence of poverty declines, so the sect itself finds the maintenance of internal cohesion more difficult to sustain.

It has been suggested that religion prospers during periods of economic depression, but there is virtually no relationship between *per capita* incomes (at constant prices) and membership statistics for various churches. In Britain there has been an overall increase in prosperity since 1925, accompanied by a decline in religion. Although some religious leaders welcomed the high unemployment of the 1930s because they felt it would produce a return to the churches, in fact there was only a slight increase in affiliation to the Church of England and the Catholic Church, and none at all to the non-conformist bodies. In the United States, by contrast, rising prosperity has been associated with the increasing popularity of religion, for all denominations and sects. Clearly economic factors are of very limited value in explaining developments in religious attachment.

As society changes, so the influence of religion alters its character. While society develops from the simple to the complex, from the preliterate to the industrialized, so religion becomes delocalized, less anthropomorphic, more separated from everyday affairs. In the primitive village, religion seems to permeate every act, whereas in the modern city it is withdrawn into a separate category of behaviour. In Britain the post-war drift out to suburbs, housing estates and new towns has had a decisive effect, not only on Christianity in general, but also on the growth of the ecumenical movement. The provision of new churches and of associated clergy has proved such a heavy burden on the churches that it has led them inevitably towards pooling and sharing arrangements. At the same time there is some evidence that people uprooted from inner urban areas to new housing developments are prepared to have their traditional denominational loyalties loosened in the process. With the growth in the separation of roles between Church and State, there is increasing fragmentation of sentiments and ceremonies.

Yet, although the process of secularization can go a long way, there is an ultimate limit beyond which it is unlikely to proceed. It is true that science, while often misrepresented and misunderstood, has undermined some of the foundations of religious belief, but many would argue that ultimately such belief is not susceptible to scientific method because it is not to be regarded as a set of hypotheses simply to be investigated then supported or rejected on the basis of empirical evidence. McPherson,[24] for example, holds that while it is perfectly proper for the religious believer to subject his beliefs to rational examination, is it also

[24] McPherson, T., *Philosophy and Religious Belief*, Hutchinson, 1974.

the case that "a religion of hypothesis, a religion of conjecture and refutation . . . would not be Christianity. Christianity involves commitment of several sorts". Theological claims are seen as based on certain verbal formulae which are "authoritatively provided by the founders of the religion". Moreover, McPherson asserts strongly that "there is no obligation on a man always to back up his beliefs with reasons or arguments". Not all theologians, philosophers or scientists would accept this standpoint by any means, but it does ultimately have to be conceded that faith is a matter of commitment—and faith based on no empirical evidence whatsoever is not the exclusive province of religious believers. Some adherence to religion, too, may be helpful in performing a cohesive function in society. Organized religion in Britain reinforces a set of values which the majority of the population implicitly accepts and which generate feelings of solidarity and unity particularly important in situations of stress, such as wartime. Participation in or even mere observation of religious rituals serves the purpose of reminding people about the values to which they subscribe, and this helps to strengthen the values themselves.

Political Attitudes and Behaviour

Political institutions provide support for both the "consensus" and the "conflict" models of society. From the "consensus" point of view, it is argued that political parties—and the other organizations concerned with the exercise of power, such as trade unions, employers' association, pressure groups and so forth—accept an underlying framework of common values. This is illustrated by the smoothness with which a change of government is achieved if an election produces a different balance of majorities; equally there is consensus over the rules of political operation. For the conflict theorist, on the other hand, consensus is a temporary state resulting merely from the successful dissemination of the ideas of the ruling group. Mass political parties are seen as important devices for assimilating deviant and dissident groups into the existing social order, by persuading such groups to confine their opposition to peaceful and therefore relatively ineffective methods. Clearly there is some substance in both of these approaches. Consensus theory helps to account for the stability and persistence of political institutions, whereas conflict theory throws some light on the sources of political innovation and change.

Like other large-scale organizations, political parties are bureaucratic in form. A strong hierarchy of centralized administration is built up, and power tends to be concentrated in the hands of a few top officials. Once the position of these leaders has been consolidated, they become established and virtually irremovable, creating a kind of oligarchical rule which Weber believed to be inevitable: "The formation of oligarchies within the various forms of democracy is the outcome of organic necessity which consequently affects every organization, the socialists or even anarchists." Why is a party organization necessary? The essential functions of a party bureaucracy are to maintain and improve party efficiency in order to secure the votes necessary to place the party in power, and also to provide the machinery essential for the two-way communication of ideas between the party leadership and the rank-and-file. In short, electoral success depends almost entirely on the efforts of the party organization.

A political party itself is a formal union of individuals and affiliated groups, having similar views on leading political questions. The party deliberately tries to gain power so that it may put these views into practice. The party system has considerable disadvantages. Once in power, the party is difficult to control, and the leadership may not always be responsive to the wishes of party members. Moreover, a two-party system—which does not mean that only two parties exist, but that only two parties are capable of forming a government— inevitably misrepresents the real attitudes and policies of large sections of opinion within each party.[25] On the other hand, effective and continuous government without political parties would scarcely be a practical possibility. Indeed, the chief advantage of the two-party system lies in the fact that, by eliminating splinter parties or groups, it almost always produces a government with an effective majority over all other groups combined.[26]

[25] For an account of some of the more radical minority groups in British politics, see Shipley, P., *Revolutionaries in Modern Britain*, Bodley Head, 1976.

[26] This remains true on a long-term basis despite the tightrope majorities of the mid-1970s.

Perhaps one of the most unenviable tasks of any party leader—apart from simply holding his party together by justifying the allegiance of his members at the extremes of the organization—is to ensure that his party presents a unified and coherent image to the outside world. People do not always look at a party in terms of a rational appraisal of the various social, economic and international issues. Studies show that people do not even select the "most important issues" in an election; by far the most relevant factor chosen is the party image, which is, in effect, a mental set or impression of "what a party stands for" gathered from impressions, propaganda and discussion. This factor is probably partly responsible for the high degree of stability in voting behaviour, because it has been found that images are extremely resistant to change. Thus, even when the accepted image of a party is untrue, the image remains. A survey of Bristol in 1955[27] showed that 85 per cent of Labour supporters identified their own party as "for the working class" and the Conservative Party as "only for the rich and big business". The figures suggested that Labour supporters are more likely to rely on a few commonly held images than the Conservatives, since no more than a third of Conservative voters subscribed to any single image of their own or the Labour Party. This may be an indication of the lack of political awareness among the working class or may reflect little more than class solidarity, but some other studies have also indicated that party images are more important to the working class than to the middle class.

While it is true that there is a large measure of stability in voting behaviour, consistent voting is far less common than was once believed to be the case. According to Butler and Stokes,[28] perhaps as many as 30 per cent or more of the electorate can be classed as in some measure floating or volatile. They are influenced by their perception of the issues, by their general feeling about the parties at the time of the election, by the extent to which they see the parties as competent or up-to-date, by the pull of leaders, and by their own general feelings of economic well-being. Between 1966 and 1970, for example, the Conservatives benefited from straight conversions from Labour, movements

[27] Milne, R. S. and Mackenzie, H. C., *Marginal Seat*, Hansard Society for Parliamentary Government, 1958.
[28] Butler, D. and Stokes, D., *Political Change in Britain: the Evolution of Electoral Choice*, 2nd edition, Macmillan, 1975.

in and out of the Liberals, and non-voting; but simultaneously they lost out on the balance between supporters who had died and new voters recruited. The Conservative victory of 1970 was due to changes in the votes of those who had voted before, rather than changes in the composition of the electorate.

There have also been developments in the class basis of voting behaviour. When the influence of social class was at its height in 1951, very nearly 80 per cent of the electorate voted for either the Conservative or the Labour party. At each subsequent general election this proportion has gone down, sometimes to the benefit of the Liberals, sometimes to the nationalists, sometimes just not voting at all, until in February 1974 barely more than half the electorate voted for one or other of the main parties. Such tendencies do not justify claims that they can be extrapolated indefinitely into the future until the connection between social class and voting is totally eroded, and there is no particular reason to suppose that the main parties will ultimately be aligned on some difference other than class. On the contrary: the relationship between class and voting is still sufficiently positive for it to be given some attention.

Even before the connection between voting behaviour and class had been objectively established, many writers had tried to show some correlation between the two. Tonnies, for instance, suggested that political affiliations are conditioned by a combination of economic factors and class/status consciousness.[29] This may have been true in the context of Germany immediately after World War I, when many of the poorer classes sycophantically voted to please their economic masters and social superiors. Tonnies questions the Marxian view that economic conflicts (leading to political disputes) cannot take place within a single class: clearly electricians on strike do not always consider the factory closures which their action may provoke. At the same time, Tonnies does not rule out economic and political conflicts based on class divisions—such as struggles between workers and employers—even if this kind of conflict is not necessarily the typical pattern. One of Marx's fundamental pre-occupations concerned the fact that the conflict in society could not become a reality until the proletariat achieved class

[29] Tonnies, F., *Community and Association*, Routledge & Kegan Paul, 1955.

consciousness and became aware of its common situation and interests. In practice such a unified identity has not been achieved. Although in broad terms the Labour Party is supported by the working class and the Conservatives by the middle classes, there is a significant proportion of deviants in both groups who do not vote according to their (hypothetical) class interests.

Bonham's analysis[30] of the motivation behind voting behaviour is interesting because he tried to unravel the various components of the class situation and estimate their relative effects on political attitudes. The first such component he takes is income, which he correlates with Conservative and Labour votes: as income falls, so the Conservative vote declines, and vice versa. Butler's short survey of the floating voter[31] substantiated this broad generalization, and also showed that house and car ownership are correlated with party preference in the expected pattern. Secondly, Bonham examined the classical Marxian dichotomy: the distinction between employers and employees or, in Marxian terminology, between bourgeoisie and proletariat. Among business proprietors, the Conservative vote tends to be maintained whatever the income. In Butler's survey, a Northampton plumber said, "Perhaps I vote Conservative because I'm self-employed", and a Newcastle publican's wife said, "We used to vote Labour, but we look at things differently now that we have our own business." Among employees, on the other hand, the Labour vote tends to rise sharply as income falls.

Thirdly, the contrast between manual and non-manual occupations displayed the fact that, even in the lower income groups, non-manual employees largely vote Conservative, while manual workers typically support Labour. A general shift from manual to non-manual occupations, characteristic of current economic changes, might be expected to favour the Conservatives, and it was widely expected that with its third successive electoral defeat in 1959, the Labour Party had entered a period of continuous decline because of its excessive reliance on support from blue-collared workers.[32] Perhaps fortunately for the survival of

---

[30] Bonham, J., *The Middle Class Vote*, Faber & Faber, 1954.

[31] Butler, D., "The floating voter", *Sunday Times*, 17 March 1963.

[32] See Crosland, C. A. R., *Can Labour Win?*, Fabian Society, 1960; Abrams, M., "Why Labour has lost elections", three-part study in *Socialist Commentary*, 1960; Abrams, M., and Rose, R., *Must Labour Lose?*, Penguin Books, 1961. According to Butler, D., and Rose, R. (*The British General Election of 1959*, Macmillan, 1960), "The swing to the

the pendulum theory of politics, the more naive *embourgeoisement* theories were exploded by the work of Goldthorpe and his associates,[33] and the Labour Party eventually secured power in 1964. Certainly Bonham concluded that proprietorship seemed to be the most important single factor influencing the Conservative vote; the others, such as industrial status, intellectual status and economic status, were merely reinforcing elements.

Blondel[34] has listed the various factors influencing voting behaviour from a slightly different perspective, stressing the social pressures which produce one pattern rather than another. Among the demographic elements in the situation, women are more right-wing than men, though the tendency is not sufficiently marked for universal suffrage to produce a permanent Conservative government. Older people also tend to be more right-wing. The reasons for these tendencies are very hypothetical: it may be that women are more isolated from a working environment and therefore less prone to develop militantly radical opinions,[35] and that increasing age causes a decline in idealism. Religion is of some significance in that Non-conformists and Roman Catholics show a slight tendency to be less Conservative than members of the Church of England,[36] but again the association may be based more genuinely on occupational differences since the Church of England is predominantly a middle-class group, and manual workers (frequently Irish immigrants) are heavily over-represented among Roman Catholics.

[33] See Goldthorpe, J. H., Lockwood, D., Bechhofer, F. and Platt, J., *The Affluent Worker: Political Attitudes and Behaviour*, Cambridge University Press, 1968.

[34] Blondel, J., *Voters, Parties, and Leaders*, Penguin Books, 1963.

[35] Even those women who do go out to work are more likely to be employed in offices where conditions are cleaner and generally more pleasant than in factory surroundings.

[36] The association between religion and voting was very marked in Glossop, but the authors of the Glossop survey stress that there were local reasons for the persistence of this religious influence. Equally, religion plays a much greater part in voting behaviour in Wales and Northern Ireland than in other parts of Britain. See Birch, A. H., *Small-Town Politics*, Oxford University Press, 1959.

Conservatives (culminating in their 1959 election victory) cannot be dismissed as an ephemeral veering of the electoral breeze". It could be traced ultimately to the chief social change of the 1950s, namely, "the gradual erosion of traditional working-class attitudes".

The political opinions of the individual voter's family, friends and associates have a more powerful influence on how people vote than any other single factor. One way in which this can be illustrated is by reference to the disintegration of party loyalties among those aged 65 or more, occurring partly because of slackening pressure from working and family relationships. The Greenwich study[37] went into this in more detail and found a definite pattern. Those whose voting intention was the same as that of the majority of their family or work group (conformists) were more likely actually to vote (rather than abstain) for that party. Those who differed from the group (deviants) were more likely to display erratic patterns of voting by changing their loyalties from one party to another, or to abstain altogether. Blondel, speaking about abstainers, says: "They are usually the most ill-informed of the electors. They are often found to have no opinion on current political issues. These perpetual and occasional abstainers are more likely to be found among women, among very young and very old, among poorer people."[38] The floating voter is much more difficult to isolate in that he is scattered randomly throughout the electorate as a whole. One of the Bristol studies[39] found that changers appeared to differ in no marked way from the rest of the electors except that the higher a person's social class, the higher the chance of his having changed his vote at some time. As Butler and Stokes[40] show, those experiencing upward or downward mobility undergo an intergenerational effect as the pull of parental partisanship works against the class basis of alignment. As far as *subjective* social class is concerned, change is relatively more frequent among the group perceiving themselves as "lower middle class".

Regional differences within the United Kingdom show that even within each social class there are significant variations in voting behaviour. The south of England is more Conservative compared with

[37] Benney, M., Gray, A. P. and Pear, R. H., *op. cit.*
[38] Blondel, J., *op. cit.*
[39] Milne, R. S. and Mackenzie, H. C., *op. cit.* Figures produced in a study of two Leeds constituencies showed that women, if disillusioned with their traditional political loyalties, tended to abstain rather than switch to some other party. See Trenaman, J. and McQuail, D., *Television and the Political Image*, Methuen, 1961.
[40] Butler, D. and Stokes, D., *op. cit.*

Wales, the north, and the north-east. In Wales, Labour generally receives almost a quarter of the middle-class vote, instead of about a sixth over the whole country, and almost three-fifths of the lower middle-class and working-class vote compared with about two-fifths over the whole country. Much of this may be attributable to the fact that "People tend to conform to the predominant influence of the area in which they live."[41]

A recent study of political behaviour in part of rural Wales has demonstrated with remarkable clarity the dangers of drawing conclusions about, say, British political homogeneity from "typical" constituencies—English, urban, moderately industrial, with a stable two-party environment.[42] In Cardiganshire there were found to be four political parties, each with substantial electoral support. The class structure was just as diverse, and there was a long list of ideologies and institutions which do not figure in most parts of the United Kingdom, such as Temperance Nonconformity, *English* immigration, the Welsh Language Society, Pacifism, Welsh Nationalism, Sabbatarianism, Plaid Cymru, and so forth. Class differences were certainly present, but they were not dominant in the context of rural Wales, and class identification was very low. Only a fifth of respondents considered themselves to be members of a social class. Even objectively the Cardiganshire farmers did not fit into any class structure, and had to be classified as a separate group. They were consistently the most non-radical group, strongly Welsh (but not nationalist), and forming the backbone of Liberal and Conservative support. Generally, however, feelings of Welsh identity were negatively correlated with Conservative voting. Labour was the working-class party in terms of support, but as in other parts of Wales, there was a relatively large Labour-voting middle-class element. Over a third of the top two classes voted Labour, well ahead of the Conservatives and other parties. Plaid Cymru supporters were too few to dominate any particular class, but they were disproportionately stronger in the lower middle and lower working classes. But Madgwick rejects any explanation of Plaid Cymru support in terms of alienation from the political system: far from being vague, negative,

[41] Blondel, J., *op. cit.*
[42] Madgwick, P. J., Griffiths, N. and Walker, V., *The Politics of Rural Wales: A Study of Cardiganshire*, Hutchinson, 1973.

destructive and anomic, Plaid Cymru voters had a relatively high level of confidence in the political system, and appeared to be much more politically aware and active than supporters of the other parties. Although Butler and Stokes claim that "a child is very likely indeed to share his parents' party preference", this was not found to apply in Cardiganshire.

It has been shown in Sweden, the United States and France that the more an area is inhabited by manual workers, the greater is the proportion of those manual workers who vote for a left-wing party. Conversely, movement to.new towns produces a dilution of traditional Labour support, and in middle-class districts like Woodford, manual workers are less likely to vote Labour. Yet evaluation of these environmental influences is complicated by another type of background factor concerned with employment. Generally speaking, it is probable that workers in large plants are more likely to vote Labour than workers in small plants—perhaps because the traditions of collectivism and group conformity are greater in the former. Stacey's first study of Banbury[43] indicated that manual workers employed in "traditional" firms were markedly more Conservative than manual workers employed in "non-traditional" firms. Trade union membership is highly correlated with support for Labour: surveys have shown that manual workers who are members of trade unions are three or four times more likely to vote Labour; manual workers who are not trade unionists are much more evenly divided. Blondel[44] summarizes the position as follows:

> The solid core of the Conservative vote is based on occupations (with reference to income and education as well). The solid core of the Labour vote is based on the membership of a voluntary association, the trade union. Admittedly, in many cases, the membership of the trade union is not really voluntary: pressure is brought to bear on workers in many factories, and family upbringing also plays its part. . . . The distinction between Labour and Conservative voters is largely one of occupation, of status, of income, when one comes to distinguish between manual and non-manual workers, between lower middle-class and solid middle-class people; it is largely based on the membership of an organization within the manual working class.

[43] Stacey, M., *Tradition and Change: A Study of Banbury*, Oxford University Press, 1960.
[44] Blondel, J., *op. cit.*

As we have already noted, the class basis of British politics is somewhat undermined by a large measure of cross-class voting. Since the third Reform Act of 1884, the working class has held preponderant political power in Britain. At that time manual workers—skilled and unskilled—made up more than three-quarters of the population, and they still comprise almost two-thirds today. Yet the Conservative party has ruled, alone or in coalition, for three-quarters of the period since 1886. This is because one-third of the working-class population consistently votes Conservative and provides that party with nearly half its electoral strength. The reasons for their political behaviour and attitudes have been the subject of two major studies.[45]

Both surveys examined party images and stereotypes held by manual workers voting Conservative. In Nordlinger's enquiry, fully half of the Conservative supporters indicated that their party is *particularly* concerned with the workers' interests, a surprising result in view of the fact that Conservative Party propangada has consistently emphasized its classlessness and its national concern for what Disraeli called "the condition of the people". Nordlinger also found that 45 per cent of his respondents did not believe that a Labour Government would be especially attuned to the wishes of manual workers, despite Labour's unmistakable appeal to the manual workers themselves. The explanation for this paradox lay in the assumed untrustworthiness of Labour politicians, who were described as incapable of keeping their promises ("it's all talk to get into power") or simply self-seeking ("they are too much for themselves"). McKenzie and Silver's sample of Conservative working-class voters, by contrast, were prepared to admit that Labour ranked higher than the Conservatives in terms of "Concern for the interests of the common man." Yet in more general terms, Labour was often seen as more solicitous than efficacious, while the Conservatives were widely seen as more efficacious than solicitous. In short, Conservatives were believed to have a capacity to get things done—a superior executive ability—which offset their lesser concern with the class interests of manual workers.

McKenzie and Silver identified two major types of working-class

[45] McKenzie, R. T. and Silver, A., "The working-class Tories", *Observer*, 6 September 1964; Nordlinger, E. A., "The working-class Tory", *New Society*, 13 October 1966.

Conservative voter. Firstly, there were those whose reasons for support-
ing the Conservative Party reflected a belief in the *intrinsic* superiority
of the party and its leaders. About 30 per cent of the sample[46] fell into
this "deferential" category, which did not necessarily imply self-
abnegation but rather the abdication of any right to pragmatic evaluation and criticism of the Conservative Party. A second group fell into
the "secular" category in that they based their support for the Conservatives, not upon any *a priori* assumptions about their innate superiority, but upon an empirical assessment of their policies and record in
office. For example, one respondent said, "They have done a better job
of running the country than Labour did after the war." Forty per cent
of the sample subscribed to these attitudes, while the final 30 per cent
gave *both* secular and deferential reasons for their support. Comparison
of the social characteristics of the deferential and secular types showed,
among other things, that the deferentials tended to have lower incomes
and to include a much larger proportion of women. This raises the distinct possibility that deference may prove to be of declining importance
in accounting for working-class support for the Conservative Party, and
the party may have to rely more on a proven display of competence in
order to justify its support among its increasingly secular adherents.
Butler and Stokes[47] see the persistent support of the Conservative Party
in the working class as the result of vestiges of an earlier basis of political
alignment before the Labour Party was fully on the political map. When
the process has fully worked itself out—those born before the Labour
Party acquired the status of a major party having died, and the effects
of parental influence having been dissipated—not only is the deferential vote in Conservative support likely to be of negligible significance,
but also the Labour Party is probably not going to be able to rely
firmly on its working-class adherents. In other words, Butler and Stokes
predict a much more volatile electorate—though, of course, this
prediction is dependent on a continuation of the decay in the class basis
of voting behaviour which was observable between 1963 and 1970.[48]

[46] The interviews were conducted in January 1963 among 35 marginal constituencies.
Needless to say, care has to be taken in drawing general conclusions from a limited
sample taken at a particular point in time.

[47] Butler, D. and Stokes, D., *op. cit.*

[48] One of the criteria used in identifying deference and secularism in McKenzie and
Silver's work was the response to the question: "Which of the following men would

Nordlinger demonstrates that the relationship between income and voting behaviour is rather more complex than a straightforward correlation between increasing prosperity and Conservative support would suggest. Indeed, since this connection is based upon a crude economic determinism, it is scarcely surprising that the hypothesis turns out to be invalid. Results among Nordlinger's sample showed that it is only after income has been related to personal economic expectations, resulting in economic satisfaction or dissatisfaction, that income helps to structure voting behaviour. The crucial variable is therefore economic satisfaction—and the reference group chosen by the individual—rather than income alone, a finding which, incidentally, endorses the refutation of the *embourgeoisement* thesis. Nordlinger also found that middle-class identification was conducive to Conservative voting: among his sample, 29 per cent of the working-class identifiers voted Conservative compared with 53 per cent of the middle-class identifiers. However, it was clear that middle-class identification was not a product of subjective status aspirations in the sense that Conservative voting could be seen as an assertion of middle-class respectability, as has been argued by other researchers. Nordlinger points to the peer-group pressures towards working-class conformity, the "staff" and "works" distinctions in the working environment, and the high acceptance barriers erected by the middle class, as forces making it unlikely that manual workers would persist for long in their strivings for middle-class status. If the middle-class identifiers were actually status-aspiring, one would expect

---

make the better Prime Minister (and why)?" Mr. A. was described as "the son of a banker who had been a Member of Parliament, attended Eton and Oxford, was a former officer in the Guards, entered the House of Commons and became the leader of his party". Mr. B was described as "the son of a lorry driver; educated at a grammar school and at Bristol University, joined the Army as a private and rose to the rank of captain, entered the House of Commons and became leader of his party". Half of the Conservative and one-fifth of Labour voters in the enlarged sample of just over 600 working-class voters preferred the Prime Minister of elite social origin. Deferential responses frequently emphasized that Mr. A was "born to rule" and that he "had breeding"; secular preferences for Mr. B tended to be in this vein: "He has struggled in life. He knows more about the working troubles of the ordinary person. Those who inherit money rarely know anything about real life. This man has proved he is clever and can achieve something without any help from others." It would be interesting, in view of the hypothesis advanced by Butler and Stokes, to analyse current responses to the same question.

them to hold typically middle-class attitudes more frequently than the working-class identifiers, but in practice Nordlinger found very few differences. For instance, one attribute of a middle-class style of life is a respect for education, as we have already seen. But when asked if they would have like to have stayed on at school longer than they actually did, the middle-class identifiers answered "yes" only slightly more often than those who thought of themselves as working class.

Some doubt is also cast on the general validity of Stacey's observation, from her early research in Banbury,[49] that employees in "traditional" enterprises are more prone to vote Conservative. Within Nordlinger's sample, the frequency of Conservative voting among workers having contacts with the head of their firm was no higher than among workers without these personal relationships. Moreover, the existence of personal relationships did not seem to be correlated with deferential attitudes. The significance of these findings is further heightened when they are related to plant size. Normally it would be expected that personal employer–employee relations in small firms (up to 300 employees) and medium (301 to 1000 employees) enterprises would be far more meaningful than in large plants. In practice, in the small and medium firms the workers coming into personal contact with the head or owner actually voted Conservative *less* frequently than did workers not having personal employer contacts in similarly sized plants.

By now it should be apparent that there is a considerable amount of information on British voting behaviour and political institutions. Unfortunately this information cannot usefully be employed for predictive purposes; in fact, it strongly underlines the argument that voting behaviour is the extremely complex result of a great number of interrelated and interacting factors. Although voting studies can discover certain trends and probabilities—each one of these trends is just a small component of the total complex of influences on voting behaviour. The situation is further complicated by the dynamic nature of the environment in which voting occurs (and where political attitudes are sustained). A recently-published second study of Banbury,[50] for example, shows that since 1960 the population increased from 19,000 to 25,000,

[49] Stacey, M., *op. cit.*
[50] Stacey, M., Batstone, E., Bell, C. and Murcott, A., *Power, Persistence, and Change: A Second Study of Banbury*, Routledge & Kegan Paul, 1975.

with a further planned increase to 40,000. New housing estates had been built, and new industries and migrant workers had moved in. During this process, Banbury became less middle class, though social cleavages as a whole had become less sharp. Social divisions based on religion, political party and social class were much less clearly superimposed upon one another; no clear-cut views of "class" and "status" were shared by the residents. The decline of the Liberal Party had meant that the Labour Party, now a contender for power in the local council, had become more integrated into the social and political structure.

Yet the Banbury research also illustrates that, in focussing on political attitudes and voting behaviour, a misleading impression of the focal points of power can be created. The rise of the Labour Party had theoretically created more opportunities for the representation of manual workers in the power structure. Yet the analysis of decision-making on the proposal to expand the town of Banbury to a projected 70,000 population indicates very well how power remains concentrated. Involved in the decision-making were the political parties and business groups. But few manual workers even attended a public meeting. Even those whose homes would have been demolished under the expansion scheme paid no attention to the issue: to them it was something remote and unreal. The actual loci of power, then, remain an unresolved issue in the field of political sociology. Dahl's conception of power—in his study of New Haven, Connecticut[51]—had been criticized as narrowly "one-dimensional" because it was confined to the visible manifestations only, in particular the actions of individuals in decision-making over public issues on which there was observable conflict. But, according to Bachrach and Baratz,[52] it neglected the other, hidden side of power involved in "non-decision making": the agenda-setting capacity to suppress or deflect potential issues from entering the political arena in the first place; the power to produce a "false consensus" by shaping people's beliefs and preferences even against their best interests; and the more subtle, unconscious domination exercised by those whose existing reputation for power induces a fatalistic compliance among others (the power of "anticipated reactions"). Thus, what may appear

[51] Dahl, R. A., *Who Governs?*, Yale University Press, 1961.
[52] Bachrach, P. and Baratz, M. S., "Two faces of power", *American Political Science Review*, Vol. 56, 1962, pp. 947–52.

to be high levels of consensus and satisfaction in a community are not necessarily incompatible with the existence of powerful elites selfishly serving their own interests at the expense of the majority. In developing this approach, Lukes[53] quotes from a study of pollution as a political issue in communities in the United States. This study showed that the emergence and resolution of the issue tended to be longest delayed in company towns, not because the dominant corporation actively intervened but as a result of its silence and inactivity, and in particular its reputation for decisive power and the operation of anticipated reactions. Unfortunately it remains very difficult to establish empirically the precise political significance of "non-decision making" and even to establish how reputations for such latent power are developed—perhaps by previous explicit exercises of power to a substantial public or alternatively because, by extension, any given corporation is automatically assumed to possess the same degree of power which has been demonstrated by other corporations in similar circumstances (in other words, the designation of power through "non-decision making" is dependent on the operation of stereotypes).

Some years ago, Butler[54] remarked that "ideas about the activity of pressure groups, the structure of parties, and the nature of elections, are radically different from those of a generation ago, simply because of the hard labour of scholars who have sought to describe and explain them". After all the elaborate and expensive sampling, the compilation and analysis of statistics, it emerges that, for the liberal democracies as a whole, the social characteristic that a party's supporters are most likely to have in common is, not social class, but religion (Catholicism or Protestantism) or its rejection (clericalism against anti-clericalism). In Canada, the United States and Ireland, social class bears almost no relationship to party preference; in Germany, Italy and the Netherlands it takes second place to religion, and in Belgium, to language. Even in Britain there are signs that social class is only significant for lack of any competing social cleavage: where religious, racial or cultural/linguistic divisions occur, the importance of class diminishes markedly.[55]

[53] Lukes, S., *Power: A Radical View*, Macmillan, 1975.
[54] Butler, D., *The Study of Political Behaviour*, Hutchinson, 1958.
[55] Rose, R., ed., *Electoral Behaviour: A Cumulative Handbook*, Collier-Macmillan, 1974.

Crime and the Penal System

We have seen already that social conformity is induced through a complex pattern of rewards and punishment. The criminal law deals exclusively in the administration of punishment for activities which are perceived to be a threat to the maintenance of social order, and in this section we shall be concerned with such problems as the definition of crime, the causes of criminal behaviour and the aims of a penal system.

It seems reasonable to accept that crime is a concept which, at least in large measure, is culturally determined. Presumably all human actions could be placed on an imaginary continuum from the most sinful to the most saintly. At one extreme of such a scale would be actions which even a society of criminals (as currently defined) would regard as unacceptable, such as sexual attacks on children, but the majority of human behaviour would be classified somewhere in the middle of the scale as neither particularly sinful or criminal, nor as particularly saintly or beneficial to society. Some actions could be seen as marginal, in ethical terms. The cut-off point for criminal behaviour may be changed from time to time, either by some specific enactment or by custom allowing statutes to lapse or by different interpretations of the language of statutes themselves.

Many people who work in offices, for example, regard it as normal practice to use the office telephone occasionally for private purposes or to divert official stationery to their own use, and such perception "legitimizes" these illegal acts in the eyes of the members of a particular culture where such actions are the rule rather than the exception.

> But behaviour "legitimized" in the "paper-using cultures" relates to paper, and the same paper-using culture would regard exactly similar behaviour on the part of those who worked with metals as illegitimate. This and all similar distinctions are not made by the law, they are cultural distinctions. Within the metal-using cultures, attitudes similar to those of the paper-using culture towards paper are, not unexpectedly, applied to metal, despite prosecutions from time to time.[56]

Over a quarter of a century ago, Sutherland[57] caused something of a stir by producing evidence to show that persons of the upper socio-economic classes commit many crimes, and while his facts were from

[56] Wilkins, L. T., "What is crime?" *New Society*, 18 July 1963, pp. 15–16.
[57] Sutherland, E., *White-Collar Crime*, Holt, Rinehart & Winston, 1949.

the United States, it is likely that the evidence for Britain would not be very different. Many of these "criminals" had violated laws on behalf of their employers, simply because they were executives carrying on a certain business activity for the purpose of profits, found themselves impeded by a specific law and so broke that law. Typical violations in Sutherland's study included restraint of trade, misrepresentation in advertising, infringement of patents, copyrights, and so on. Caught out in such practices, the executives typically did not suffer ostracism from the business community but were comforted by phrases from the general ideology like "business is business". Indeed, sharp practice on behalf of a company may actually enhance a businessman's career: such offenders rarely have difficulty in finding a job (or, more exactly, rarely lose their job) when their improper activities come to light. A different sort of reaction, however, is evoked by the individual performance of "ordinary" crime in a paper-using culture, like embezzlement. As Sutherland stresses, "the ordinary case of embezzlement is a crime by a single individual in a subordinate position against a strong corporation. It is, therefore, one of the most foolish of white-collar crimes", though not all offenders have their offences publicized or suffer the stigma of a criminal conviction for their "foolishness". As Martin[58] has found, wherever possible companies neither prosecute nor call the police, but deal with the matter themselves. As a consequence of these various practices, the statistics invariably understate the incidence of white-collar crime, but by precisely how much it is impossible, for obvious reasons, to say.

Such viewpoints merely reinforce the need to reiterate the earlier argument that, contrary to Merton's assumption of common norms and values, society contains a "plurality" of norms and values, differentiated on class, ethnic, religious, occupational and other grounds. This being so, what is considered "right" and "legitimate" is bound to vary from group to group. Crime is not an absolute but rather a relative definition of behaviour, and crime exists only when a society has defined certain actions as criminal. Crime cannot be considered independently of social structures and while it can be argued that a series of constant concepts of crime can be observed in all societies—respect for property,

[58] Martin, J. P., *Offenders as Employers*, Macmillan, 1962.

life, sexual rights, and so forth—there can be no crime until an act has been the subject of social evaluation. As Morris has written, "the criminal law, far from being a mere repository of immutable social values, is increasingly a set of rules governing contingent situations that change as the needs of society change. The history of the criminal law over the past century is a history of continuous adaptation".[59]

Illustrative of this process is the development of the law regarding rape. In 1976, 1100 rape cases were reported to the police in England and Wales, compared with 422 in 1963. On the other hand, the incidence of rape (at least in terms of reported cases) had not increased at the same rate as the rest of violent crime which, between 1969 and 1973, rose by three-fifths to about 33,000 cases a year. In the same period, rape cases rose by about a tenth to almost a thousand. It is likely, however, that recent changes in the law may lead to an apparent acceleration in the number of rapes. Until 1976, the law was governed by a traditional common-law definition of rape as unlawful sexual intercourse with a woman without her consent, by force, fear or fraud. With the Sexual Offences (Amendment) Act emerged a new definition: a man commits rape if he has sexual intercourse with a woman who at the time did not consent to it and he knew that she did not consent, or was reckless as to whether she consented or not. This change of emphasis—towards lack of consent rather than violence—has been accompanied by a right of anonymity for victims of rape and defendants (until found guilty). The Act also protects women from intensive and painful interrogations on their sexual history, except at a judge's discretion; this practice was often used by the defence to cast doubt on a woman's moral rectitude, and hence, so the argument ran, on the likelihood that she had been raped. If such reforms do lead to more reporting of rape cases, it would clearly be a mistake to interpret rising figures, by themselves, as evidence of any specific increase in rape offences.

The process of adaptation in the criminal law is exemplified by the more general trends in crime statistics. In the nineteenth century, committals for crimes involving assault and drunkenness declined in times of depression and increased in times of prosperity, whereas committals for offences against property "increased in depression and diminished

[59] Morris, T., "The sociology of crime", *New Society*, 29 April 1965, pp. 7–10.

with prosperity". By the 1880s, this contrast was weakening as patterns of crime began to approximate to the twentieth-century position in which property offences increase in times of affluence and diminish in times of depression. In the latter part of the century, too, criminal activity steadily declined, owing to the twin pressures of improved policing and reduced poverty. By 1890, the proportion of indictable offences known to the police was much lower than it is today. Furthermore, by that time the prison population was ageing, and was becoming increasingly distinct from the community at large because of its relatively poor education and relatively frequent previous convictions. Thus "proportionately more offenders later in the century came from a hardened and perhaps an experienced criminal class than was the case in earlier decades".[60]

In Britain there has been a virtually uninterrupted increase in reported (as distinct from committed) crimes since 1926, disturbed only for a decade after the end of World War II. In 1966, Avison[61] reported that

It has taken 20 years for the number of persons proceeded against for non-indictable (i.e. lesser) offences to double; but it has taken only 8 years for the indictable crimes reported to the police to double. . . . These indictable crimes are generally regarded as the more serious; they include the graver offences of violence against persons, sexual offences and offences against property. Recently, however, some non-indictable offences akin to indictable crime—like taking and driving away motor vehicles, and malicious damage of a not very costly kind—have apparently been increasing at more than the rate of indictable crime.

The Chief Inspector of Constabulary noted in 1965[62] that the rate of increase in indictable crime had fallen slightly to 6.2 per cent, and subsequent figures showed further marginal reductions to 6.1 per cent in 1969 and 5.8 per cent in 1970.[63] But for the first time since the Home Office began to record criminal statistics, the number of indictable crimes reported to the police in England and Wales exceeded 2 million in 1975. That figure represented an increase of 7 per cent over the

[60] Wrigley, E. A., ed., *Nineteenth Century Society*, Cambridge University Press, 1972.

[61] Avison, N. H., "The new pattern of crime", *New Society*, 8 September 1966, pp. 358–60.

[62] Her Majesty's Chief Inspector of Constabulary, *Report for 1965*, H.M.S.O., 1966. This report deals with all police forces in England and Wales, with the exception of the Metropolitan Police which covers Greater London.

[63] Her Majesty's Chief Inspector of Constabulary, *Report for 1970*, H.M.S.O., 1971.

previous year, but when this was followed by a rise of only 1 per cent in 1976, it generated hopes that the incidence of crime had reached a plateau. Such hopes were shattered when it became clear that, in the first quarter of 1977, the figures were up by a tenth over the same period in 1976; for the second quarter of 1977 the increase had accelerated to 12 per cent compared with April to June, 1976.

Such increases cannot be correlated with changes in population. There were 250 crimes per 100,000 of the population at the beginning of this century and 2374 per 100,000 in 1965. If the rate of crime prevailing before World War I had continued, there should be no more than about 200,000 indictable crimes a year; in fact there were 2,105,631 recorded instances in 1975. Yet within these broad figures there have been significant changes of emphasis. Offences connected with larceny of and from motor vehicles are only of significance from 1930 onwards, but now exceed 200,000 a year. Study of crimes of violence shows that the increasing incidence of such crimes is largely confined to malicious woundings and not to the more serious felonious woundings, a direct consequence of changes in police methods of recording crime which in turn derives, at least in part, from decreased public tolerance of crimes of violence. Since more of the non-indictable type of offences are being recorded as indictable malicious woundings, this should be paralleled by a fall in the numbers of persons proceeded against for non-indictable assaults; indeed, figures from the Metropolitan area support this. At the same time nothing can conceal the marked increase in crimes of violence and vandalism. In 1975, the number of cases of violence against the person rose by 11 per cent and criminal damage by 17 per cent; it was noted that criminals were increasingly resorting to violence when committing "traditional crimes" like burglary.[64]

Other trends include a reversal of the tendency for burglary and robbery to be less popular. Whereas burglary showed a 1 per cent drop in April to June 1976 compared with the same period the previous year,

[64] Her Majesty's Chief Inspector of Constabulary, *Report for 1975*, H.M.S.O., 1976. See also, *Criminal Statistics, England and Wales*, Comnd. 6566, H.M.S.O., 1976. It might appear from the homicide figures —which include murder, manslaughter and infanticide —that there had been a slight drop in extreme forms of violence. In 1975 there were 515 violent deaths in that category, compared with 600 in the previous year. But there were 499 cases of *attempted* murder, an increase of 128.

in 1977 the equivalent second quarter showed a 15 per cent increase. Something similar happened to robbery figures over the same period: a 6 per cent drop followed by an 11 per cent increase. The general rise in crimes of dishonesty was reflected in a 13 per cent increase (for April to June 1977) in theft and handling stolen goods, reported cases of which rose by only 2 per cent in the same period of 1976. That these are not merely ephemeral movements is indicated by the 1975 figures, which indicated a 31 per cent rise in robberies over 1974, an 8 per cent increase in burglary, and a 7 per cent increase in theft and handling stolen goods. In numerical terms, burglary accounted for more than 500,000 cases. Theft and handling stolen goods, including shop-lifting, totalled 1,267,674 cases.

One noticeable feature of the statistics about criminals is the increasing proportion of women. In 1965, 31,011 women appeared in court for indictable crime; 10 years later, 86,304 women were in court charged with serious criminal offences. The incidence of vicious crime perpetrated by girls up to the age of 17 has risen sharply. In 1965 they numbered 86 for the whole year in England and Wales; in 1975 that total had jumped to 555. Such figures have to be interpreted against a context in which, for 1975, a total of 402,500 people were found guilty of indictable crime, and where the total number of crimes solved (excluding the Metropolitan Police district) was 49 per cent. The number of reported sexual offences has tended to fall—they were down by 4 per cent in 1975 compared with 1974—but possibly, given a more permissive moral climate, this reflects an increased toleration of minor assaults which might earlier have been notified to the police.

Drug addiction itself is not criminal, but unregistered addicts, and people taking marijuana or drugs of the amphetamine class, are thought to commit crimes to acquire money for the purchase of their drugs. Proceedings under the Dangerous Drugs Act, 1951, numbered 614 in 1964, and have since risen considerably. As the Chief Inspector of Constabulary commented in 1970:

> Over the past 5 or 6 years prosecutions for few offences have increased more rapidly than those involving drugs. In 1965 there were only 834 prosecutions, whereas in 1970 there were 9897. While this increase reflects the spreading of the drug habit, part of it is attributable to police expertise and activity, including the comparatively recent introduction in most forces of specialist drug squads.

Unfortunately nothing very precise is known about the proportion of drug-taking which remains unknown to the police, though there is reason to suspect that it is limited to metropolitan centres and occurs among young people who have left home and are to some extent living relatively disorganized lives on the fringe of the urban underworld. Indeed the so-called iceberg effect—the extent of unreported crime—applies to many other types of illegal activity. There is often unwillingness to prosecute on the part of the victim, or the offence is considered relatively trivial. The result is that the statistics on theft, which it is in the interest of the property-owner to report, are far more reliable than the statistics on hooliganism and wanton damage. Even so, the number of criminal damage cases rose by 29 per cent between the second quarter of 1975 and the second quarter of 1976, and by a further 27 per cent in the next 12 months.

With regard to non-indictable offences, the problem in assessing the trends derives principally from the fact that published statistics do not give details of the numbers of such offences reported to and investigated by the police. Instead, the criminologist has to be satisfied with figures representing the numbers of people proceeded against, and these show that the overall picture is not one of marked increase. If traffic offences are excluded, in fact, the general trend seems to be downward. In a few cases, this fall is a reflection of legislative intervention. Betting and gaming prosecutions have dropped from an average of 12,000 persons annually in the late 1950s to a current rate of less than 2500 a year; offences by prostitutes have declined from 14,000 annually to just over 1000. Other offences show only minor changes which are sometimes difficult to understand. For example, non-indictable thefts have shown a slight decrease compared with the sharp rise in indictable thefts. Perhaps Avison's explanation for this curious phenomenon is the most accurate: "the thief today is searching for money, or goods which can easily be converted into money, and so will but rarely turn his attention to trees, shrubs or animals as objects of his crime".[65]

Another aspect of defining criminal activity accurately is the problem of establishing, from a piece of behaviour, whether or not a genuine case of deviance from societal norms has occurred. In some situations

[65] Avison, H. R., *op. cit.*

the citizen is uncertain whether he is confronted with a clear-cut case of rule violation or merely by something which "looks like" an offence but which is, in reality, a joke, a trick, which need not be taken seriously. A policeman encountering a fight between two youths must often use his judgment, based on "common sense", to determine what actually happened. If one of the combatants is a coloured youth from an urban slum background in which it is known that the stimuli for and approval of law breaking are considerable, the policeman is more likely to interpret his behaviour unfavourably than if the fighters are white boys from middle-class homes. In the latter case, it seems plausible to assume that the policeman will more readily accept their explanation that the fight was just "high spirits" and legal action is unlikely to follow. All this implies that there is a bias in law enforcement practices against the lower classes, and certainly there is some evidence to support such a belief. Russell[66] has suggested that the bias reveals itself, perhaps unconsciously, in the way complaints against the police are handled. It seems that certain complainants are "discredited" by the police and that the more they are discredited the less likely are their complaints to succeed. In fact the success rate of complainants is strongly affected by certain background characteristics in the background of the complainant, with the result that complaints from middle-class people are far more likely to be successful than those by the working class.

The earliest research into the causes of crime[67] established that criminal activity is not randomly distributed throughout society, but is concentrated in particular geographical areas and among some sections of society more than others. Some observers saw crime as a rational response to social conditions, and this has found particular expression

[66] Russell, K., "Police v. public: the rules change", *Sunday Times*, 21 March 1976. Russell was permitted access to the complaints files of two English police forces; in addition he interviewed more than 200 police officers and questioned a random sample of more than 500 members of the public on their relationships with the police.

[67] Such empirical research should be distinguished from the construction of typological theories of criminal behaviour based upon, say, anthropological deviance, mental subnormality, emotional disturbance or constitutional inferiority. Such theories suffer from the fact that these phenomena can equally be found among non-criminals. Given that crime is not an objective variable but rather a special form of anti-social behaviour relative to society at a given moment in time, it can hardly be isolated by reference to bodily forms, shapes of heads, or neurotic traits.

in the hypothesis of a connection between poverty and criminal behaviour. The difficulty with this approach, however, is that not all criminals are poor (though poverty may be associated with certain kinds of crime), and as the proportion of offenders in poverty declines, the hypothesis declines in its explanatory usefulness. There are other objections on methodological grounds. As we have seen already in the chapter on social class, poverty is a relative concept, and it might therefore be more useful to correlate crime with subjective feelings of poverty, which would themselves be dependent on the reference points chosen by the individual. Unemployment, too, may be more meaningful than poverty or absolute income levels. In England and Wales since World War II, adult crime rates have continued to rise—and juvenile delinquency rates have increased even faster—during a period of full employment. It hardly seems possible to explain the enormous incidence of property offences—larceny and breaking and entering—among juveniles aged between 14 and 20 by reference to poverty, particularly in view of the published evidence of spending power and economic independence among teenagers; on the other hand, high levels of prolonged unemployment, especially for school-leavers, are closely associated with relative poverty and also leave the individual with adequate free time to undertake criminal acts. Yet this would not explain those crimes which have no immediate economic significance at all, like violence against the person or sex offences.

Another possibility is that criminal tendencies are learned as part of a process of cultural transmission.[68] Sutherland's theory of differential association, for example, argues that people become criminals because of exposure to criminal behaviour patterns and relative isolation from non-criminal patterns. People therefore behave in the manner to which they have grown accustomed by their social milieu; in the urban slums it is commonplace for children to be aware, at first hand, of the realities of crime. As Morris puts it, "The juvenile court is likely to be as real as the welfare clinic, and they will know of brothers who have been 'put away' in detention centres and approved schools, as well as fathers who have 'done bird'. They will have as much precocious knowledge of the

---

[68] One weakness of this approach is that it cannot explain the reasons for the initial existence of criminal tendencies other than by acceptance, in some form or other, of the poverty hypothesis.

criminal behaviour of their elders as they do of their sexual behaviour."[69] But it has to be remembered that such slum environments are a comparative rarity in the national picture, and therefore such explanations of criminality can only be partial.

Undoubtedly the opportunity to commit crime is a very important factor leading to criminal acts. If the majority of criminals are assumed to be fairly rational people (and there is little reason to suppose otherwise), then it is likely that before engaging in criminal behaviour they weigh the opportunity against the risk. Increasing affluence means greater opportunity: if society facilitates the legitimate transfer of goods it seems that simultaneously the facilities for legitimate *and* illegitimate transfer are increased. Britain's entry into the European Economic Community has generated its involvement in a completely new type of crime, illustrated by Mack's example[70] of salesmen from France, Germany, Yugoslavia and Rumania collaborating to send a large consignment of butter on a European tour by ship and train.

> While the butter was being transformed, whether in the course of nature or by fiscal fiction, to butter-fat, the butter-fat to mayonnaise, the mayonnaise to fat for industrial use (e.g. soap), the industrial fat to seasoning sauce, the series of export or import subsidies was paid for each transaction until 10,000,000 Deutschmarks compensation money was accumulated on this one consignment.

The circulation of money similarly implies a higher probability of monetary thefts (offset partially by the increased use of credit cards, though they too have sparked off various frauds); more cars means more stealing of and from cars. Indeed, from 1938 onwards there is a close correlation between the number of motor vehicles in Britain and the number of thefts from motor vehicles. Vehicle thefts in London have gone up as London streets at night have become, more and more, open-air car parks. Perhaps, too, the growth of larceny from impersonal organizations like chain stores, British Rail and supermarkets could be interpreted, not only in terms of the increasing impersonalization of social relationships, but also in terms of available opportunities for theft and damage.

[69] Morris, T., *op. cit.*
[70] Mack, J., *The Crime Industry*, Saxon House, 1975.

Another element in calculating opportunity for crime is the likelihood that the crime itself will remain undetected, or the offender will not be caught. As Wootton has suggested, "So long as less than half the crimes known to the police are 'cleared up' (and clearing up does not necessarily mean that the offender is brought to justice), crime offers at least as good a chance of easy money as does membership of the Stock Exchange."[71] Sprott has expressed a similar point of view:

> Crime for the offender is more rewarding than respectability, otherwise he would be respectable. To lure him into the paths of virtue we must offer better prizes. If only we could discover how to make law-abidingness attractive to offenders, we would not send naughty boys to detention centres where the Spartan regime is hardly calculated to demonstrate the dazzling charms of being good.[72]

In practice, people who are caught can be broadly divided into two groups: those who are merely caught because they are "unlucky" but who are nevertheless representative of the uncaught or undetected criminal, and those who are, in psycho-social terms, "inept". This latter class is composed of people so inadequate they cannot even make a success of a criminal career, people who actually wish to be caught and punished, and people who are so inexperienced in crime that they are easily discovered. Walker[73] has shown how the chances of being detected rise rapidly for each criminal who persists in his criminal activity. Assuming an initial chance of one in two of avoiding detection, "the probability of his committing two thefts and remaining undetected is only one in four, and if he commits three thefts, one in eight". From these figures Walker concludes that "there can be very few persistent thieves who have not at some stage become known as such to the police". Yet it is possible to be far less sanguine about these findings. For some classes of theft in the Metropolitan Police area (Greater London) the clear-up rate is under 10 per cent. If this is applied to the criminal who persists in crime, statistically he could commit 20 crimes before his chance of escaping detection fell as low as one in eight.[74] Such figures are by no means impossible. It is highly significant to note that robberies involving sums of £100 or more have risen at a faster rate than

[71] Wootton, B., "Crime and its rewards", *New Society*, 23 September 1965, pp. 17–19.
[72] Sprott, W. J. H., *The Howard Journal*, Vol. 10, No. 4, 1961.
[73] Walker, N., *Crime and Punishment in Britain*, Edinburgh University Press, 1964.
[74] Avison, N. H., *op. cit.*

any other type of robbery, and that such crimes produce a clear-up rate of around 30 per cent. The increase in well-organized and lucrative crimes suggests the existence of a fairly small number of persistent professional criminals, caught infrequently if at all.[75]

Merton's explanation of deviant behaviour as a reaction to blocked opportunity is also relevant in any discussion of crime. Those who are denied access to the legitimate means of attaining socially desired goals may react in two ways. First, they may retreat from the effort to attain such goals. Since the goals of society, in Merton's terms, are those of material success through occupational advancement, this group turns to pop music, alcohol, drugs and other manifestations of the youth culture. A second alternative is to innovate by resorting to illegitimate means of goal attainment, and it is in this social context that the in-crease in crime—principally acquisitive crime, but also violence and vandalism—can be understood. Industrialization presupposes an en-hancement of individual motivation, towards both occupational advancement and private possession of goods, which is bound to gen-erate discontent and frustration among those who are less successful in satisfying these criteria. As Durkheim pointed out, such "failures" are likely to feel more resentment at this state of affairs than do men in a society where opportunities are fewer and the emphasis on achievement lower. Moreover, the disparity between aspiration and real opportunity may well be greater among people of working-class origin, since characteristically they have fewer opportunities for advancement and are less well informed on how to make use of the opportunities available. Not only is frustration generated by the awareness of failure in such circumstances, but Pym[76] has shown that manual workers generally feel more frustrated about their work as such, when compared with other types of employee, and are more likely to display the kind of aggressive behaviour associated with poor or inadequate socialization.

Support for these hypotheses can be derived from the fact that in the United States, where the ideology of success (whether defined in occu-pational or purely materialistic terms) is more deeply rooted than in Britain, the rate of violent and acquisitive crime is far higher than in

[75] For an analysis of the characteristics of this group, see Mack, J., *op. cit.*
[76] Pym, D., *Occupational Psychology*, Vol. 37, No. 3, 1963.

this country. According to Goldstein,[77] the homicide rate in the United States per 100,000 is 23 times that of England (and up to 70 times that of some other advanced industrialized nations); 20,000 Americans are shot to death and over 200,000 seriously wounded each year; in 1972, 34 per cent of all adult women in one New York district were the victims of serious crime. On the other hand, society's goals—even in the United States—are by no means as explicit as Merton has assumed. Others have argued that it is not so much material wealth but rather status which is the relevant factor. The working-class youth, socialized into the acceptance of status through achievement as a desirable aim by such external agencies as the educational system, is at the same time denied access to the means of achievement. As a result he develops his own internal status system among his peers,[78] which may require demonstrations of prowess in delinquent activities. This idea is attractive because it helps to explain the prevalence of vandalism and other offences which juvenile crimes are committed by members of a gang or group rather than by isolated individuals.[79] Yet the status theory does not explain why delinquency tends to peter out in adulthood. Little[80] has said that even if the chances of males below the age of 20 committing at least one indictable offence were very high, the probability that they would commit more than two such offences was very rare—no more than 1 or 2 per cent. At the same time it is important to catch these offenders early in their criminal careers, for statistics show that the more

[77] Goldstein, J. H., *Aggression and Crimes of Violence*, Oxford University Press, 1976. Of the nine million serious crimes in the United States in 1972, only 50 per cent were reported, 12 per cent led to arrest, 6 per cent to conviction and 1.5 per cent to incarceration. A Philadelphia survey indicates that of murderers found guilty, 33 per cent were sentenced to 1 year or less. Yet curiously, Goldstein rejects the leniency shown to offenders and the chances of escaping capture altogether as contributory causes of the crime rate, and favours explanations based on social learning reinforced by the effects of the mass media, alcoholism and drug addition.

[78] This phenomenon has already been discussed in the non-delinquent context of the school as a social system. See Lacey, C., *Hightown Grammar*, Manchester University Press, 1970.

[79] The annual reports of the Commissioner of Police of the Metropolis show that, of people under 21 arrested for indictable offences, about 60 per cent are operating with other persons normally within their own age-range.

[80] At a meeting of the British Sociological Association on juvenile delinquency reported in *New Society*, 20 May 1965.

crimes the offender can commit before being caught, the more likely he is to revert to his criminal behaviour.

Delinquent behaviour may have been facilitated by the growing impersonality of society and its institutions, to which reference has already been made. In a speculative article on this theme, Wilson[81] argues that "social policy itself has promoted the decline of the locality as a significant social phenomenon: the centralization of schools, the creation of large housing estates, the promotion of social mobility have all weakened community allegiances". Schools have become larger and more impersonal; teaching more instrumental and less concerned with imparting moral values; teacher mobility has increased. The consequence is a breakdown of the nexus between school and home,[82] with conflict provoked by the clash between parental and educational values in the socialization process. Associated with these trends towards impersonality is the growing institutionalism of modern society, expressed in terms of companies, public corporations, schools, universities, the media of communication, and so forth. These agencies become more routinized, formalized and rationalized in their operation—in a word, they acquire the conventional features of bureaucracy. Wilson sees delinquency, in part, as a rebellion against the specialization and professionalism characteristic of bureaucratic forms. "Deviance becomes intrinsically satisfying as an evidence that one has defied the whole complex of social organization—an expression in the fight for emotional freedom and survival against the meaningless complexity of institutionalized society." Not all the activities of the youth culture are delinquent, but many of them could more appropriately be described as delinquescent, representing behavioural standards characteristic of the age level but at variance with the patterns demanded by society. The creation and maintenance of these standards has undoubtedly been assisted by the redistribution of income to younger people, and particularly to unskilled

[81] Wilson, B., "An approach to delinquency", *New Society*, 3 February 1966, pp. 8–12.

[82] This could be especially significant in the case of immigrant children. In a study of immigrant school pupils (Townsend, H. E. R., and Brittan, E. M., *Organization in Multiracial Schools*, National Foundation for Educational Research, 1972) more than 100 schools reported problems with Asian mothers, most of whom spoke little or no English. Most secondary schools reported they saw less than 1 in 10 Indian or Pakistani parents even once a year. More generally, *Britain's Sixteen-Year-Olds* (National Children's Bureau, 1976) indicated that only about 20 per cent of parents showed no interest in what their offspring did at school.

workers. As Morris comments: "High-powered motor bikes are in keeping with the aggressive masculinity that is commonplace among young males from female-dominated lower-class milieux."[83]

Having considered the range of possible causes leading to criminal behaviour, with a natural emphasis on sociological considerations, we must finally turn to the functions of a penal system in controlling and preventing such behaviour so that the accepted fabric of society is sustained. In doing so, it is worth recalling Durkheim's suggestion that crime fulfils a positive function in society: were it not for larceny and published information about arrests and convictions, the courts would not have the opportunity daily to reinforce the values that surround the institution of property.[84] Thus society's real objective is not to eliminate crime altogether—which would be an unattainable aim in practical terms—but rather to contain it within "reasonable" or "normal" proportions, such proportions being defined by society itself. One of the aims of a penal system therefore becomes that of showing society's abhorrence of crime, which is a disguised version of the extreme form of retributivism which claims that offenders should atone by suffering. Unfortunately, whole-hearted retributivism suffers from two major disadvantages. Firstly, it often involves measures—such as the pillory—which expose the offender to unofficial retaliation;[85] and secondly, it may imply the imposition of penalties which are counter-productive in that they actually increase the probability of the offence being repeated, as in the case of imprisoning homosexuals.

Whereas retributivism implies that the punishment should fit the crime—that is, the penalty imposed should match the harm done or intended—the principle of deterrence demands that the punishment should exceed the crime. There is undoubted evidence that deterrence can be effective, particularly in cases of inter-racial violence, but the

[83] Morris, T., *op. cit.*

[84] The corollary of this argument, of course, is that frequent exposure to information about deviant behaviour—not only actual cases, but also fictional incidents portrayed on television and the other media—encourages imitative crime. It seems likely that the way the crime is delineated, and the penalties of capture, are more significant influences than the mere fact of publicized crime itself.

[85] There seems to be general acceptance for Montero's view that a penal system must protect offenders and suspected offenders against unofficial retaliation. In accordance with this principle, juvenile offenders are given some anonymity to protect them against stigma. See Walker, N., *James Seth Memorial Lecture*, Edinburgh University Press, 1967.

whole question is far more complex than it may at first appear. In some instances (such as driving on the left-hand side of the road) there is sufficient consensus for deterrent penalties to be unnecessary, while in others (such as parking and minor motoring offences) it is clear that mild penalties do not deter people from committing crimes about which they feel no guilt. Yet the same mild penalties—a suspended prison sentence, a fine, probation, or even a short prison sentence[86]—will be reasonably effective in maintaining a low incidence of, say, larceny. Obviously the restraining force at work in such instances is not fear of the penalty itself, but rather social pressures or internalized inhibitors expressed through the super-ego or "conscience". It is probable that if penalties were more severe (and consistently so) they could deter more potential offenders, but this would not be a proposition susceptible to empirical study and in any case society may find extremely deterrent punishments intolerable and therefore unacceptable. As Wootton remarks, "The prospect of being boiled in oil might well be a splendid deterrent, but it is unlikely to be acceptable."[87]

The third major function of a penal system is the reform and re-habilitation of offenders. Here again the evidence of effectiveness is not clear-cut. The research suggests that persons convicted of breaking and entering are more responsive to probation, but that probation (perhaps not surprisingly) is relatively ineffective in cases of fraud. In particular instances, however, it is singularly difficult to determine whether an offender is "amenable" to reform or should be treated in some other way; and if so, what sentence to impose. In considering such issues the concept of "justice" is invariably introduced but, as Miller[88] has recently shown, the idea of justice is surrounded with apparently irreconcilable conflict and paradoxes. Justice incorporates not one but three distinct principles: to each according to his rights, to each according to his deserts, and to each according to his needs. These three principles do not harmonize easily: for example, when we assign priority

[86] There is accumulating evidence that the deterrent effect of a period of imprisonment, especially for those experiencing it for the first time, is at its height during the first few days when the impact of the transition from freedom to incarceration is naturally greatest. Diminishing returns (in terms of deterrence) set in if the sentence exceeds 7 to 10 days.

[87] Wootton, B., *op. cit.*

[88] Miller, D., *Social Justice*, Oxford University Press, 1976.

according to desert we do not act as we do when we assign priority according to need. The man who most deserves is seldom the same man who most needs.[89] Need, rights and desert are competing criteria, and if justice requires all three, then justice cannot be satisfied. Miller's socio-historical account of the development of justice, however, suggests that different types of society have emphasized different principles of justice. Feudalism saw justice mainly as the correct ascription of rights; "market" (or bourgeois) society saw justice mainly as the correct acknowledgment of deserts; while the mixed-economy or welfare-state society sees justice mainly in terms of distribution according to need, hence stressing reform rather than retributivism or deterrence. But even if it is true that some people are unresponsive to, or even made worse by, punishment it is still arguable that such people should occasionally (if not always) be punished in order to deter others (in other words, a penalty exceeding the offender's deserts would be awarded).

Thus it is extremely hard to select a punishment that will fit the crime *and* the offender. Courts deliberately try to equip themselves with information that will enable them to reach a rational decision on such matters, but it is doubtful whether relevant and irrelevant data can be separated effectively. In an American experiment[90] it was shown that the people who write case histories (probation officers in this country) and those who have to act on them do not agree on the respective value of the various items of information which they contain. Nonetheless there has been significant progress more recently towards scientific sentencing, with the growth of training for magistrates and the use of indeterminate sentences, the actual duration of which is decided by those who can make close and continuing observation of the offender concerned.

In the background of such developments is the humanitarian principle that the penal system should be such as to cause the minimum of suffering (whether to the offenders themselves or to others) in its attempts to achieve its fundamental aim of ensuring the maintenance and survival of society. This could be seen, in fact, as a somewhat diluted

[89] For example, if Nobel Prizes were given to the poorest scientists, they might never go to the most accomplished.

[90] Wilkins, L. T. and Chandler, A., "Confidence and competence in decision-making", *British Journal of Criminology*, Vol. 5, No. 1, 1965.

interpretation of Bentham's straightforward but influential view that the penal system should be designed simply to reduce the frequency of the types of behaviour prohibited by the criminal law.[91] Cohen and Taylor, for instance, have argued that prison sentences in excess of 10 years have doubtful efficacy on this score; indeed, they generate problems because of the psychological and physical deterioration[92] which takes place during that time.[93]

Apart from the more obvious measures such as imprisonment, supervision, deterrence and so forth, Bentham's approach also justifies social hygiene (such as slum clearance and integration of immigrants[94]) and reduction of the opportunities for crime by, say, encouraging the practice of paying wages by cheque and the more widespread use of credit cards. At least such strategies help the community to avoid the depressing implication that the mere existence of a penal system is an admission that more positive social controls are not entirely sufficient in themselves.

[91] Bentham, J., *An Introduction to the Principles of Morals and Legislation*, 1780.

[92] The evidence on this is disputed. Smith's findings (presented at the International Congress of Psychology in Tokyo, 1971) indicated that the I.Q.s of long-term prisoners did not deteriorate with time, nor did they become more neurotic. But they did tend to become more introvert and their reaction times slowed down (possibly a consequence of increasing age rather than imprisonment).

[93] Cohen, S. and Taylor, L., *Psychological Survival: The Experience of Long-Term Imprisonment*, Penguin Books, 1972. The authors identify five styles of coping with their long sentences: body-building or mind-building (perhaps exemplified by devouring as many as 15 books a week); campaigning by writing letters of complaint to the outside world; hunger strikes; confrontations with the prison authorities; and escapes. Choice of these modes of adaptation tended to be related to the kinds of crime committed outside; thus the escapers and the confrontationists had often been involved in "confrontational" crimes like armed robbery, and the campaigners were more likely to come from the world of organized crime and protection rackets.

[94] In a study of violent crimes committed in England and Wales between 1950 and 1960, McClintock finds that "the proportion of immigrants (from the Republic of Ireland and the Commonwealth and Colonies) who are convicted of crimes of violence is far greater than that found in the indigenous population. They were responsible for 40 per cent of the offences committed during domestic squabbles in 1960, 33 per cent of the attacks on the police, and just over 20 per cent of the public fights (which mainly involved unskilled labourers against unskilled labourers)". As McClintock concludes, "Most of the crime is not committed by criminals for criminal purposes, but is rather the outcome of patterns of social behaviour among certain strata of the community." See McClintock, F. H., *Crimes of Violence*, Macmillan, 1964.

Suggestions for Further Reading

General

CENTRAL OFFICE OF INFORMATION, *Britain: An Official Handbook*, H.M.S.O., annually.
KLEIN, J., *Samples from English Cultures*, Routledge & Kegan Paul, 1965.
SAMPSON, A., *Anatomy of Britain Today*, Hodder & Stoughton, 1965.
FRANKENBERG, E., *Communities in Britain*, Penguin Books, 1966.

Chapter 1

REX, J. and MOORE, R., *Race, Community and Conflict*, Oxford University Press, 1967.
BANTON, M., *Race Relations*, Tavistock, 1967.
McKEOWN, T., *The Modern Rise of Population*, Edward Arnold, 1976.
TRANTER, N. L., *Population Since the Industrial Revolution: The Case of England and Wales*, Croom Helm, 1974.
OFFICE OF POPULATION CENSUSES AND SURVEYS, *Population Trends*, H.M.S.O., quarterly.

Chapter 2

STONE, L., *The Family, Sex and Marriage in England 1500–1800*, Weidenfeld, 1977.
MITCHELL, J. C. (ed.), *Social Networks in Urban Situations*, Manchester University Press, 1969.
NEWSON, J. and NEWSON, E., *Infant Care in an Urban Community*, Allen & Unwin, 1963.
CLARKE, A. M. and CLARKE, A. D. B. (eds.), *Early Experience: Myth and Evidence*, Open Books, 1976.
MUSGRAVE, B. and WHEELER-BENNETT, J. (eds.), *Women at Work*, Peter Owen, 1972.
OAKLEY, A., *The Sociology of Housework*, Martin Robertson, 1975.

Chapter 3

GOLDTHORPE, J. H., LOCKWOOD, D., BECHHOFFER, F. and PLATT, J., *The Affluent Worker: Industrial Attitudes and Behaviour*, Cambridge University Press, 1968.
WEDDERBURN, D. (ed.), *Poverty, Inequality and the Class Structure*, Cambridge University Press, 1974.
REID, I., *Social Class Differences in Britain*, Open Books, 1976.
ATKINSON, A. B., *The Economics of Inequality*, Oxford University Press, 1975.
WILLMOTT, P., *The Evolution of a Community*, Routledge & Kegan Paul, 1963.
WEIR, D. (ed.), *Men and Work in Modern Britain*, Fontana, 1974.
GIDDENS, A., *The Class Structure of the Advanced Societies*, Hutchinson, 1974.

Chapter 4

DOUGLAS, J. W. B., *The Home and the School*, MacGibbon & Kee, 1964.

LACEY, C., *Hightown Grammar*, Manchester University Press, 1970.

HALSEY, A. H., *Towards Meritocracy? The Case of Britain*, Oxford University Press, 1977.

NEAVE, G., *How They Fared: The Impact of the Comprehensive School upon the University*, Routledge & Kegan Paul, 1975.

WILLIAMS, G. and GORDON, A., *Attitudes of Young People to School, Work and Higher Education*, University of Lancaster, 1976.

JENCKS, C. *et al.*, *Inequality*, Basic Books/Allen Lane, 1973.

HUSEN, T., *Social Background and Educational Career*, O.E.C.D., 1973.

BOYD, D., *Elites and their Education*, National Foundation for Educational Research, 1973.

KELSALL, R. K., POOLE, A. and KUHN, A., *Graduates: The Sociology of an Elite*, Methuen, 1972.

FORD, J., *Social Class and the Comprehensive School*, Routledge & Kegan Paul, 1968.

Chapter 5

SCHOFIELD, M., *The Sexual Behaviour of Young People*, Longmans Green, 1965.

DUMAZEDIER, J., *The Sociology of Leisure*, Elsevier, 1975.

FOGELMAN, K. (ed.), *Britain's Sixteen-Year-Olds*, National Children's Bureau, 1976.

PARKER, S., *The Sociology of Leisure*, Allen & Unwin, 1976.

Index

277